MASTERING EMBEDDED SYSTEMS WITH UML STATE MACHINES

Designing Embedded Systems Building Robust Embedded Systems Using UML

BY

Nishimoto Takehiko

TABLE OF CONTENTS

INTRODUCTION TO FINITE STATE MACHINE 6
MEALY AND MOORE MACHINE 13
MEALY AND MOORE STATE TRANSITION TABLE 20
EXERCISE-0001 LED CONTROL MEALY MACHINE EXAMPLE 24
EXERCISE-001 LED CONTROL MEALY MACHINE IMPLEMENTATION PART 1 33
EXERCISE-001 LED CONTROL MEALY MACHINE IMPLEMENTATION PART 2 48
EXERCISE-002 LED CONTROL MOORE MACHINE IMPLEMENTATION..... 53
EXERCISE-003 PRODUCTIVITY TIMER DEMO 58
UML SIMPLE AND COMPOSITE STATES 63
UML STATE MACHINE INTERNAL STATE ACTIVITIES(ENTRY EXIT DO)...71
UML STATE MACHINE TYPES OF TRANSITIONS 76
EVENTS AND SIGNALS 86
EXERCISE-003 STATES AND INITIAL PSEUDO STATES............................ 90
EXERCISE-003 DEFINING STATES ENTRY AND EXIT ACTIONS................ 96
EXERCISE-003 DRAWING STATE TRANSITIONS 101
EXERCISE-003 IMPLEMENTING TIME_SET STATE 107
EXERCISE-003 IMPLEMENTING PAUSE STATE.. 111
INSTALLING MICROSOFT VS CODE AND PLATFORMIO EXTENSION 120
EXERCISE-003 CREATE NEW PROJECT... 122
EXERCISE-003 DATA STRUCTURE EXPLANATION 128
EXERCISE-003 DEFINING INITIAL TRANSITION FUNCTION.................... 133
DIFFERENT APPROACH TO IMPLEMENT STATE MACHINE.................... 135
EXERCISE-003 NESTED SWITCH IMPLEMENTATION OF AN FSM PART 1 136

EXERCISE-003 NESTED SWITCH IMPLEMENTATION OF AN FSM PART 2 144

EXERCISE-003 HARDWARE CONNECTIONS 152

EXERCISE-003 IMPLEMENTING EVENT PRODUCER CODE 157

EXERCISE-003 DISPATCHING TIME TICK EVENT 164

BUTTON BOUNCING EXPLANATION 168

EXERCISE-003 BUTTON SOFTWARE DE-BOUNCING IMPLEMENTATION 173

ADDING ARDUINO LIBRARY TO PROJECT IN PLATFORMIO 180

EXERCISE-003 IMPLEMENTING LCD FUNCTIONS PART 1.....................184

EXERCISE-003 IMPLEMENTING LCD FUNCTIONS PART 2.....................186

EXERCISE-003 HELPER FUNCTION IMPLEMENTATION 193

EXERCISE-003 IMPLEMENTING INITIAL TRANSITION ACTIONS 196

EXERCISE-003 TESTING ON HARDWARE 197

FUNCTION POINTERS IN C 201

PASSING FUNCTION POINTERS AS FUNCTION ARGUMENTS...............208

EXERCISE-004 IMPLEMENTATION USING STATE HANDLER APPROACH 214

EXERCISE-004 STATE TABLE APPROACH FOR IMPLEMENTATION OF AN FSM PART-1..224

EXERCISE-004 STATE TABLE APPROACH FOR IMPLEMENTATION OF AN FSM PART-2..228

2D ARRAYS IN C...230

EXERCISE-004 STATE TABLE APPROACH FOR IMPLEMENTATION OF AN FSM PART-3..238

EXERCISE-004 STATE TABLE APPROACH FOR IMPLEMENTATION OF AN FSM PART-4..244

HIERARCHICAL STATE MACHINES(HSMS) 249

RUN-TO-COMPLETION AND QP™ FRAMEWORK 255

DOWNLOAD QP™ NANO ARDUINO LIBRARY... 264

HSM TRANSITION EXECUTION SEQUENCE TESTING............................ 266

EXERCISE-006 TEST HSM TRANSITION EXECUTION SEQUENCE ON ARDUINO... 270

ADDING FILES IN QM TOOL... 272

ADDING CODES TO FILES USING QM TOOL 284

ADDING A CLASS ATTRIBUTE 290

ADDING ASSERTION FAILURE CALLBACK 302

QHSM_INIT() AND QHSM_DISPATCH() APIS.. 303

EXERCISE-006 TESTING 306

EXERCISE-006 TESTING HISTORY STATE... 318

EXERCISE-007 CLOCK ALARM INTRODUCTION 326

EXERCISE-007 CLOCK ALARM DEMO 328

EXERCISE-007 STATES, SIGNALS AND DATA STRUCTURE USED........... 336

EXERCISE-007 DRAWING AN HSM 342

EXERCISE-007 ADDING MAIN APPLICATION OBJECT AND CONSTRUCTOR... 347

ATMEGA328P TIMER PERIPHERAL EXPLANATION.............................. 352

ATMEGA328P TIMER REGISTERS AND SETUP CODE........................... 361

EXERCISE-007 ADDING CLASS OPERATIONS 365

EXERCISE-007 DEFINING INITIAL TRANSITION ACTIONS..................... 369

EXERCISE-007 CODING FOR THE TICKING STATE 374

EXERCISE-007 ADDING FREE OPERATIONS.. 380

EXERCISE-007 READING CURR_TIME THROUGH CLASS OPERATION ..382

EXERCISE-007 HANDLING TICK EVENT IN TICKING STATE AND TESTING 383

EXERCISE-007 DRAWING CLOCK_SETTING STATE 387

EXERCISE-007 IMPLEMENTING CLOCK_SETTING STATE PART-1 389

EXERCISE-007 IMPLEMENTING CLOCK_SETTING STATE PART-2 397

EXERCISE-007 IMPLEMENTING CLOCK_SETTING STATE PART-3 403

EXERCISE-007 IMPLEMENTING CLOCK_SETTING STATE PART-4 412

EXERCISE-007 UPDATING REAL TIME 417

EXERCISE-007 ALARM_SETTING STATE...422

EXERCISE-007 IMPLEMENTING ALARM_SETTING STATE.....................425

EXERCISE-007 IMPLEMENTING ALARM_NOTIFY STATE 431

INTRODUCTION TO FINITE STATE MACHINE

Now in this project, let us understand what exactly is a state machine? We also quieter an FSM finite state machine. A state machine is a software computation model. It's just a model to solve a complex application, and it comprises a finite number of states and cities also called out finite state machines.

What is a state machine(FSM) ?

- A state machine is a software model of computation, and it comprises finite number states. Hence it is also called a Finite State Machine(FSM)
- Since states are finite, there is a finite number of transitions among the states. Transitions are triggered by the input events fed to the state machine(FSM is an event-driven system).
- A state machine also produces an output. The output produced depends on the current state of the state machine and the input events fed to the state machine.

So states are nothing but situations off your application in different situations. Since states are finite, that is a finite number of transitions among the states that transitions are triggered by the incidents or what we call an input event threat to the state machine, basically, and FSM is an event driven, reactive system. So we will understand more on this later about states and transitions and what exactly are events, etc. We are going to discuss a lot of things about these technologies with various examples. A state machine also produces a sound output. The output produced depends on the current state of the state machine, sometimes and sometimes it also depends on the input Iran's threat to the state machine. So here is an example where you are seeing a flat state machine. There are different types of state machines like flat state machines, hierarchical state machines and various other things. So we will discuss all those things later. But just to show you the feel of an FSM here, you can see that there are various states which are interconnected, right? And the state. They represent different situations of the application. The application or the problem? What do you need to solve? This situation is represented as a state in the state machine diagram, which handles different events, and it may produce different outputs. And you see there are various interconnections between the states. These are called transitions. And transitions are caused because of an event which is received by the state machine. Since the application months between different states producing various outputs and processing various events, this may be called a machine, a state machine. But we'll see how to draw these diagrams later.

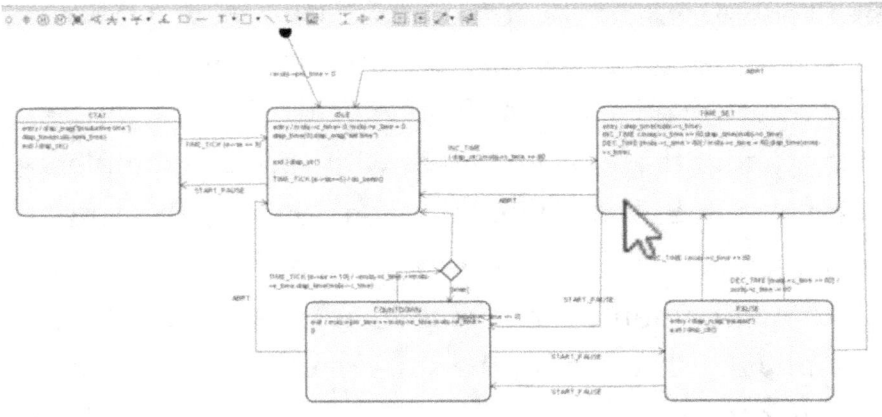

Basically, this is drawn using the syntax up. You are most state machine specification and will be using the umph specification throughout this course. Now, let's get back to our project. What are the benefits of using state machines? State machines are used to describe situations, as I explained, are different scenarios of your application to be precisely state machine models. Different scenarios of the application, object object in or terminology that is object oriented terminology is nothing but an instance of a class or an instance of a structure in C I application maybe having different classes. So a state machine actually belongs to a class. If your application has many classes, then that could be many state machines. Not necessarily. Lifecycle of every class has to be modeled by means of a state machine. So thumbs are helpful in modeling the life cycle, react to objects to interconnections of state here, object is nothing but an instance of a cloth. And FSM is helpful to model complex applications that involve lots of decision making, producing different outputs and processing various events. So, you know, many times or heightened by the complexity of the application, the application sees various asynchronous events to various synchronous events entrapped, and the application looks very tedious because it produces various outputs. And when this event is received, that action should be taken. And when that action happens, this event should be produced. All these things which are in your mind, you can express it through the state machine diagram what we call a state chart, and it will help you to visualize the problem more clearly. And you can decompose the complexity. Or you can narrow down the complexity to state level complexity. And you can add to the problem with much more clarity. And you can't work efficiently, so one of the biggest advantages of using FSM is that it helps you to decompose your complex application into smaller situations. And you can think about solving that situation and then you interconnect all the situations to finally think of your problem. And state machines are realized through state machine diagrams in the form of state charts. This helps to communicate with non-development and Olympus that is one of the advantages of expressing finite state machines in the form of diagrams. FSM makes it easier to visualize and implement the changes to the behavior of the project.

Benefits of using state machines(FSMs)

- Used to describe situations or scenarios of your application(Modelling the life cycle of a reactive object through interconnections of states.)
- FSMs are helpful to model complex applications that involve lots of decision-making, producing different outputs (actions), and processing various events.
- State machines are visualized through state machine diagrams in the form of state charts, which helps to communicate between non-developers and developers.
- Makes it easier to visualize and implement the changes to the behavior of the project
- complex application can be visualized as a collection of different states processing a fixed set of events and producing a fixed set of outputs
- Loose coupling: An application can be divided into multiple behaviors or state machines, and each unit can be tested separately or could be reused in other applications
- Easy debugging and easy code maintenance
- Scalable
- Narrow down whole application complexity to state level complexity, analyze and implement

Tomorrow, if you want to incorporate any other changes or if you want to add any new features, then it is very easy or straightforward to make changes to the existing FSM diagram. Complex application can be visualized as a collection of different states, each state processing a fixed for events and producing a fixed set of outputs, Luf coupling and application can be divided into multiple state machines, and each unit can be tested separately or could be reused in other applications. Easy debugging. There's also the advantage of solving a problem. Using Epatha scalable and troubleshooting becomes much easier than implementing the same problem using traditional procedures based on step by step implementation of what we have been doing so far too late. When we implement some applications, you'll definitely appreciate the idea of finite state machines. Now, let's move forward. There are different types of state machines. First one is mainly machines such as Harold St. Charles and Umstead Machine. Some of these state machines are used for software engineering, and some state machines are still being used in these electronics, VLSI design, etc.. In this course, we are interested in Umstead machines, because this debt machine is predominantly used in software engineering to model the software engineering problems, and it is influenced by David of State Chart Formalism explained by this research paper, which was published in 1980. And in the market, there are various tools available which can interpret your email, state charts, and it can generate the base level code. So that's the advantage of using AMP specification basic state machine diagrams. You can auto generate the code in C or C++ or Java using some of these tools. So these tools from IBM are Quantum Leap, and that is one more tool quality akin to state charter. Some are paid tools and some are Open-Source.

UML Modelling tool and code generator

- Rhapsody® by IBM®
- QM™ Model-based design tool by Quantum Leaps, LLC
- Visual State by IAR
- Yakindu state chart tools by Itemis AG

So these tools can interpret your model and it can auto generate the code later. Part of the course will be using quantum leaps, kewpie framework and Q modeler tool to implement nested hierarchical state machines. From the next project onwards, that expert, what exactly the milling machine is, how it is different from war machines, and we'll also explore the umph specification about driving the UMF tape machines. I'll see you in the next project.

MEALY AND MOORE MACHINE

In this project, let's explore what exactly a media machine is and how it is different from a war machine. The difference between a machine and more machine life and how exactly the output is produced in the machine. Now first, let's explore the media machine in the media machine. And what happens is the output produced by the state machine depends on the input events, threat to the state machine and present active state of the machine. The output produced depends on two factors: the input events affect the state machine and the present active state of the state machine, and we should also remember that the output is not produced inside the state. That means the output is produced along the transition from one state to another. This is a generic model of the media machine that says you have to state, let's call it at state one and state two. And this is called a transition, and this transition is happening from state one to state to. When this input is referred, the machine moves from state to state to produce the output. As you can see here, output is mentioned during the transition, not inside the states. In the media, machine output is represented along with each input separated by a flash character, so output is also called as action. And in the m.E model, the output is also called as input action because when the input is received, the action may happen where the output may happen. And that will be a state transition.

Mealy machine

- In this machine, the output produced by the state machine depends on the input events fed to the state machine AND present active state of the state machine.
- The output is not produced inside the state

George H. Mealy
American mathematician

George H. Mealy was an American mathematician and computer scientist who invented the namesake Mealy machine, a type of finite state transducer.
Wikipedia

1) Output is represented along with each input separated by '/'
2) An 'Output' is also called 'Action.'
3) In the mealy model, the 'Output' is also called 'Input action.'

Generic Mealy model

That's why in the media machine, all you need to remember is output is not produced inside the state, but along the transition. Here is an example of a flight control application: a flight control application has a forced state of state that demonstrates medium brightness, state and the brightness that is the full brightness state. A state can be drawn at a circle or as a rectangle or as a rounded rectangle. It doesn't matter. You can draw it in any way you want, but in particular your MS specification base of the state machine diagram, then it should be a color rectangle toward which you are talking later. Because we have not yet gone into understanding the specification of

UMC state machines. So but you are just modeling your application using different states, then you can either use a circle or a rectangle. No problem for later with seeing how to arrive at a different stage than how to do interconnections and various other things. I'm just giving an example here, so don't worry too much about all of these things. We are going to understand everything about these technologies, like Iran's transition stage, the entry actions, exit actions, so all those terminologies will be explained with proper examples. This is a simple light control application which has got four states, and these are the interconnections. So this state machine is used for events. Let's say there are two buttons on the light or on the light stand or whatever. Let's imagine something like this. Let's say this is a light stand and this is a light. You are studying light, table light or whatever, that state has two buttons here. And this is the off button, I just write f here off. And this is on this on button. This is power. So when you give power to this table lamp, initially the application will be in off state when you press the on button, the on event is delivered to the state machine so that the on event. And when you press the off button, the event is delivered to the state machine. And as I said, when you first give the power, the table lamp software gets into the initial state off. And when you press the on button, the on event is delivered to the software and it takes a transition. So the state of the software will be changed to dim, and along this transition, it produces the output, dim the light. So the light will be turned on, but the intensity will be dim. As you can see, this is a mini machine, right? Because the output is the action is probably along with a received input event that means along with a transition. Now, the software is in dim state, and when it gets into the dim state, it doesn't do anything in the media machine. It just waits in the dim state. When you again, press the on button one more time and the state machine receives the event and the state machine morphs from dim state to medium brightness state, and it produces the output medium brightness. As you can see, she is at this event. The actions taken are different, right? The event is the same here. That's right. Based on the current state, the action taken what's different here for the retired event. So that familiar machine? Now, the software is in medium brightness state, and again, you press the on button, it receives the on event and it produces some other output. So like that? And when the state machine is in any of these states, when the user presses the off button, the off event is received and they actually go back to the state.

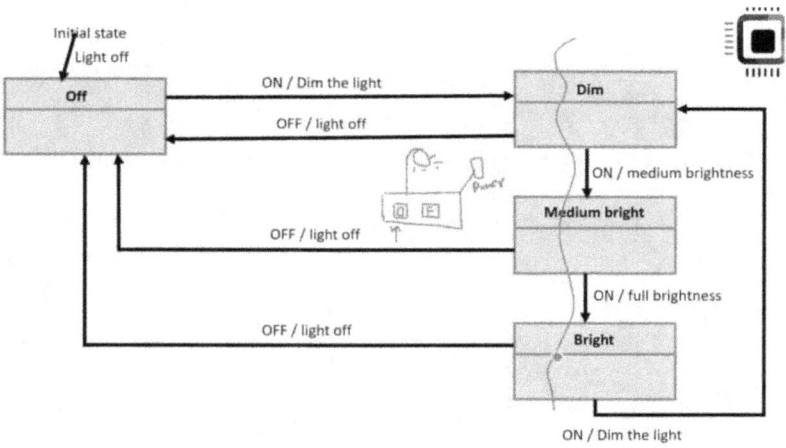

And a longer transition, the action taken was lights off. This is a machine. And now let's see what more machines are? Very simple. In the machine, no output. During the state transition, there is no output here. The output is determined only by the president acting state after state machine and not by any input events. So all you remember is the output is probably inside the state, the not during transition from one state to another output is represented inside the state. Output is also called as an action in the motor model. The output is called an entry action. Here you can see in this model. Just look at this part of this diagram that is a transition. Let's say this is state one. This is state two. So that is a transition from state one to state two. And also, there is one self transition here.

Moore machine

- In this state machine, the output is determined only by the present active state of the state machine and not by any input events

- No output during state transition.

Edward F. Moore

American professor of mathematics

Edward Forrest Moore was an American professor of mathematics and computer science, the inventor of the Moore finite state machine, and an early pioneer of artificial life. Wikipedia

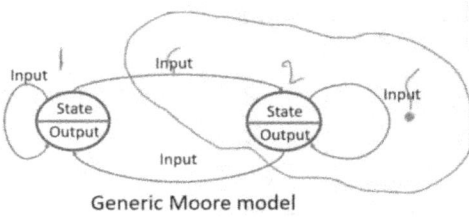

Generic Moore model

- Output is represented inside the state
- 'Output' is also called 'Action.'
- In the Moore model the 'Output' is also called 'Entry action.'

So it doesn't matter what this input is, so regardless of this input, when this date is entered, this output is produced. That's why this output has got nothing to do with these inputs. When the state is entered, that output is produced. That's why the output produced only depends on the present active state. Hence the output produced. It is also called an entry action. So we convert our previous example light control application to more machine type. Very simple. What you need to do is just move. All those actions are output to, you know, you move all those actions within the states that fit. Let's say when the initial state was off or when the initial state office is entered, the entry action gets executed or the output is produced, that is lights off. And when the user presses the on button, the state machine receives the on event and when the state machine receives on event it Morse to. Dim state. It enters the dim state, and when it enters the dim state, the entry action gets executed that is dim, the light and like that. So the media and war machines are not quite famous in software engineering, tomatillo or software engineering problems, but they are still being used.

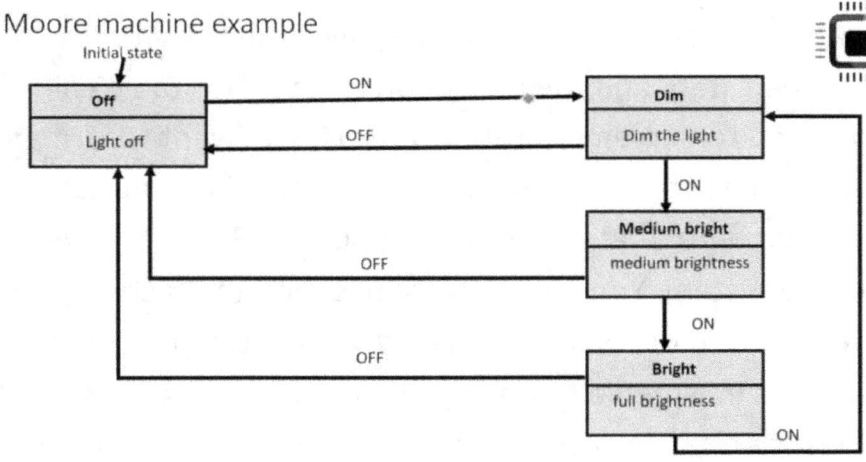

It has its application areas in the circuit design, the VLSI System design, etc. So it will not be using more machines or merely machines in this course. But we use its advanced version, which is proposed by David Harrell. In his paper, which is later incorporated in the Human Stick machine. So in the machine we call the output producer of entry actions. In this example, the end reaction thought lights off, take the light, make the light dim, make the light medium brightness, make the light full brightness. All these are entry actions, and there are two events in the system that are on and off.

MEALY AND MOORE STATE TRANSITION TABLE

So now let's look at the state transition table for our light controlled media machine. A state transition table is nothing, but it's a table which explains the transition between state and the output produced. This table will help you to implement the code. So if you want to write a state transition table for a mini machine. Then you can see that here, that is a column of output. For every event up the system. You know, the application that actually went on and off. Hence, there are two output columns. Because in a media machine, the output from others depends on the present state as well as the received event. So this column shows the present state and there are multiple columns, each for one event. Now, how to understand this. Very simple, so let's take this question. That we understand this rock. When the state machine is in upstate. And if you event on the third date machine produces the output, make the light dim and it makes that transition to the dim state. That's the next state. So that's what you should understand. And when the state machine is in our state, if an input event is received, then that event asks for our application. It is ignored. I mean, no output is defined.

State transition table
Light control Mealy machine

Present state	Next state			
	Input events			
	OFF		ON	
	Next state	input action (output)	Next state	input action (output)
Off	off	--ignored--	Dim	Make light dim
Dim	Off	Light off	Medium	Make light medium
Medium	Off	Light off	Bright	Make light bright
Bright	Off	Light off	Dim	Make light dim

When the state machine is in 'Off' state and if
- Input event 'ON' is received, then state machine produces the output 'Make light dim' and makes a transition to 'Dim' state
- Input event 'OFF' is received, the event is ignored

So the event is ignored and the next step will be the same as the present state. There is no state change that helps you understand this state transition table. So the only point you should remember here is there are multiple output columns. One for each event of the system. Now, let's see how the state transition table of life control machines looks like here, that is only one column which explains the output because the output is not depending on the received events. So that's why you see only one output column, and that is one column which explains the next state. That's how to understand this table. Very simple. Let's understand this raw. When the state machine enters the state. It executes the light of entry action and waits until an input event is received. If the input event received is on the state machine most to the dim state and if the input event refute is off, then that event is ignored as per our application.

State transition table
Light control Moore machine

State	Entry actions (output)	Next state	
		Input events	
		OFF	ON
Off	Light off	--ignored--	Dim
Dim	Make light dim	Off	Medium
Medium	Make light medium	Off	Bright
Bright	Make light bright	Off	Dim

- When the state machine enters the 'Off' state, it executes the 'Light off' entry action and waits until an input event is received.
- If the input event received is 'ON', the state machine moves to the state 'Dim.'
- If the input event received is 'OFF', event is ignored

So that's about the state transition table. And now let's understand her real estate charts. So in 1984, David Harrell published a paper on the paper and I mean visual formalism for complex systems, so this is publicly available online. You can download and read it. And in this paper, he introduces the concept of state charts. So the state charts extend conventional state transition diagrams with essentially three elements dealing, respectively, with the notions of hierarchy, concurrency and communication. The state charts proposed by him consist of features from both Milling Machine, More Machine. And on top of that, he adds a lot of other features. So some of the interesting features of the state chart are it introduces the concept of such state and super state composite state history, state or tonality and communication between state machines, conditional transition entry and exit actions for a state or for a composite state activities inside a state parameterized state, overlapping state records state chart. These are some of the features introduced in the state judge. And later, this has been incorporated into the human state machines. If you read the latest UML specification from OMG, then you can write. It says that the specific form of financial statement I used in, erm, is based on an object oriented variant of David Harold State Chart Formalism. However, readers who are familiar with that formalism should note that there is a small number of semantic differences that distinguishes the human version from the very. So in this course I will be learning the grammar state machine, which is specification oriented. And whenever I want to explain something, I would be referring to the specification itself and the specification number is 2.5 one.

EXERCISE-0001 LED CONTROL MEALY MACHINE EXAMPLE

Alright, so now let's see one code implementation in this exercise. We are going to implement the light control milling machine. And this is a state machine diagram. So we will use one entity to control its brightness. For this exercise, you need an Arduino Uno board and one for Amnesty so you can take whatever color you like and queue jumper while. In this course, I'm not going to argue that you already know about the Arduino UNO board and its programming framework, so that's why I would also talk about the art, you know, board it, the Fed floats and its programming interfaces, and some of the API use it to control the pedals, etc.

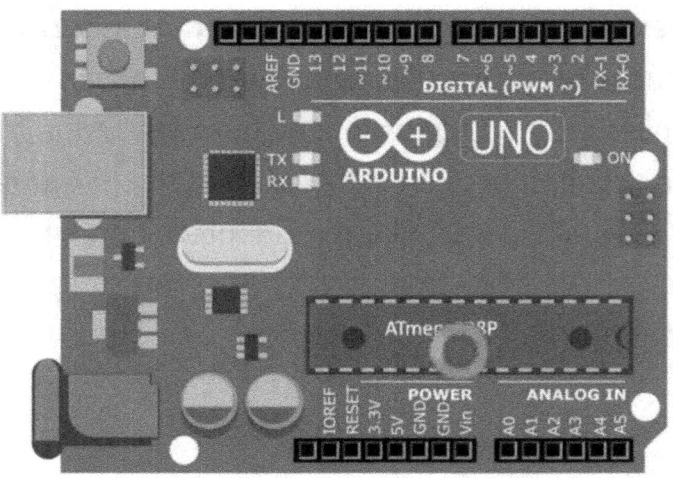

And I would also explain the API provided by the Arduino community to do various things. In this application, we are going to change the intensity of an edit of our light. And for this, you have to control the voltage which you feed to the entity, right? How do you control the voltage or how do you ready the voltage, what you feed to the energy through programming? You can modulate or you can use the P.W. well, though you can pulse through it modulation. That is what P.W. aim is. And by controlling the duty cycle of the P.W. This way, you can control the intensity of the energy. The Arduino Uno board has many pins. You can see it, so there are a couple of holes here and here as well. These holes are connected to the microcontroller, which is on the Arduino Ono board. So this is a microcontroller and it is at Mega 328 PPI microcontroller, which is actually a eight bit microcontroller from automatic. So now it is a microchip. Here are these digital pens, so not death from zero to 30. There are around 15 digital pens and there are few analog pens. If you have any analog sensors or if you are doing some project related to the luxury token water or digital to unlock and water, then you can use Bradford's analog petrol's at these pins. These are just digital pens. And out of these digital pins, though, there are few P.W. on pins, so you can see the pins, which are marked with the symbol tilde. So these are. P.W. Pince. The, you know, board has around six P.W. and beneath the digital pin numbers, three, five, six, nine, 10 and 11 are P.W. opinion. What exactly is the meaning of P.W. and PIN that means on those pins, the microcontroller can generate P.W. signals. Or you can say something like this. These beans are actually connected to the microcontroller's internal P.W. am a signal generation engine for what the frequency is that way? The P.W. arm, where it is for 90 knighthoods on three nine 10 11. And it is 980 Hudson pin number five and six. So we'll use one pin. Let's say we'll use pin number nine. So you have to change the duty cycle of the P.W. Way and to do that. The Arduino framework gives one API analog, right? That's it. You just have to use that when you use analog, right? So you can see that you can change the duty cycle, the wave. For example, when you supply zero to this analog right, that is to say, zero percent duty cycle. That means the signal is always at zero. That means it's denote. And when you want to create P.W. a way with a 55 percent duty cycle, that means 65 percent of the time it will be on and 75 percent of the time it will be off. It's like that and it's. Time period is won by, let's say, for 90. Because the frequency is 490 us, so that comes around two milliseconds. So two milliseconds is the time period of the P.W. underway, and out of that two millisecond, 25 percent of the time it will be on. That means the signal will be fired and the rest of the time it will be zero. So if you take the average voltage, it comes around 25 percent. That's the average shortage, and that much voltage is a. And it's like that.

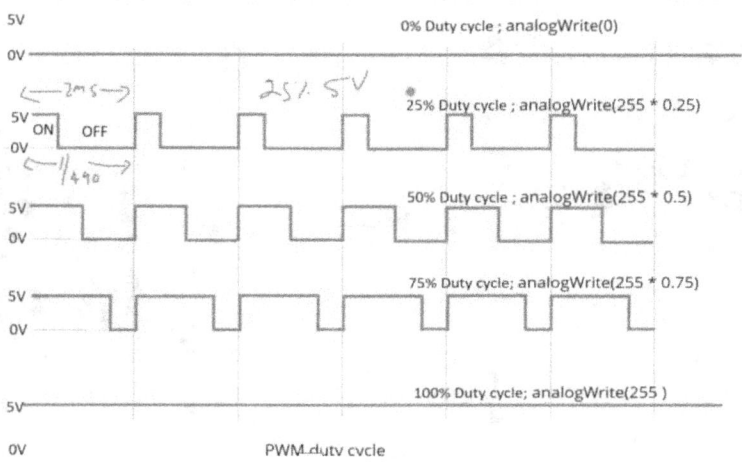

Similarly, by varying the value of what you supply to this API and low right, you can change the duty cycle of the P.W, and the concept is very simple. And for this exercise, we need a two button one button is to send the on event and a button is to send the off erector instead of using the button. We will send on and off commands to our events through the Arduino Kriol interface. We will send the commands from the host. What we do is this is our host, that is our computer and this is our target. But we can't do a feeble communication between the USB cable or what you use to connect the Arduino board to the computer. The same USB cable can be used for the purpose of powering this board.

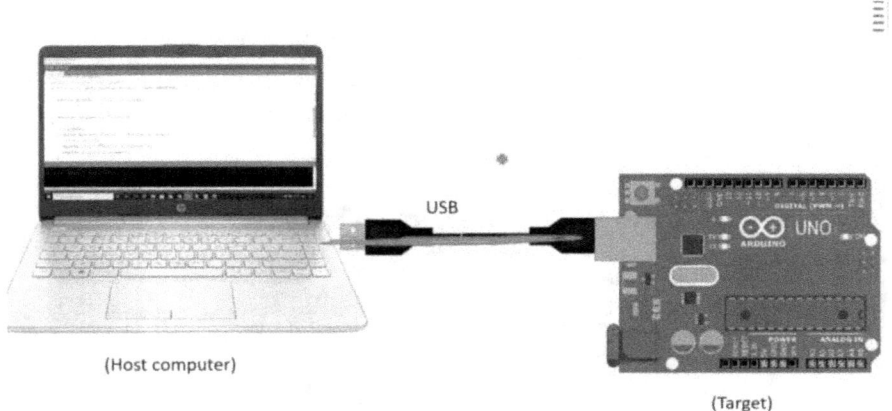

Arduino serial(UART) communication with HOST

As well as this, the USB cable can also be used for the video communication between host and the target and that is what we call the UART communication. When you connect this board to the computer through the USB cable. Our show COMPORTE is created by the host. That's because if you check the Arduino UNO board, this is our main microcontroller. And that is another microcontroller, actually. So this one, you feel that it's one more microcontroller. This is a secondary microcontroller, and that microcontroller is at Mega 16 U2. This access, the USB to you, is a converter. It has its own firmware, which converts the UART signal to USB signal. And because of this, this board enumerates it as a virtual comm port on the host site. And that's why whenever you upload any code from the host, it actually takes this part. It goes to this microcontroller and from that microcontroller is the form that the code is received by the bootloader of the main microcontroller and that so you program the flash memory of the main microcontroller.

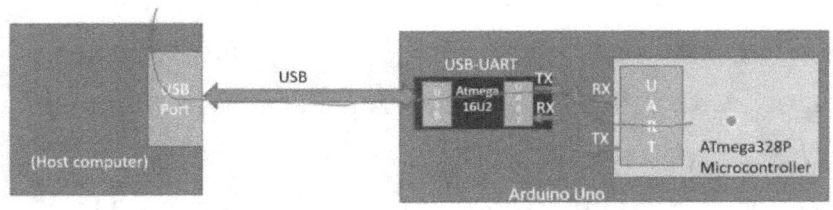

Arduino serial(UART) communication with HOST

So that is what happens when you upload a code and the same port can be used to send some data or commands to the Arduino program. While it is running through the host computer. So what you do is instead of using buttons, you just send the on off you rent. Or where the communication fits. Now, let's get started. Now let's create one new project, and let's start coding. So just open the Arduino IDE, and let's first save this project. So just create one folder. I just created a folder state machines underscore project. And under that, I'm going to save all my projects of discord. First, let's start with the number zero zero one. I call this light. Control mainly, let's click save. So we are just using one entity with this project, and we are controlling that entity using the API analog. Right? But we don't know how to use the analogue right to understand that. So let's go to the official documentation of Arduino dot org and we'll learn something about that. Now I am on the official website of Arduino and go to documentation, and here is the reference. And here, just check analog, right? So the analog write function is exclusively used here to generate P.W. way with the desired duty cycle. So the description says it writes an analog value to a pin. This can be used to later alight at varying brightness or drive a motor at various peaks. Basically, this function generates a steady, rectangular wave of space by duty cycle until the next quarter and log writer digital functions. Please note that on Arduino Uno, the function and log right has got nothing to do with the internal analog. Like Athie, because the Arduino owner doesn't have the DAC Belfort DSD peripheral, it doesn't have that at all right function just to configure the timer patrol up to microcontroller in such a way that you just control the on off period of a pin by using a timer in such a way that desire duty cycle is achieved. So that's why it has got something to do with the time our up to microcontroller or the timer has associated P.W. Generation Unit, then the P.W. MBA is generated using that instead of the DAC Bedford. So here you can see that in some other words, in addition to the P.W. capabilities on this piece, the MKR nanoparticles, the IOTA and zero votes have true analog output when using analog right on the DSP, but it is not the case with the audio board and that you also have got true analog output. True analog output means using the internal DSC preference. So far, you know, you know, dysfunction just produces a rectangular wave of desired duties. And here, the description also mentions that you need not to call PIN mode to set the pin as an output before calling analog, right? So you just straight away, you just use analog, right? So the API will do all the necessary initialization. But the Angelo Reid function is different, the analog read function uses the ADC better because the analog read function converts the applied input voltage to a digital number.

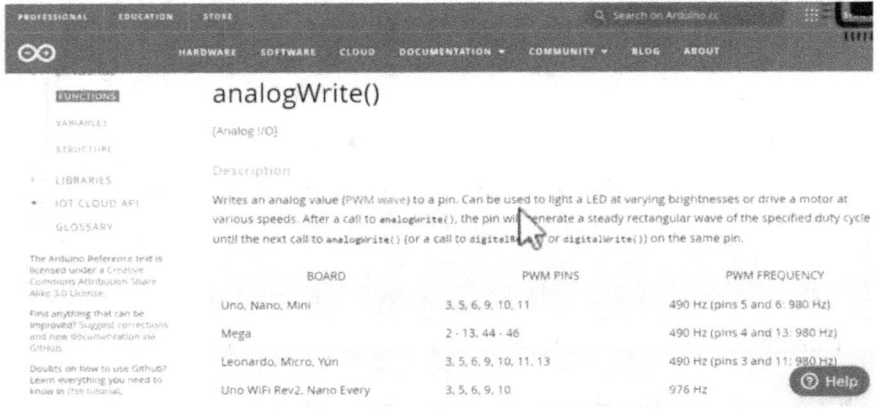

No, it's analog to digital conversion, so hence the analog read takes the help of the owner's ADC better, and when we need it, has the added benefit. How to use this function, very simple, the syntax is very simple. You just have to mention two parameters with this function. The first one is a pin number, a PWI pin number, you should mention. And by using this value parameter, you can control the duty cycle. What's the valid values for this parameter? You can see here the values between zero two 255 zero zero percent duty cycle, 255 min, 100 percent duty cycle and any in-between number you can use to achieve different duty cycles up to P.W. Anyway, I'll use this function in our project.

EXERCISE-001 LED CONTROL MEALY MACHINE IMPLEMENTATION PART 1

Now in our application, we also have a couple of states, right? We have got four states here and a couple of events on and off. So now all this information is defined in their application. I'm going to my project. Now let's use these enumerated data types to define the details. Let me use Enum. You went. And let's define on and off. So these are events. In this course, I'll also explain some of the key concepts, what we missed in our earlier course on microcontroller emergency. So in that course, I didn't cover Inam side code, the function pointers and various other things. Let me take this opportunity to explain all those concepts. First of all, let us understand what exactly is enumerated should our enemies be seated? It's a very simple concept, and let's understand what is that? Enumeration and see. So an item or any mention in C or C++ is a user defined data type. You can use it to create your own user, define it our time by using Enum. You can define your own data type. It provides some clarity to your program, so to use Enum, you should give an enumerated list. So the enumerated list must be known in advance. Enumeration of a list is nothing but a finite list of named integer constant values. Data type can take on. Let's see an example. Let's say I want to create a data tie to represent the day of a week. So basically the idea here is to create a named integer constant like here, for example, Sunday, Monday, Tuesday. These are labeled when you use a label. You know it. Add some clarity to your program instead of calling zero one two three. You call it Sunday, Monday, Tuesday. So it adds some clarity to your program. But these are not just labor. These are actually named integer constants. So that's how Enum binds those named integer constants or labeled integer constants.

Example

I want to create data type to represent the day of a week.
```
enum Day_of_week
{
   SUNDAY,
   MONDAY,
   TUESDAY
};

enum Day_of_week whatIsToday;
whatIsToday = MONDAY;
```

For example, here I create a couple of Labor's four days off a week like Sunday, Monday, Tuesday and other days you can add separated by a comma. So this is called and enumerates the list, and this is actually defined inside an enum tag. This is the Inam keyword and this is enum tag or this is also called as an identifier. So this enumerate means you have to place inside the braces. This whole thing is called in the declaration. After that, you create a variable of this animation type. So this is a data type. This is a variable. And with that variable, you use any of these values. Now, let's see some examples of using Inghams in different possible ways. Now, let's dig the earlier example in. Day after week. Sunday, Monday. This is a valid declaration for the last member to terminate with a comma, no problem or usually we don't give a comma here. This is an item declaration and after that you can create a variable of this type. For example, what I created today is equal to Monday or something like that. So this is valid. Variable creation and initialization, that's compile this. So it's actually giving some warning on news radio about. In C programming, this is how you create a variable of NMDA type. You have to mention the keyword mentioned the tag or identifier and then create a variable. It's like that. But in C++, if you are using it, then this is actually not required. So if I made this, then also it will compile. I think you may be knowing this fact, Arduino. AC + + program, so the compiler is C++ compiler. That's why this also compares fine. No problem here. But if you compile the same thing on a C compiler, then you would see errors. So let me bring that killer back. So this is one way of using DNA. Now I will just tell you another way. So let's say. I created another one. Cloudy, sunny. This is also another decoration.

```
10    CLOUDY,
11    SUNNY
12 }
13
14 #define PIN_LED 9
15
16 void setup() {
17    // put your setup code here, to run once:
18    enum Day_of_week today = MONDAY;
19    int climate = |
20
21 }
```

C:\Users\nieki\OneDrive - BHARATI SOFTWARE\Workspace\StateMachine_projects\00
C:\Users\nieki\OneDrive - BHARATI SOFTWARE\Workspace\StateMachine_projects\00

It doesn't have any tag a tag list declaration, so I can't, you know, even use such. Ms. I create one variable, let's say climate is equal to funny. So just typecast these things too wide, the compiler warns. Now let's compile. Sorry, I just did not add the semicolon. This also works well, I mean, such unions are not so youthful. But you can use such tactless enemies as a replacement for preprocessor directive like fort preprocessing directives such as Ash Defiance. So if I had to write harsh defiance for the same thing as I did, I'd have to find a way to insulate it to zero. And I have to define zero here and hash define. Cloudy like that. So I had to write so many things instead of that, you can write something like this. Now in the beginning, I said these are named integer constants. What integer value it takes. Now, let's see the specification work specification says so on the specification phase, I have taken this process vacation through 1990 specification. Here it is, an numerator with assignment operator defines enumeration constant as the value of the constant expression. So you can use the assignment of next year to mention the initial constant value for like 30, let's say it's value 30. Each subsequent person returns? OK. With no assignment operator. Defines the enumeration constant as the value of the constant expression obtained by adding one to the value of the previous animation constant, its value becomes 31. Implicitly, its value becomes 32. Like that, you can print them and your fee automatically.

```
 4    MONDAY,
 5    TUESDAY
 6 };
 7
 8 enum{
 9    RAINING = 30,
10    CLOUDY,
11    SUNNY
12 };
13
14 #define PIN_LED 9
15
```

Sketch uses 438 bytes (1%) of program storage space. Maximum is 32256 bytes.
Global variables use 9 bytes (0%) of dynamic memory, leaving 2039 bytes for local vari

These labels get a value one added to the previous one. And this also says that if the first enumerate has no assignment operator, the value of the enumerate should be zero. Let's say in this case, the Sun Labor has the integer constant. Zero zero one two like that. So this is the second time we are using animation in the sea. Now let's look at the third way. So here you see, while creating a variable of this type, you have to use the keyword as well right here. You cannot permit this in the% now to escape from that in order to get rid of using this enum keyword. What you can do is you can go for Typekit, wash it off enemies. How to do that? Let's see. Very simple. You just write in them. You know, you're right. So let's say I just write these labels. And after that, you just add the keyword Typekit here. So this actually doesn't have a tag nor tag here. And after that, just mention here the typed up alias name activity and Scotty, let's say and terminate the declaration with a semicolon. This is Typekit. After that, what you can use after that, so you can use this type of alias name and create one variable activity is required to meet. Now, you no longer have to use the key word here. That's it. So now let's say I, instead of storing this value here, I stored some integer value, let's say 55. What would you think it would compile the compiler through and add it? Let's see what happens here. So that is a problem. Let's see what this is. This is an error warning, so warning it safe, invalid conversion from into activity. You fear the C++ compiler won't feel that you have used it. Our data here is a value here, which is not bad in the enumerate, at least after animal activity and difficulty. What happens if I use, let's say, three? Orders still give that warning. Let's see. It would still give the warning because it's saying you are trying to use an integer value. You are not using these labels, but this would be fine if you compile the same statement with the compiler. So if you are going to check the specification here, so if you had compiled that on a C compiler, the C compiler wouldn't have given any warning because this is what the specification says here that each enumerate type shall be compatible with. Here, you can see that the expression that defines the value of an enumeration constant shall be an integer constant expression that has value represented as an INT. You can use that value if it is compatible with cat assign integer type or an unsigned integer type. As long as the value is what you mention, do these types cat into your type or an unsigned integer type, then it would be fine for a C compiler. But a C++ compiler has some issues with that. So it wants you. What if I use a floating point number four, I use three point five. Then it would break the specification and it would throw an ETA. This is an error because. This has to be in integer constant. All right, so that's about enemies. And one more point I want to mention. Let's say you have enough declaration of something like this. So here I have internalized this label, 220. Now, if you print all these labels, then you would see something like this. The first one is zero. It is automatically initialized to zero. Second one is one, the third one is 20 and the fourth one is 21. Remember that because it takes the value by adding one to the previous value. So you just remember that. Now let's use Enum to capture different states and different events, the information in our project. Just delete all the things. So I just use an item with a tag, you know, event. And after that, let me create another Inam state or light state. What is the state we have? We have dim state, medium brightness state and full brightness state. So just right off dim, medium and full. And after that, let me use a global variable to hold the current state of my application. So for that, let me create a variable of this type I would just write in. State. Current state. Or you can convert this to a typedef. I can remove this tag and put it here like a life state under Scotty, and I just can't use this.

This is also fine. The tea signifies that it's the up watch, and I'll initialize this variable to Obstet initially. That's fine.

```c
enum event{
  ON,
  OFF
};

typedef enum {
  OFF,
  DIM,
  MEDIUM,
  FULL
}light_state_t;
```

So now there is a problem with two labels with the same name. That is the label of their label of such conflict is not allowed. So while using multiple enum declarations not to enumerate, you can't have the same name. You have to modify this. I will change this to, let's say. I'll do something like that. Make this light of light, dim light, medium light for. That would be fine. And I turn this to light off. So now let's create one more function. I'll call this a light control or light state machine. And this state machine and the things that you rent. So let's create one parameter. Let me use you in eight underscore events. Now, let's use the Switch case to switch between different states. Not to implement the state machine or state machine handler, there are many ways you can use nested speech or nested if health is an effective bladder. So that is something called the state table approach and state handler approach. To adopt this three state handler approach is more efficient, and it helps you to implement a less redundant code. And so we'll explore all these three options in this course. But as a starting point, let's just use methods which are nested a fail safe ladder for this project. Now, let's get back to the court, so let's do the switch case, which is the current state. If the current state is. So in an effort switch, what happens is there will be one upward switch which switches you between different states and that will be another Nestor switch, which switches you between different events. All right, so now this is the auto switch. These switches have switched between different states. The cases of this, which will be four different states for the state machine. So we have got four states right, the first case for state one. That is our light off. Let's create a case and immediately add the brake statement. So now we have got four different states. Four times we have to write this case. Copy and paste. So this is for light. Tim, this is for light. Medium. This is par for. Let's get inside this state when the current state is light off. Then we have to process a couple of events, so that's why I give you one more switch case or methods which are nested effects or you can also use the latter no problem. Let me use another Switch case to switch between events. What's the case? Cases on. So just add the BRICS statement. And another case is. That fit. Let's do one thing, so let's copy this to every state. Just copy this. Right here. Now, let's save this and try to compile. That is a problem. Light to medium was not declared. So like the media. That was compiled. No problem. Now, let's get back to our state transition diagram. So when the state is off. It doesn't process the off event, it doesn't affect that ticket. It just processes the on event. So when the state is this one, when the audio rented received, it produces this output and it makes a transition to demonstrate, let's implement that. So when the state is light off, it doesn't implement off, let's say modest. For here, light change intensities, some function, we have it. What is the change in intensity? The pin, you have to mention, is pretty. And the intensity rallied, right, a value to feed to the analog write function. So what I'll do now is I'll just define these macros with these numbers. To control the duty cycle of the GWM, think that. As you can hear, this label, R255 helped me to produce the P.W. and signal our 100 percent duty cycle. So like that, this is for them. This is for medium, this is for full brightness and it is to turn off, of course. Now let's go back here and let the youth dim here. And after that, there is a transition where the current state is changed. So our current state, wary of a current state, becomes light, dim.

```
38      {
39          case LIGHT_OFF:{
40              switch(event){
41                  case ON:{
42                      light_change_intensity(PIN_LED,LIGHT_BRIGHT_DIM);
43                      curr_state = LIGHT_DIM;
44                      break;
45                  }
46              }
47              break;
48          }
49          case LIGHT_DIM:{
50              switch(event){
```

Sketch uses 438 bytes (1%) of program storage space. Maximum is 3
Global variables use 9 bytes (0%) of dynamic memory, leaving 2039

And it breaks here. Now let's program this state. So when it is in them, when the EN event is received, it produces the output and most of the medium state. Let's do that.

Let's copy this code. It goes to medium, and the brightness value is for medium. And it goes to the. Media and when it receives the off event. It produces this output, and most of the. So let's make this entity bright. And this goes to light off St. Cloud state becomes light upstate. And likewise, you had to call for these two states. Let's do that. So as you can see, the quick implementation looks messy, isn't it? This is not a good method, but it's OK for the sake of exercise, we can use this. This is the definition of the light change in density function, which just takes the intensity here and uses analog right to control the intensity of the entity which is connected to the spin. And now let's try to compile. It's fine. No problem. Now we have to call the state machine function whenever we receive any rent. By the way, I have to add the prototype of these functions. Let me add the prototypes here. And a prototype of this as well. Right. So now how to receive that you will receive that you rent from the host over the communication that I will cover in the next project, for that to have to refer to the RV now CEO object. So for that to go to documentation reference and the serial object you can access here. So this is a surreal object, and its related epitaph, our function. So before using a serial port you are prepared for serial communication. You may be knowing from earlier courses that we have already covered this. You are communicating on a Stanford microcontroller. You have to configure the bar rate. No, I'll bet you want to send it as a payload. No, stop it, etc. So all those things can be done in one go by using a function called Begin. Here it is. The trial begins. The trial begins in two flavors here, so you have to mention the serial object and its associated method like that you have to use because, as I said, it's a C++ framework. So you just have to mention the board right here, that's it. Or if you have any special requirements regarding star orbits and the payload weight, that means no update orbit you want to send in, you are free, then you can use any of these values, for example. This is, by default, a database. You know you are free, no parity and one stop it. For any reason, if you want to change it, if you want to use parity and in parity, if you want to use even pattern or parity or if you want to change that number of databases, then you can't use any of this value. But I don't think we need to do that for this exercise or stick with the theory. And one of the borders, it's possible there are many borders. It's possible like they have mentioned here. Let's use this. Let's go back to the court and keep that in the head of function. All SAP related activities you have to do in a set of functions because the setup function executes only one time when you give power to the Arduino board. The microcontroller first jumps to the setup function and it executes the setup related activities here. And then it goes and hangs in a loop function until the low function is executed repeatedly. Begin for latitude when boarded 11 five two zero zero hour, any values like nine six zero zero four eight zero zero are one MVP, up to two MVP, if you can use, I think, for you or not. And in the next project, let's see how to get the commands from the host so that I would cover them in the next project.

EXERCISE-001 LED CONTROL MEALY MACHINE IMPLEMENTATION PART 2

So now we understand how to set up the border for the UART communication, using a method of the serial object of Arduino. And now we were in this project to understand how to receive the data from the host in our Arduino code. For that, that is one more method available that is called a reed, just open this it reaches the incoming serial data and watch it returns here today. The first bite of incoming serial data, it returns to minus one if no data is available. So that is one more API to check whether the data is really available or not. Here it is. The example code shows that before using serial read, read the data, you can check whether the data is really available or not. Using Serial Dot available, let's explore the available Ettridge and number of bytes available to read. So if it's 10 zero, then there is no data. Now, let's use this map that stopped a serial object to program. To implement our project. So let's get back to the court and in the law function, what you do if. I'll just check for if. Is greater than zero. Then we will read about it. We can just create one temporary variable you and eight and T input something like that. Or I'll just call you rent. So the event is equal to. TD-LTE read. Just you have cereal, right? And if the event is equal to, let's say, a character or lowercase or.

```
28      // put your setup code here, to run once:
29      Serial.begin(115200);
30    }
31
32   void loop() {
33      uint8_t event;
34      // put your main code here, to run repeatedly:
35      if(Serial.available() > 0) {
36          event = Serial.read();
37          if(event == 'o'
38      }
39
40   }
```

Sketch uses 438 bytes (1%) of program storage space. M
Global variables use 9 bytes (0%) of dynamic memory,

Ben considered it as the only event. If the event is equal to all, then you should send the on event to the light state machine. Right on. You have to fend. Event. Is the court illegal to let the F R X versus the X? Then you should send off your. That's it, that's about receiving the events. So actually speaking, we should implement this using partners. So if you want to print a message from your Arduino code to the external world, then that is one API for that. There are a couple of APIs, so you can see that there's a function called print. So this prints a message without the new line character and prints a line that is printed with the new line character. And that is also right. Let's use print, Alan. So, Prince, that data to the airport and airport, so as a human readable ASCII text, followed by a Kabbage written character, it actually upends half Q30 or slash art that the carriage returns and a new line connects the two characters that attach to the message. Slashdot, followed by Flash. And So. Print, Ellen. I'll just send one message light control application. That's it. Now, let's compare this. No, it is.

```
void light_change_intensity(uint8_t pin, uint8_t intensity);
26
27 void setup() {
28    // put your setup code here, to run once:
29    Serial.begin(115200);
30    Serial.println("Light control application");
31    Serial.println("--------------------------");
32    Serial.println("Send 'x' or 'o'");
33 }
34
35 void loop() {
36    uint8_t event;
37    // put your main code here, to run repeatedly:
```

Now let's test this to test this. You can use Tiger Cat Web Web-Based simulators for small exercises, you can use this. So first, let's try with the simulator so you can just create one account and tinker cnet.com. And then after you log in, just go to the circuit and create a new circuit. So our circuit is very simple. We just need to kind of run it, take one breadboard here. And take one lead. And take one. Are we not? So I just placed a third party on the breadboard. And this is actually the captured capital. You just connect to the ground. And after that, take one resistor. So this is true value, let's keep that pool to all. So just place it here at A. And take one wire from here and connect to pin number nine. That's a pretty pin. And connect the ground here.

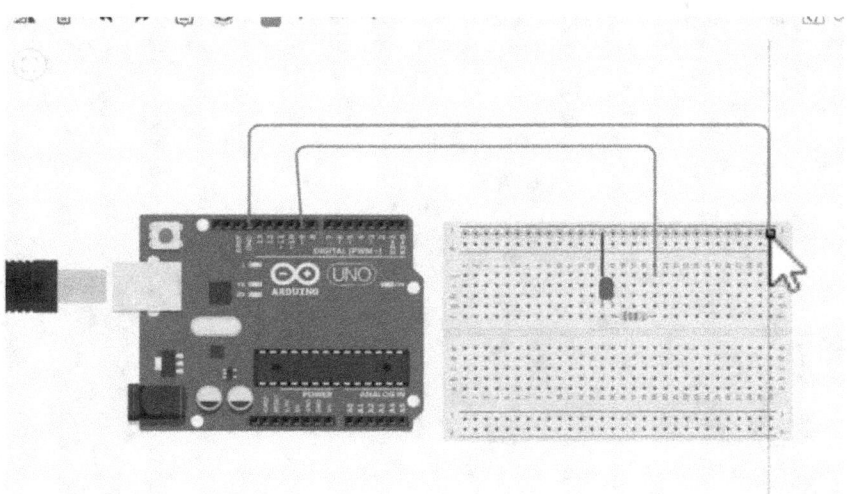

I just cannot ground up the Arduino to ground up the breadboard. That's it, that's your circuit. Very sympathetic to them. Now go to court and go to text here. Continue. Copy and paste, you are called what you wrote in the Arduino edy, but copy and paste the copy paste should work. Let's see. Start the simulation. And so they'll monitor. Send X or. That send or send. You see, the lady actually is in a dim state and spends one more time or. You can see that the intensity slightly increased. They can see it and send it one more time. They can see that intensity is changing. Now, let me fend off. It turns off. All right, so it seems to be working. So now you can try this on an Arduino board if you want and you should see something similar. So that's a flight control application implementation using Amelia's tech machine. And in the next project, we will slightly refactor the code so that we will implement that in a more state machine fashion. I'll see you in the next project.

EXERCISE-002 LED CONTROL MOORE MACHINE IMPLEMENTATION

So in the previous project, we implemented a simple milling machine for our flight control application. You can treat these exercises as just some pilot applications. So literally do more complex applications using the state machine diagrams of UML. So we will start exploring the UMC specification to draft day diagrams, and we will explore other methods to implement the state machine like the state table approach and a standard approach. Now let's, for the sake of completion, let's implement the same application using more machines. You know that that is no action during transition, right? The action or the output is produced inside of a state. What we call us entry actions are for entry actions here.

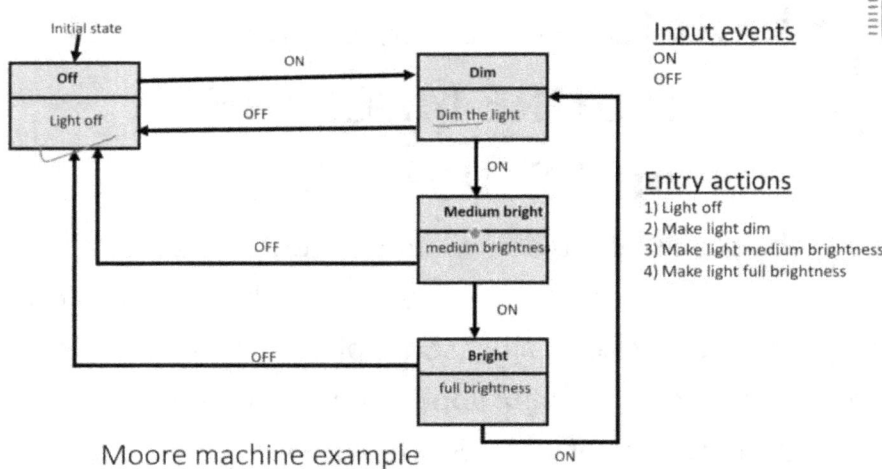

Moore machine example

And you can see here whenever the State Office enters the entry action is turned off and these are the entry actions for these states. So just create a new project and name it. Zero zero two Light control more. And here I have already implemented the code almost the same as the previous. So you have this animation for capturing events and this is part state and same global variable here.

```
1
2 enum event{
3     ON,
4     OFF
5 };
6
7 typedef enum {
8     LIGHT_OFF,
9     LIGHT_DIM,
10    LIGHT_MEDIUM,
11    LIGHT_FULL
```

Sketch uses 2168 bytes (6%) of
Global variables use 258 bytes

But I have not initialized this, so I have done that separately. And these are some macros. The new thing here is I have given a new function, run and reaction for this function. You just have to pass the state and ask for the state. This function executes the entry action. In the function here. I first need the light state machine.

```
31      run_entry_action(LIGHT_OFF);
32 }
33 void setup() {
34    // put your setup code here, to run once:
35    Serial.begin(115200);
36    Serial.println("Light control application");
37    Serial.println("-------------------------");
38    Serial.println("Send 'x' or 'o'");
39
40    light_init()
41 }
```

Sketch uses 2168 bytes (6%) of program storage spa
Global variables use 258 bytes (12%) of dynamic me

This function is to fit the first state, the first state is that if the initial stages light off when you first set the state, as for this diagram, you have to execute this entry action. So that's what I call a run entry action, and I supply that as a state and the run and reaction is right here. So a very simple switch case statement and it implements the entry action for each state. That's it. When you have to call this run reaction function, when there is a transition, so when there is a change in the state variable, that is a new function. And the loss function remains the same. I have not modified this whenever the character is received. You call this function light state machine, it means that you rent and that you rent comes a year. And for example, let's say you're a theater that you rent on here, and the current state is, let's say, light off. And if Iran is received here, then the state changes right here, the state changes. This is a transition. State changes. So before that, I actually put the current state into a temporary variable or previous state just to check whether that is any state change. Yeah, that is a state change. At the end of this function, I just compare whether the previous state is equal to the current state, if the previous state is a failed state, if it is not equal to the current state. That means that the state changes. If there is a state change, then we have to run the entry action of the new state. That's why I ran the entry action on the new state of the current state. Very simple. And there are many methods to implement the same thing. So instead of creating this run and reaction function, you can do one more trick that if you just implement one more event called entry here. You can create one more event card entry, which is an internal event, and you can implement a case on case entry like that. You can do that as well, but you have to slightly modify the application. So that's about the more machine, the output remains the same. There is no change in the output. So with that note, I would like to end this project. And from the next project onwards, let's explore the UML state machine diagrams and I would see them in the next project.

EXERCISE-003 PRODUCTIVITY TIMER DEMO

Hey, welcome back to the project. Let's do one more exercise and exercise. Name is productivity timer, so I call it a pro timer. This application tracks productive working time. That means, let's say the one use case of this application could be it tracks how many hours in a day you study or you work productively. Let's say before you start studying or while you are working, you set a time. How many minutes do you want to study? And then you can start the timer and you study hard until the timer expires and the application tracks the projected time, and at the end of the day, you will come to know how many minutes or how many hours you spent productively in a given day. But what is the fair use case of this application? And so we are going to build this application in this court using the state machine approach. Before that, for now, let us know what are the requirements we need to implement in this application. I will explain the requirement by giving you a small demo. So whenever you reset the application, as you can see it beeps, the application beeps and it asks you to set the time. Here you can see that it is asking you to set the time.

So there are a couple of components in this application. All these components are actually connected to the Arduino on board. And here you can see that it's 16 crosses to Alfred. There are three user buttons, a couple of resistors to interconnect all these components. That is a buzzer, an actual buzzer, and that is potentially a meter. Its purpose is just to set the contrast for the LCD. And now let me explain about the three other buttons for this button is increment time, but this is deployment time button and this is start or pause the timer button whenever I press this button. You can see that. You know, the minute field actually increases for here on the timer display, it has two sections. This section is for second and this section is per minute. There is no other field in this

display. So whenever you press this button, increment time. The number of minutes. Increases when you press the second button. It actually meant the minute filled. So like that, let's say you set the timer for 20 minutes and you can use this button to start the countdown. Like that? And if you want to pause this timer, let's say you want to take a break, then you can pause this timer by pressing the start or pause button. It pauses and if you want to continue again, then you can use the same start button and it continues from that. After that, if you want to abort this operation. Then you can do that by pressing these two buttons simultaneously like this. You can see that it went to the initial mode and it started beeping again.
Now if you want to know the product, two time statistics. When the application is idle more, this is idle mode of the application, when the application is idle more, you can use the start or pause button to know the product do time you have spent.

You can see that that time is just 38 seconds. And that's about this application. So let's first implement this application using flat state machines, and the state machine comprises a couple of states. You can visualize a couple of states here. First of all, this state, the initial state, is nothing but the ideal mode. Or you can consider it as the ideal state. Right? The ideal state for when it is in the Iowa State, it just beeps for a few seconds, and it took off the user to set that time. And whenever I press these buttons. So this could be more. timeThat more or something. Here. In this mode, it's actually a response to the events generated by these. Increment time and deployment time buttons. And after that, when you hit the Start button. The countdown starts. For this can be visualized as the applications. Counting down, Morgan. Our countdown mock. And when the timer is counting down, it doesn't respect the inclement time or decrement time event generated by these buttons. Of course, buttons are the bones to using soft ready bombs. So I have not used any hardware and the bouncing components here. When it is counting down, it doesn't respect these differences. And then when it is counting down, if you press the starter button here, it pauses. This could be another mod or another state in the application like that. And whenever I press these two buttons simultaneously, it generates that event and everything starts from the beginning like that. I hope now you understand about the various requirements we have to implement in this project. And don't worry about the circuit diagram, so I will show you how to make a circuit for this application in later projects.

UML SIMPLE AND COMPOSITE STATES

All right, so now you saw the demo. So these are our project requirements. There will be a plus button, which is used to intimate the time the number of minutes should increase. Whenever you press that button and the minus button, then I get two buttons that should decrease the time the number of minutes should decrease. And the third button is the start or pause button that is used to start or pause the countdown. And it can also be used to show statistics. When the countdown is passed, the time settings can be done, that time can be modified. Press the plus and minus button simultaneously to about the running timer. So the application must be fought 20 times when it returns to idle mode and when the application is in idle mode. Pressing the start or pause button should show the start for one second, and it should auto return to idle. So don't worry, all these things represent using state actors. First of all, what state? So we are going to model this application using many states. But before doing that, let's explore what exactly the state is and how you arrive at fixing a state for your application. What is the state? A state represents a distinct stage of an object lifecycle. Here, an object is nothing, but it's an instance of a class or it's an instance of a structure. So you can imagine something like that in a programming language that has no concept of classes. You can think of it as an instance of a structure. Basically, if the terminology used in all that is object oriented programming and object in its lifecycle can process through a number of stages in an application in a formal specification 2.3.1, the specification phase a state model, the situation in the execution of a state machine behavior during which some invariant condition holds. In most cases, this condition is not explicitly defined, but it is implied usually through the name associated with a state. Now how do you arrive at fixing a state? One technique is to map different scenarios through which an object lifecycle passes into a number of states. For example, in our time or application, we have seen the demo right. And in the demo, we have seen our application process through many stages, and we can imagine these scenarios in our application. Sometimes the application is in idle mode when it is in idle mode. It just asks the user to set the time it shows some initial display. It beeps and it may blink some text. So that's the idle mode and then a user starts adjusting the time. And that could be a time set scenario. So that's the scenario that the timer is actually down counting. And then there is a path scenario, and in one scenario, it will be showing the statistics. So these are the different scenarios through which the pro timeout application object lifecycle passes through all these scenarios. You can map into different states in a state machine diagram.

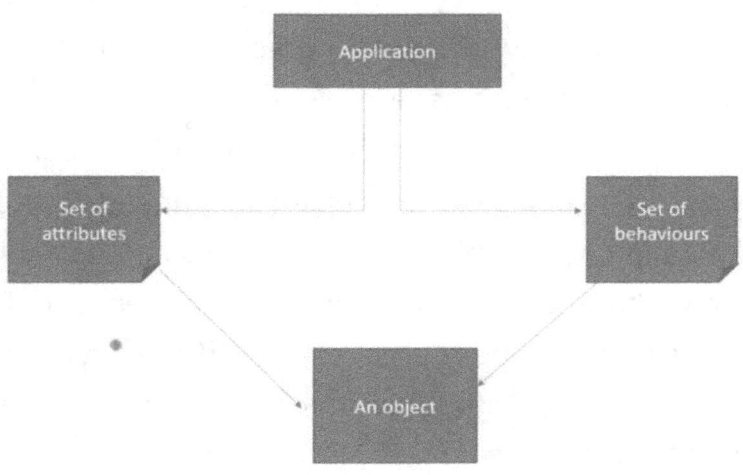

So not that all these states belong to an object, an application may have different objects, have that said, an object is nothing but in C programming language, you can just think of it as an instance of a structure. An application may have different objects, so an application also definitely will have one associated object. That's why states are associated with the lifecycle of an object and an object is nothing but its collection of set of attributes and said behavior attributes are nothing but structure are class member elements. For example, in their application, there could be a few structure or class attributes to track the current time elapsed, time to time, etc. An object also comprises set up behaviors or matters, or you can call it as member functions, and those functions act upon those attributes. Basically, what I want to clarify here is that a number of states belong to a lifecycle of an object, and an application may have different objects. And for each object, that could be a separate state machine model. So now how do you create a state? Very simple. As for the mass spec. Draw around the current rectangle, create a horizontal name compartment and give a name that is unique within the state machine diagram. Very simple. Now let's draw it. And there are also different types of state as per the specification. So one is a simple state component state, a submachine state for this exercise will just be a simple state. So they're not bothered about using a compounded state. But comparing the state actually makes our state machine diagram much simpler. You can reduce the clutter in the state machine diagram using composite state, but we'll keep that for separate discussion for this exercise with just you, simple state. And whenever I explain various transitions and other things while doing this exercise, all those terminologies are with respect to a simple state. So what is a simple state if a state doesn't have any such states transition regions, sub machines, then it's a simple state. So now let's go to the statue and let's draw a couple of simple states for a project. So these are different scenarios for soccer applications. Now let's consider these as our states in our state machine diagram for this application. I'm going to use the Ashtar tool, and here you can create a new project after that. Go here and click on this and go to create a diagram. And like the state machine diagram here, and let's rename this. So I'll just give the probe time. Now, let's create five simple states for all these situations. Application. What you do is here in this panel, you'll get various elements to draw UML state machines so you can pick one. So here I would love to go for a simple state. Simple State is also simply called as a state whenever I call a state. It just means that it's a simple state. So just select that by clicking on it, and then you just click on this canvas that fits. So this is a simple state with a name compartment. Now, let's give one name for this. Let me call this aside. And we actually need five simple state threats. Just arrange something like this. This is one state. Second state. I'll call this as I state and the third state, you can just copy and paste it. And. Another state. And another state like this, I'll call this as I do, and I will call this time set. And this is a countdown. And this says pause, let's say. And this has stepped. So we actually created five simple states for our application. So a simple state can have two or more compartments. What we draw here is a simple state with two compartments. This is a named compartment, and the name compartment should hold the name of the state as a string. And that name should be unique within the state diagram. You cannot duplicate the name of a state, nor can two states have the same name. Now what is the composite state? So a state which has such a state is called a composite state. A composed state contains at least one region.

There are two types of composite states. One is a simple composite state and another one is an orthogonal state. Or you can call it an orthogonal composite state. A simple composite state has exactly one region. By using composite state, you can express a state hierarchy in your state machine diagrams using composite state makes you a state machine. Diagrams are simply what we call a state chart more comprehensible by reducing the number of transitions between states. You can use a composite state to reduce the clutter of your state machine diagram. It makes a state machine less messy. Now, let's see some examples here. If not, this state is a simple state. It has got no region and it has got no such states. That means it has got no child state inside of it. All it has is two compartments. The first one is a named compartment. Second one, we call it, have activity compartments about which are tabulators. So whereas S1, here is a composite state. Why? Because it has got child states.

Example

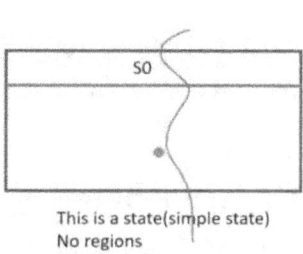

This is a state(simple state)
No regions
No sub states

Any state enclosed within a region of a composite state is called a substate of that composite state [OMG® UML 2.5.1]

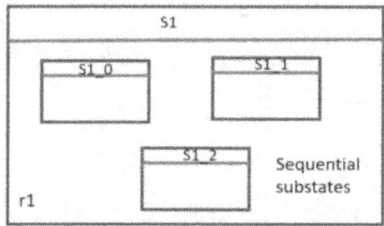

S1 is a composite state
S1 has 1 region
S1_x are sub states of S1
S1 is a superstate of S1_x
S1_x are simple states

All these are child states, are we call it out, substate whenever such states appear. It forms a region, so that's why we can call something like this if one has one region identified by Ottawa. As per the specification. So this is what the specification says about a composite state here S1 is the composite state. S1 has one region to host or to enclose the sub state. And all these. States are substates of F1, so these are nothing but simple states in nature. These are states of F1. F1 is also called the super state of these states like that, here F1 has exactly one region. That's why it is also called a simple composite state. Now, let's see one more example. So here again, F1 is a simple composite state white because they have got one region and F1 zero F1 underscore one and F1 underscore two. All these are sub states of F1. And here these two are simple states, or you can call something like this. So these two are simple substrates of one, and if you want to underscore two is a composite substrate of S1. Here is what underscore two is a simple composite state, and it is also a fact state op ed for. And if one underscore, too, is a superstate of these two simple states and yes, one under Scotty has exactly one region. So this is a region of this compounded state and this is a region of this composite state. And here these are called as direct substate al S1, and these are called direct substrate of Air Force One underscore two. But these two states are also called as indirect substates of S1. So these are some of the terminologies involved while describing a composite state. So more on this. We'll see later.

UML STATE MACHINE INTERNAL STATE ACTIVITIES(ENTRY EXIT DO)

Hey, welcome back to the project. In the previous project we explored the simple state, the composite state, and we also understood how to draw a simple state, its name compartment. And now let's explore the internal activities compartment. We know a state mission diagram if you just consider the state. Here, you can mention the internal activities. This is an internal activity compartment. Now, let's understand what exactly is an internal activity. So what are these internal activities, the internal activities define the internal behavior of a state. Each state can have its own internal behavior. And the internal activities compartment, a whole list of internal behaviors associated with the state. Now how to represent the internal activity of a state. So very simple. The syntax is something like that. First, you have to write the behavior type label. Or this is a label for the internal activity, followed by a flash character. And then you had to write that behavior, expression, behavior, expression is nothing, but it's an action. It could be any programming expression or any executable programming statement, or it could be a function called something like that. So in a simple form, this is nothing but a label. Class action. So something like that. What are the labels entry exit to do are internal activities. Labels are keywords defined in the U-M's specification.

Internal activities compartment

- This compartment holds a list of internal behaviors associated with a state
- Each entry has the following format:
  - <behavior-type-label>['/' <behavior-expression>]
- Example :
  'entry,' 'exit', 'do' are internal activities labels or keywords defined in the UML. Do not use these keywords to represent events in the state machine diagram

And these labels should only appear in the internal activities compartment. You should not use these keywords outside the internal activities compartment to represent application specific events. So these are meant to represent internal activities. Now let's understand what these entries exist and do? Label internal activity labels. These labels identify the circumstances under which the behavior specified by the behavior expression is executed. I mean, the label decides when this action or the behavior expression should be executed. Now let's understand the entry level behavior identified by behavior expression will be executed upon entry into the state. Whenever you are object lifecycle, let's say, enters into a state. At that point, the behavior expression identified by the entry level will be executed in chart use. The entry keyword if the state has an entry, action and reaction is a thing, but it's an action which will get executed when the object enters into the state. It's the one time execution. Now, exit labor behavior identified by behavior expression will be executed upon exit from the state, using the exit keyword if a state has exit action, so whenever the object leaves the state, then the exit action will be executed and the exit action is identified by the internal activity label exit. And now let's understand that due labor behavior identified by the behavior expression will be executed as long as the object is in the state or until the computation specified by the expression is completed. The due label represents ongoing behavior, whereas entry and exit actions are executed only once their due label represents an action, which is ongoing as long as the object is in the state. Now, whether you are really required is an internal activity or not. That depends on your project and how you design your state machine. All these are optional, actually our state Minotaur entry or exit actions. It may just have to do action, or it may not have due action. It may have just been an entry action. These are all optional things that you can do inside a state. Is an example of the internal activity compartment, so we are going to do this next in our state machine diagram. But I'm just giving you an example. So don't worry about this transition, and also everything will be explained later here.

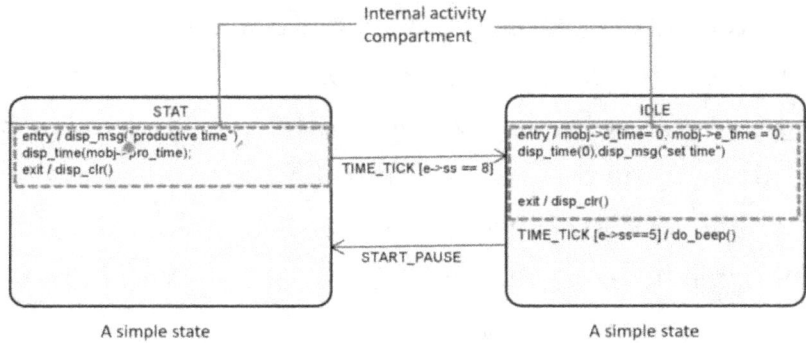

You can see that when the object is in that state, this is a reaction to these to our end reaction separated by a comma. These entry actions are identified by the label and. And that is the exit labor and the action displayed clearly. Whenever the object enters into this state. So what it does is it displays a message onto the LCD. This is a message. And it also displays a value of one variable onto the display, and whenever the object leaves the state, it clears the display. That's the exit action for the state. Similarly, here, when the object enters the idle state, it actually insulates some variable to zero. So these are actually objects attributed to all these objects. As I mentioned in the previous video, an object is nothing but a collection of attributes and methods or behaviors. So this is a main application object that is the main application object and these are its variables and it's being initialized that faint reaction for the state. And it also displays the time at zero and displays the message set time. So all these are entry actions separated by commas. And when this state is left, this is exit action and exit action is displayed clearly. And this is something different. This is an internal transition. So this is not an internal activity. This is an internal transition and about which I will talk later. The internal activities are always identified by the labels. These are the labels. And in the next project, let's understand about internal transitions. I'll see in the next project.

UML STATE MACHINE TYPES OF TRANSITIONS

In the previous project, we explored the internal activities and the entry exit. All these are internal activities of a state and now in this project, let us understand the internal transition. So the internal transition is a way of executing certain actions which are identified by the behavior expression. So when a certain trigger happens, a certain trigger happens in the system and when that guard condition evaluates to be true, if the guard condition is mentioned, the trigger here is nothing. But if the cause is that incident, you can consider it as an event. The internal transition syntax looks something like this. We can simply write something like this T in the bracket. This guard condition is actually optional and then the action. So if the event occurrence matches the trigger and guard of the internal transition evaluation to be true, then behavior identified by behavior, the expression will be executed without exiting or re-entering the state in which it is defined. So in the internal transition, the object doesn't leave its current state. There is no exit from the state when there is no exit from the state. Of course, there is no question of re-entering the state. So that's what we call internal transition. So when the trigger happens, the trigger is nothing, but it's a different event. Another name for trigger is event. An event could be an asynchronous event, or it could be a synchronous time based event or something like that when this event happens. And when the guard values to be truly predictable, then this action will be executed without exiting or re-entering the state. Now, let's see one example. Here we have a state called idle. And you can see that in this compartment, so you can imagine it here. You can call this the internal activity compartment, so all the internal activity entries are mentioned first and then this compartment, you can call it the internal transmission compartment. And here is an example where you can see this is actually a trigger. This is the guard and this is the action. So when this trigger happens or when this event happens in the system, and if this guard turns out to be true, then only this action will be taken without equity or reentry into the state. There is no exit from the state, so that's what we call the internal transition. What the statement says here.

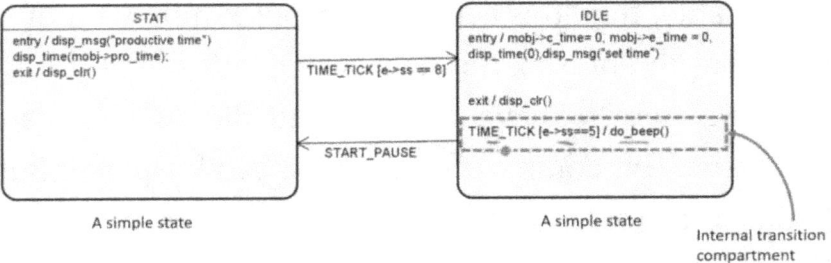

So whenever the time to happen and if some variable value is fire, then just do a beep that fits. It's like that. Let's understand exactly what the transition is. Now let's understand types of transitions as part of a specification. There are different types of transitions external, local and internal for what we just explored was internal. Now let's see what exactly is an external transition in the external transition. The source state is exited due to the incident of trigger. The optional action associated with the transition is executed, followed by execution of exit action ops estate developer. An external transition signifies a change of state or an object situation in the object lifecycle. When the state is changed now, the object is ready to process new set up events and it can now execute new set up actions. Transition thought denoted by lines with arrowheads leading from a thawed state to a targeted state. For example, all transitions, whether it is the local transition, external transition, internal transition, the general syntax is the same. This is a syntax and this can be in short, you can simply write like this. When the event happens and then the guard condition, which is a Boolean expression. This is a Boolean expression. If this condition evaluates to be true, then the action will be taken. So this event is also called Death Trigger. In this example, you can hear when the current state of the object is countdown, let's say the current state is countdown. And if the event starts, pause is refuted.

Transition

- Transition syntax :
- {<trigger>}* ['[' <guard>']'] [/<behavior-expression>]
- {<trigger>}[guard]/action
- event[guard]/action

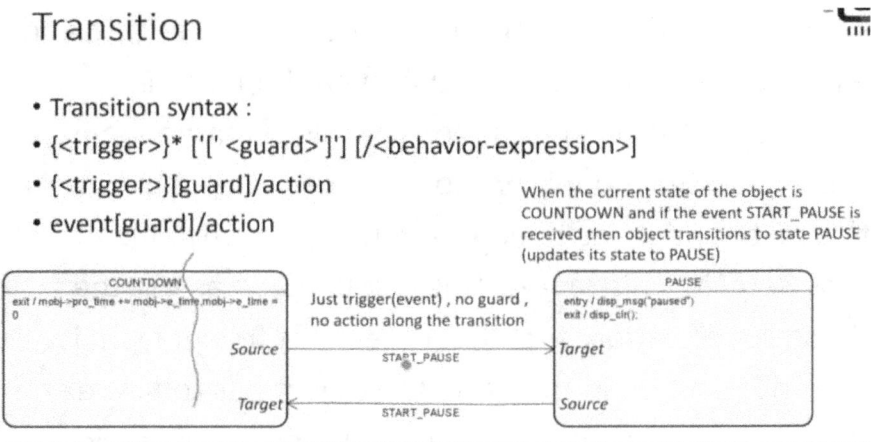

We know that when we press the start pause button, the state machine receives the start pause event, so how to do that later? And if the object stays, the current state is a countdown, and if the start paused event is received, then that is actually an external transition for an external transition to the past state. What do you mean by a transition transition is a program which is nothing, but it's just updating a state variable once a variable state changes to path. It's like that. So after the transition, the exit action of this state will be executed by the exit action of the Fourth Estate. You can see that this is just a trigger. This is just an event. So there is no God condition that is no action. Such transitions are possible. The guard and these actions are all optional. Even the trigger is optional, so any combination could be possible. So now let's see one example for external transition. Consider this example here. There are two states: idle and time set. So now let's assume the object currently is in idle state and when it is denied the state, this event happens in inclement time. Event happens. If this event happens, there is no God condition, so the object has to exit from this state and it has to go to the new state. That is the time set with this target. This is sought. So as per the Yuma specification, first, the object has to exit from its current state. So in this case, the object has to first exit the idle state. So exit means completing its exit action when the exit actions are completed. That means the object has fully exited from its state. That's why first, the exit action will be executed right, followed by the execution of that transition action. So this is a transition action. Second, this will be executed, followed by executing the entry action of the newly entered state. This executes at the end. That's how the transition takes place. This is also mentioned in the Yuma Spec. Let's go to the specification at page number 360 here, so you can read about this transition execution sequence at this section. Here it is. There is a diagram and you need not remember all those things. So you just come to the specification and you just look at this picture. And here they have shown one compound transition example. So don't worry, it is very simple. Here it is. That is one one, one simple state. So let's assume that the object is currently in one simple state and the trigger happens to trigger a thing. When this happens here, the object has to leave the state S1 one. So this is the order of execution of action. First x f one one is executed x F1 one is nothing but exit action that is executed first, followed by the transition action D1. The T1 is executed next and after that, what happens? It goes out of this composite state S1. So if one is a parent or it's a super state of S1 one, right? Exiting this composite state also means that exiting from this F-1 composite state, that's why exit action of this state is executed, that is X-1 here. So that means ask, but the specification bag with ActionScript executed right from the innermost state. This is a normal state to exit actions are executed beginning from innermost to outermost state. And after that, it goes to the exit point. This notation will explode later. And after that, too. OK. And now it enters a new composite state. That is one.

And here you can see that its target is actually this state at one one one. That's the target state.

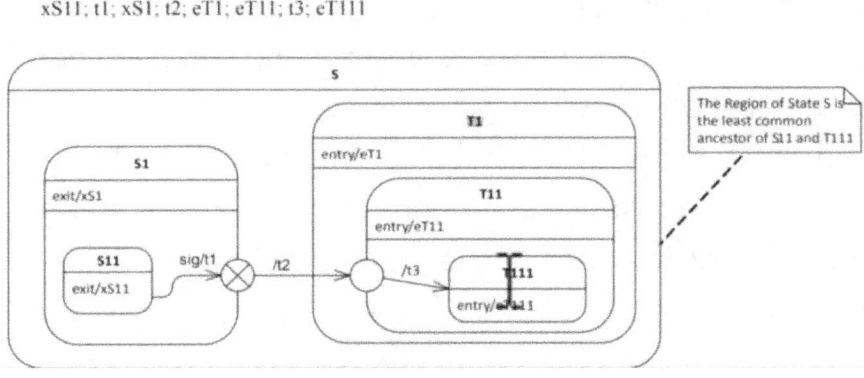

So before reaching the targets, it has to go through all these other intermediate states and it executes all the entry actions which come along the way, it executes the reaction action one. E one one. T3, that transition action A. one, one one. So now you can understand from this picture that. Bench actions are executed right from the outermost state toward the innermost state during entry into a competitive state. So whereas exiting a for the state involves executing exit actions right from the innermost state towards the outcome of state. Now, let's see one more example. So let's consider this transition here. Let's assume the object is currently in a poor state and the decrement time event happens. When this event happens, it is actually guarded by this guard condition.

The guard condition, which is written inside the square brackets and guard, is nothing, but it's a Boolean expression and it must evaluate to true for transition to fire. If this condition becomes true, then only this transition will fire. That means that action will be executed first, then the transition action, then the entry reactions. Only if the God condition evolves to be true, so if the God condition evaluates to false, if this event happens, then that is not transition at all. The object will not leave this state. No exit from the state. No exit means no execution of transition action, no entry to the new state. It's just like this event is ignored and sometimes external transition may happen just because of a trigger. The guards and the transition actions are optional, actually. Here you can see that this is just a trigger only trigger that may also cause the transition. And sometimes transition may happen just because of a trigger and got that transition action, maybe absent here. So when the time ticked you and happened, that transition happens only if this guard conditioned your values to be true. The next type of transition is the internal transition about which I explain in the earlier project. The internal transition for the specification says this kind of transition can only be defined if the source. What is a state? It could be a simple state or a composite state or a submission state. What the specification says is internal is a special case of local transmission that is the transition fact that the state is never exited. And that's not re-entered, which means that no exit or entry behaviors are executed when this transition is executed. In this example, this is an internal transition. And here this is an internal transition. This is an internal transition. So we'll try to use this transition when we attempt to dry the state pension diagram, part of a project. So now let's understand what local transition is.

Types of transitions

- Local: local is the opposite of external, meaning that the Transition does not exit its containing state (and, hence, the exit Behavior of the containing State will not be executed). However, for local Transitions, the target Vertex must be different from its source Vertex. A local Transition can only exist within a composite State. [OMG® UML 2.5.1]

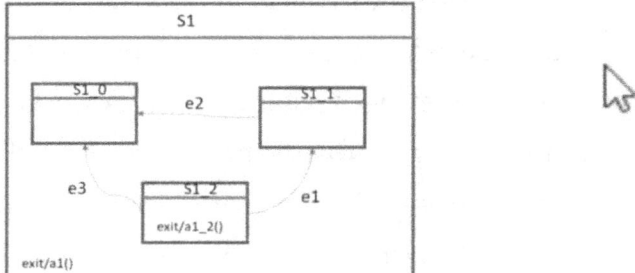

Please note that local transition applies to a composite state. So in this diagram, you are seeing S1, which is a composite stage, and this composite state has three such states. So these are three substrates, and all these transitions are local transitions of S1. The specification says something like this local is the opposite of external meaning that the transition does not exist. It's containing state and hence the exit behavior of the containing state will not be executed. However, for local transition, the target vortex must be different from its source vortex. A local transition can only exist within a composite state. These are local transitions off S1, and these transitions will not cause. Exit off S1. And there is no question of executing the exit action fast one. But these are, of course, the external transition for the substance and for local transitions. The target vortex must be different from its source. What watch here, for example, in this case, though, this is a source vortex. This is the target vortex like that so few points to remember here. Please note that due activity behavior commences execution when the state is entered only after the state entry behavior has completed. If your state has both do activity, behavior and entry behavior, then entry behavior has to be completed first before commencing the do activity behavior. So entry exit cannot be associated with any transitions. You cannot transition during internal activity and after that, if all transitions into a state, perform the same action, push the common action inside the state to make it an entry action. For example, here there are three transitions e 183 into this state and all these transitions. They have a common action F1 instead of writing death. You can transform this diagram into this one. You push that common action inside the state to make it an entry action. So this actually looks a lot neater than this diagram. And also, you can get rid of code duplication, and the core maintenance becomes easier here. That is one place you have to maintain rather than at three places, as it was before. So that was one hint when you have to implement the entry action. Similarly, power transitions leaving a state. Far from the same action, Bush, the common action inside the state to make it an exit action. For example, here. These are the living transitions from this state, and they perform the same action, one instead of that, you push all those actions inside the state to make it an exact action. So that's the hint when you have to create the exit action.

EVENTS AND SIGNALS

Now in this project, let's understand what exactly is an event, or you can also call it as a trigger. So even for nothing, what incidents are stimuli by which a state machine can be triggered? Basically, the asynchronous incidents are synchronized incidents up to application. It can be abstract as an event in the state machine. As you have already seen, events may cause transitions, and a transition could be an external one, or it could be an internal one. Let's take an example of a microwave oven. You open the door to open it. And when that incident happens, event will be generated and it will be transported to the farm where inside the oven and the firmware asks for its current state may take some actions, such as it may turn the heater off, turn the light on, etc. and closing of the door is another incident, and it may have its associated set of actions. Set the timer, use the button given in the control panel of the I want to set the timer to start our operation, etc.

Events(Trigger)

What is an event?
Events are incidents or a stimulus by which a state machine can be triggered; Incidents are abstracted as events

In state machine events cause transitions(external or internal)

Incidents in the operation of a microwave oven
1) Opening door; Heater off , lights on
2) Closing door; lights off
3) Set timer;   manage time
4) Start ; heater ON

So all these are events and events may cause transition after the state machine diagram, and it may have its associated set of actions. An event usually has two components. One is a signal component and another one is signal parameters. Or you can also call that signal values. The second component is actually optional. Let's see some examples. If you consider the application, we have got three buttons plus minus and a third button start are part pressing of these buttons to generate events. So when you press the plus button, let's say it generates one event, and that event has two components. One is a signal component, so pressing the plus button generates the event. Signal is increment time. It is just a name, the name you have chosen after your convenience. Here, this event signifies Byte Signal attribute that the user has pressed a button which increases the time, and the signal doesn't have any associated signal values that parameter.

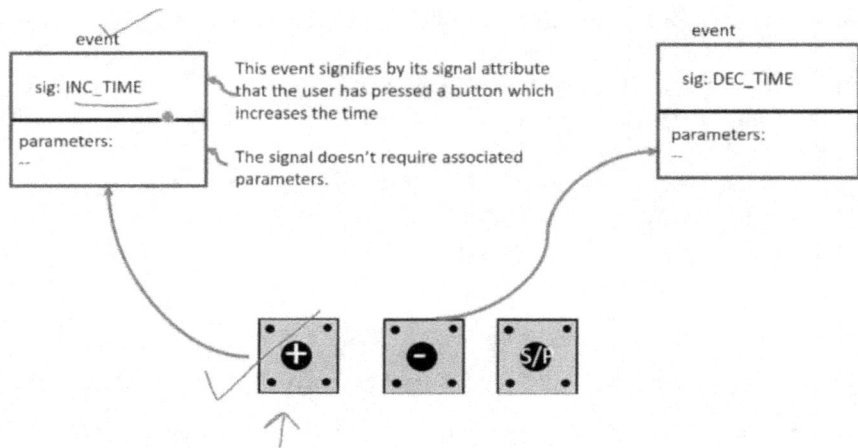

That's fine, because that is optional. And similarly, if you press the minus button, it generates another event to signal decrement time. And in this case, this event also doesn't require any parameters. Or you can write that you want something like this, let's say it doesn't matter which button the user presses either plus button or minus button, you generate the event time change, so you generate that event to signal Lamees. Let's say time underscore changes and then use the parameter, let's say direction to indicate which button really has been pressed by the user. So you can create an enumeration and you can distinguish by using these values up or down.

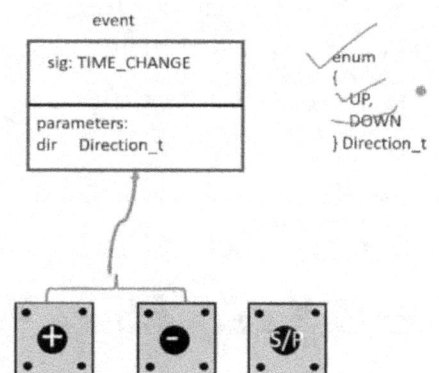

- This event signifies by its signal attribute that the user has pressed a button that changes time.
- The signal has an associated parameter that encodes whether the user has pressed a button that increases time(UP) or decreases time(DOWN)

So these will become the signal values. This event signifies byte signal attribute that the user has crafted a button that changes to time, and the signal has an associated parameter that encodes whether the user has pressed a button that includes time or decreased time. So you can also do something like this. Let's take another example of a calculator. Calculator has got its number pad, and on the number pad it has got, you know, 10 digits, zero to nine couple of operators. And the result button, cetera. So how do you encode pressing of any digit? You can do something like this. You can generate one event. Only one event will signal them is that they digit zero to nine and the parameter to signify which digit has been pressed by the user. So instead of creating one event for each digit, you can collectively generate one event and use the parameter component of the event to distinguish between which digit has been pressed by the user. Similarly, you can keep one event to signal the pressing of the operator's button. So like in programming, you can use structures in them to model events off your application.

EXERCISE-003 STATES AND INITIAL PSEUDO STATES

All right, so now let's continue our exercise. Number two, OK? The productivity timer application so far we have understood that equipment, the project requirements and these are the project requirements. I have already shown you the demo. And these are the different situations and we are converting these situations into states. So we have already drawn this on the software. And now let's look at the various events which you are going to use for this application. So the user activity when the user processes the plus button that you can generate is increment time so that you won't name the signal name.

Events

User activity	Event generated : SIGNAL	Parameters	note
Press '+' button	INC_TIME	none	This event gets posted to the state machine whenever the user presses the + button
Press - button	DEC_TIME	none	This event gets posted to the state machine whenever the user presses the - button
Press S button	START_PAUSE		This event gets posted to the state machine whenever the user presses the S/P button
Press + and – button together	ABRT		This event gets posted to the state machine whenever the user presses the + and – buttons together
	TIME_TICK	ss (sub second)	This event is system generated for every 100ms ss parameter value can vary between 1 to 10

And it has no associated parameters. And when the user presses the negative button, the event would be generated and its signal name is decrement time, and it has no associated parameters. And after that, whenever a user presses the starter pause button, the signal generator starts with a difficult pause. And users can press plus and minus buttons simultaneously, which is about. And also that is one more event time underscore tech. OK, so this is not a user generated event. This is system generated. And it has got one associated parameter F stands for for a second this event, the system generated for every hundred milliseconds. So the f parameter value will be in between one to 10. One means 100 milliseconds, 10 mins. Thousand milliseconds, that means one second. Well, explore more on this later. Only time in Iran has got one associated parameter, that is effort. Also, we need to use some extent to state variables in this application, so extreme state variables are nothing but those variables which appear throughout the state machine diagram. These variables will help us to capture various data, and it will help us to, you know, take decisions on the state. Machine diagrams help us to draw state machines in such a way that we can reduce the number of states used and we can implement various decision making on the state machine, etc.. I'm going to take three variables for this application. The current time variable holds the time that the user has selected. You know that the user can select the time using the plus or minus button, right? So that's a user effect time. OK, that's the current time. Next variable is elapsed. The time variable holds the number of seconds that's been elapsed. And after that pro underscored time, that's another variable which holds the product to time spent by the user front desk or time used to show the statistics. You can use more variables if you want to, but currently I just stick with these three variables and all these variables we keep under this structure. The main application structure, I call it astro timer and difficulty. So all these variables will be kept under this structure, and this structure may have more variables. So we'll see when we need any variables. So we will put that variable in this structure. All right. So the state machine, what we're going to draw now is for this application object. The state machine, the various states, which have been included in our state machine diagram, traces the life cycle of this application object.

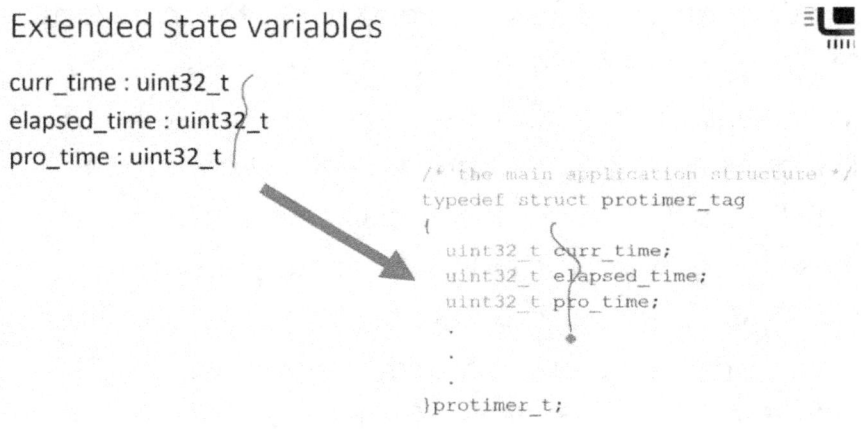

OK, and now let's get back to the software and let's complete our state machine diagram. Now let's get back to the software and this is our state machine. And we have already named all these states. But what is a first date when you give power to this application or when this application runs for the first time? Initially, which state it comes to that is very important that can be designated by using this symbol here, a black dot symbol circle filled with black color so that what we call in the umph specification, it is called as initials Utah State. We'll explore more on that later. So just click on that, and after that, you just select the appropriate place here and place that initial pseudo state. And after that. You just use this arrow and you just pull towards the state, which has to be the initial state of your state machine diagram, and for our application, the idea state is the initial state that I would just put towards that state, OK? When you look at this diagram, the signify fact idle state is the initial state. OK, so now let's begin drawing the transition for internal transitions, internal activities right from this state. OK. There are many feudal states as falsification, and the initial state tries to join the state history. So let's plot these things when the right time comes, okay? But what exactly is the initial pseudo state? This is the specification facing the initial pseudo state that represents a starting point for a region. If it is the point from which the execution of contained behavior commences when the region is entered, the world region comes into picture, then that is the relationship of super state and the substitute, right? But our state machine, we said that it is just a flat state machine, which consists of a couple of simple states. But if you look at this software, it actually places all these simple states inside a super state right there, the super state and outer shell. You can see it when you zoom out right? That's why this becomes the region. This is a region. And when this region is entered from the external world, this initial pseudo state signifies that this state to be entrusted, our initially this state should be entered okay. So that's the meaning of that. Let's go back to the definition. It is the thought for, at most one transition. Remember that drawing another transition from here to here is not possible. OK, so that gives you the idea, though it says that an initial zero state can have, at most, one outgoing transition. So this software actually does all this safely. So which may have an associated affect behavior, but not an associated trigger or guard. So in this diagram, this is called the initial transition and the initial transition cannot have trigger, cannot have guard. And when you select this transition, you can see that at the. Left-Hand side, you can mention the trigger guard and action for this transition, but this transition is the initial transition, right? This transition is originating from the initials Utah State and asked by the specification you cannot have associated trigger our guard. So that's why the far easier transition you cannot use trigger guard perfection here, you can only mention the action. So what could be our initial action? We may have to initialize our extended state variables, so what we do is. I'll call the main object an object. OK. An object is the main object, our pointer to the main object, and we are writing the state machine for this object. So the action for the initial transition could be left to initialize the state variable value to zero. I would just make the current time equal to zero. And more B.J. lapsed time is equal to zero, and ammo B.J. product to time is equal to zero. These are the actions associated with the initial transition. The object and these are the attributes of the object, I just initialize them to zero.

EXERCISE-003 DEFINING STATES ENTRY AND EXIT ACTIONS

So to reduce the clutter on the diagram instead of using full variable names, I'll just call this as feed time each time and Pete Time. I'll just use chart names. Now let's design this idle state. As per the demo, whenever you give power to the application. So the LCD display should display that time, and the time component shows zero eight zero zero minute. So that's why whenever the application comes to the idle state, it should display something. That's why we will now define the entry activity for this state, either state. So just click on that state and here at the left side, you can see entry to exit. Now let's define that entry action. One entry action could be. Display the time on the LCD, I'll just call display time, display time is helper action. It's a function. It's a helper action or just an action which displays the time. But initially, whenever the application is in the idle state, it should display zero. So that's quite the argument. I sent just zero. The display time function displays. As for the argument being passed to the argument being passed in zero display time and also, as you can see in the demo, it also shows one message to the user right set time display message that Anna the helper action function. And here, display the message, I'll just send the message at a set time. So these are the two and two. And what could be the next entry action? We should also make our mortgage. Current time is equal to zero and also a mortgage. Lapsed, the time is equal to zero.

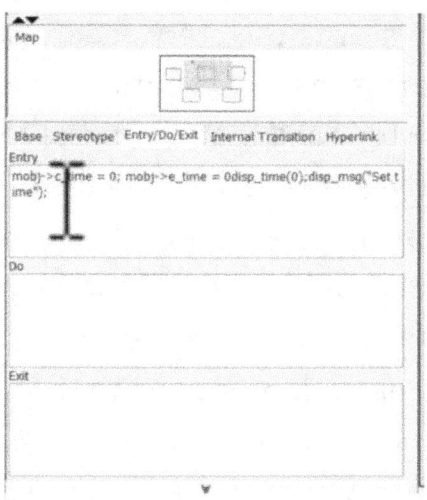

Because it's in the eye of the state, that is why I would say these are the entry action and Amobi current time is equal to zero elapsed time is equal to zero and display the time at zero and display message set time. So these are the interactions and scenes that we are already doing. See, time is equal to zero, each time is equal to zero, he added. Is not required. That's very modest. I would just make part time equal to zero here. That's our reaction to this. That's great. So now we finish the interaction for the state. Now let's go to that state. So whenever the application comes to the timethat state it should display the current time. So let's define one entry reaction for this. Just select the state, go to the entry and here entry action will be displayed. Time. And you have to just display the current time, see time. So whenever an application comes to the state, it displays the time that was set. Now let's write the entry action for prostate. So whenever you press the pause button, you can see here the countdown stops and that is a message passed. Now, let's do that in the pause state. Now the reaction for this would be. Display message. And it doesn't respect the countdown so that we'll see how that happens later. But whenever the application comes to this date, it should send a message past. Now, let's go to the countdown for the countdown. It should countdown every one second. So that means whenever the state receives the Typekit rent, there will be a counting down process. That's why I have no idea whether this requires the end of the action or not. So if you don't have any idea, then you just leave it. But I don't want to find any reaction to this. Now let's go to the fattest state fat state, as you can see in the demo.

So whenever you press the starter pause button, it shows the product to your time, and it also displays the message product to time. That makes it clear that you have to do something in the entry of this state. So that's why I like this and got the reaction. What shall we do here? As you can see in the demo, it should show the productive time in the first line of the display and it should send a message at the second line. That means we have to take action for you. So display time and mobile. Peter Pan of Time and Gil Chroma display. Message. Product tour time. So whenever you have two or more actions to do, then you can do one thing and each action with the semicolon. That looks nice. So here. So after this line, that one action, you give a semicolon the second action. I'll just give a semicolon. And then the third and fourth action. So here also. He just terminated this with a semicolon. Now, let's define some exit actions. Let's start with. So the ideal stage during the entreat is to display something, and when the applications receive some event, it goes to some other state and it may display something else. That's why I think whoever displayed something on the display, they should clearly so while exiting that state, the state has to clear whatever message it has displayed on the display. So that's why I would define the exact action for this state act. OK, I'll just go to the exit section here for the exit action of display clear. Let receive whether more actions are required or not, but currently I can only think of clearing the display whenever this state is left. And for the fat state, also the exit, that action would be displayed clearly. And what about the times that state? It may be required, so for the time for that, I'm not going to define any exit action for the time being, so see later for the pause. Also, it has displayed something. Pause it right? So it should clear it up. So I would define an exit action for this. Display clear. And for the countdown, also, I'm not sure whether I have to define any exit action or not ventilator. Now we have partially implemented the entry and exit actions. Let's do some transition.

EXERCISE-003 DRAWING STATE TRANSITIONS

Welcome back. In the previous project, we brought some entry and exit ActionScript to various states. Now let's implement that transition, and the number of transitions we draw per state depends on the number of events the state left to the state processes, and how many events we have in this application. I have already shown this table to you. We have got five events so that fly at maximum that could be five transitions from each state because there are five events. Now let's start with the Iowa State, and you have to check whether that state really processes a particular event or not. It doesn't trust us, or if it doesn't respect that event. Then you can just ignore it. You need not define it. Now, first, let's start with inclement time in the case of idle state. Now the application is in an idle state.

Events

User activity	Event generated : SIGNAL	Parameters	note
Press '+' button	INC_TIME	none	This event gets posted to the state machine whenever the user presses the + button
Press - button	DEC_TIME	none	This event gets posted to the state machine whenever the user presses the - button
Press S/P button	START_PAUSE		This event gets posted to the state machine whenever the user presses the S/P button
Press + and – button together	ABRT		This event gets posted to the state machine whenever the user presses the + and – buttons together
	TIME_TICK	ss (sub second)	This event is system generated for every 100ms ss parameter value can vary between 1 to 10

Whenever the inclement time event is refute, it should go to the time fact state because the user wants to fact the time right user wants to set the time. That's why you have pressed the plus or minus button. So. We'll take one transition here. Or you can also draw like this, go to this panel here, select this transition, and you can draft from wherever you want. Like this? Something like that? I would just move this here. So this is not a. I'll just delete this. This is a transition. And the trigger is the erent name that is increment time. Any guard is required. So currently, I don't give any guard for this. Whenever the plus button is pressed, it should take a transition and what could be the action for this transition? By the way, if you want to get this window, I'm defining the properties of a transition. You should select this line. At the left hand side, the property window shows up, and now the action is. The user has pressed the plus button. We have to increment the time details. That's why action could be bigger. Currently, sea time has to be increased. Plus. Is equal to 60, 60 seconds, I have to add to the current time variable because whenever the plus button is pressed, the minute should increase, right? So that's why I'm adding 60 to that variable 60 seconds. That's the action associated with it. You can think of some guard here, but I'm currently not putting any guard to keep everything simple and to reduce the explanation that could be some bug in the state diagram. But you can easily trace it and you can easily fix it. So that's the beauty of state machines. If I'm doing anything wrong, you come to know because, for example, here I am adding something without checking the boundary conditions, right? That may be quiet. If teatime is already at the highest level or the peak level, then you can just ignore it and you don't do any transition as per the guard evaluation. But those small things you can always implement. But I would just do this. Yeah. So it adds something to this and that is being displayed at the entry level in that new state. So whenever it wants to display something new not to worry about the state of the display because the state of the display is already clear due to the egg reduction as of specification, what happens plus the eggs that action will get executed. The display will be clear. The display is ready for the next state.

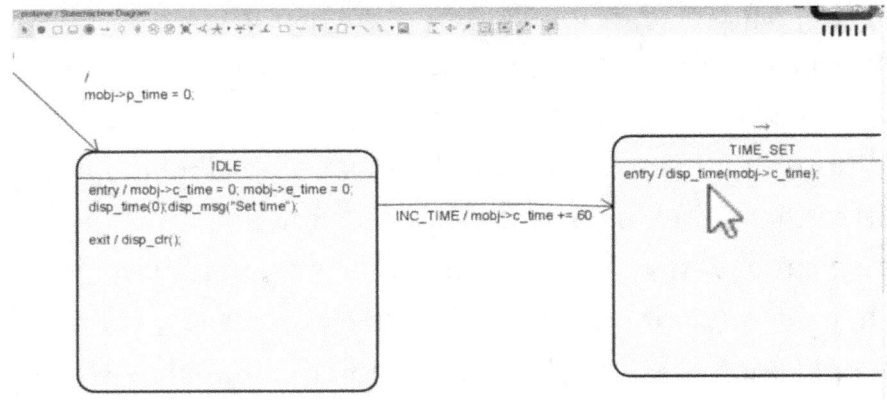

This action takes place and the new value is printed and displayed here. Now, let's stick to this state only now less processed the next event that decreases time. So the decrement time when the free time is equal to zero. The decrement time has no meaning, right? The user cannot crash the negative button when the time is zero because we don't use the negative time in this application. That's why this state ignored doesn't respect the decrement time event. You just forget it. Now what is the next one? What about the Bart tank? There is nothing to abort because the operation has not yet started. When do you use abort when something has started? Nothing has started in this state, so that's why it doesn't affect the abortion event. Also start and pause. There is nothing to pause, and the start actually doesn't happen from here to start something. The time has to be set fast. That's why it only happens in other states, not in the ideal state. So that's why it doesn't respect the start and cause event. Also, this state? Just look at this state. Don't worry about other states. I'm just talking with respect to this state only. Now, let's go to the next event. That is the time to correct. So we have one project requirement, the requirement says the application must be 20 times when it returns to the iDEN. What? Now, let's consider this requirement, something like this. Now, let's say for every final millisecond, the application has to beep. Let's say this is fine in a millisecond. So this is one two, three, four five, this is time, this duration is by hand MF. This is a five hundred millisecond duration forever defined in milliseconds. The application has to beep beep part, let's say 10 milliseconds. A sharp beep. This is be. So like that, it has to do 20 times and then it should go to the silent mode. I mean, no more BP, this thing can be easily implemented in our framework. That's why you can see that. This happens whenever the picky rent is received, so whenever the ticket rent is received, the ticket rent is received for every 100 milliseconds. Whenever the United receives, some action has to be taken, but that is no transition. That means this is actually an internal transition, so it will implement this as an internal transition in the ideal state. Now let's go back here and select the idea more and now go to the internal here.

Internal trigger set that trigger. You just click on add here, trigger time underscore, take that fact trigger.

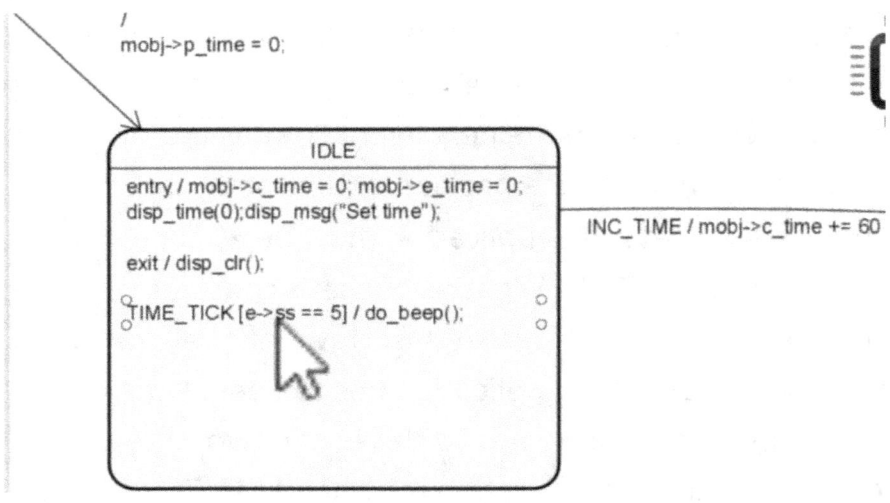

And this event had a parameter parameter, you write in parentheses, open a parenthesis if. That triggered what the guard guards when access is equal to prior court, I would find in a millisecond if it is equal to five means that the final minutes seconds action is to be. Function. Or it can also be written like this instead of using this for many more things. Here, let me change this to E D referencing SS. You mean you want to refute that at the time, tick and its parameter SS subsequent when that is equal to five. It does a beep like that for internal transition. Now we took care of all the rent for any state. So now let's go to that state and you just think how you wish to process all the events in this state. So just think of this state only and I've seen the next project.

EXERCISE-003 IMPLEMENTING TIME_SET STATE

Now, let's process all the events for this state, considering the state. Now the application is in time sat state and let say that inclement time event is received inclement time. You have to increment the time, the fee time ready. But let's do that. So now the increment time should happen inside this state. This is a state which takes care of setting the time. That's why obviously it cannot transition. It should take care inside of it. Hence, increment time and decrement time will be internal transition for this state. It cannot ask someone else to do increment time or deployment time. It's this state responsibility. So select this and go to internal. The trigger is implementing guard. OK, let's forget about the guard for timing action is what action, if the same action this one. And that is one more action. That is, it should show they implemented time on the display cell display time. Albie K c underscored time, let me remove this guard, okay, for the time being. That's not required. So whenever inclement time, everything just does plus to feed time and then displace the modified time, that's it. Very simple right now. Let it process that increment time. The decrement time is also an internal transition. Now let me add one more internal transition decree. Men Time Guard is what could be the guard. Let's think about that later. What is action now you have to do minus your Amobi J. He underscored time. Minus is equal to 60. You you modified the time for display the time. OK. I'm Beech eight. The Time that fits. So what could be the guard here, you should make sure that you don't go below zero, right? So guards. Amobi, get seat time should be greater than or at least is equal to 60. Right? That's the guard. OK, so this is a Boolean expression. A Boolean expression will be false if the time is less than 60. So please note that using increment time and decrement time, you can only increment or decrement the minutes, not the second. So this has no effect on a second. So I hope you can understand this. Now we process it for you, Grant. Let's move to the next event. That is Albert. Now you have set something and you abort everything and you want to go back to the idea of what you can do. So when that is about the event. It just comes back to the. I state I'm in no guard, no action, nothing. OK, so like just a BRT, when the Abbott event is reviewed, it comes to the idol stage.

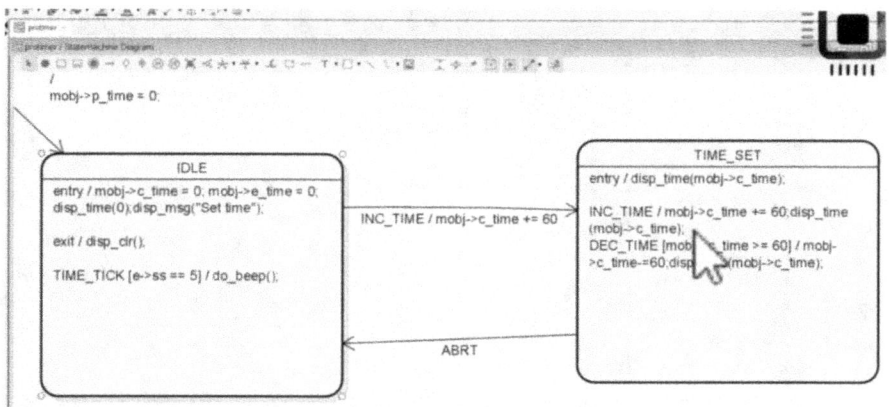

But it has displayed some things that need to be clear. That's why you can argue and take that action here like that action is. Display clear. And when it comes to the ideal mode, it sets everything to zero and it displays the theater and sends the message set time. Now the next event has started. Pause right now, you have done the time settings. So now the user presses the star pause. Button, so the countdown has to be started, right? And that happens in the countdown state. That's why now there will be one transition from the time state to the countdown state. So let me write one transition here. So let me just implement that here. I'll just call this trigger as start, pause. OK. And what could be the guard? You see, the countdown cannot begin if minutes are zero.

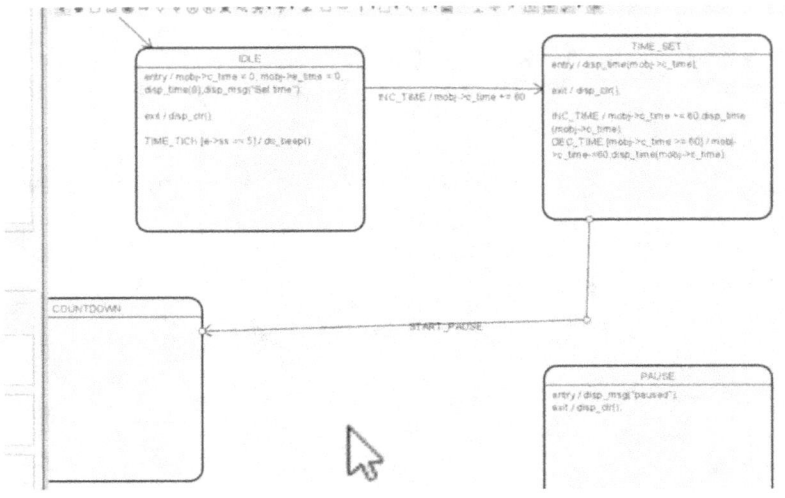

That's why a guard would be InMobi J. Seat time should be greater than or equal to 60. That's the guard for this transition to happen if this condition is not true, then this transition cannot happen. So that's our. Stock the rent now, let's move to the next rent. All right, so now the next event is time to give rent when the application is in time, said state. So it doesn't actually process the time ticking event. I mean, there is no action, which is synchronous with the time, because the time set merely does modification to the time variable for the plus or minus button pressed by the user. That's why it has no time based on an action defined. That's why let's ignore that event in the state. Now let's move to the next state that is poth. And you just think of what you can do here and you try to draw your stuff. And I will cover this in the next project.

EXERCISE-003 IMPLEMENTING PAUSE STATE

Let's implement the paused state. In the products equipment it is mentioned yet, when the countdown is paused, time can be modified. That means when the application is in call, the state time can be modified. That means it respects the increment time and deployment time event. So when we are in pause state and now let's assume we receive the increment time event, so we should of that right. We should go to that time set the date. I just called the south in three men time. And what would be the action Amobi gets the time plus is equal to 60. OK, so that faction along the transition? And also, there is one more transition. Let's draw one more transition from here to here. For the decrement time. So this trigger is decrement time Gardez. You know, already InMobi day of the time should be greater than or equal to 60. And action is a Mobike of seat time. Minus is equal to 60. That's the action. All right, so that's how the prostate processes implement time and increment time events next start underscored path. So what is the positive thing about the countdown has passed when the countdown has paused, the application isn't posted. And if it again receives. Start port event, then it should resume the countdown, right? So that's why it should go back to the. Countdown State for the trigger is nothing but stock. That fit. And how about a party event? Everything must be aborted. It should go back to the idle mode. So let's draw one more transition from here to here.

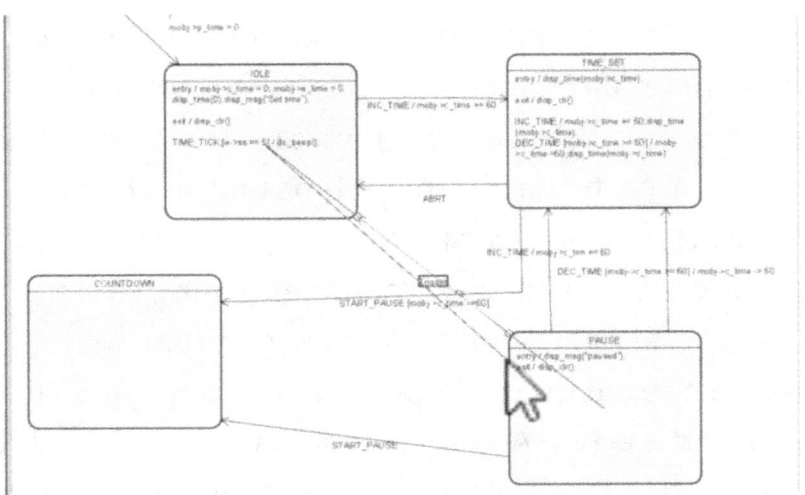

You can draw something like this. Or something like this? OK, so this is about. That looks good. So an application isn't part of the state, so it doesn't process the time tick event. That's right that it is not the time to event. Now let's move to the next state. That is the countdown. So when the time is counting down, you cannot modify the time that two hour increment time and decrement time events are not processed in this state while in the state. We can't ignore them the next few days, start, pause. You rent. That is actually processed whenever it receives stock because they rent it, it must go to it. So that's why that must be one transition from here to here. So this is. Tarte undiscussed cross. How about Abbott, you can afford it. So just draw this transition here. So this is about. So now how about the time tick event while in the countdown state? Whenever the time to event happens. And when the subsequent field is 10, that means a thousand milliseconds has elapsed, then we should diclemente the current time by one second. So the countdown happens for every one second. Now, let's do that. So now, first of all, will you implement it as an external transition or internal transition? But actually go for internal transition, OK, I'll just go for internal transition here. Let me add an internal transition time. Take. So guarded when you went parameter, second is equal to 10. And what is the action? We have comedic cement ammo, B.J. time, it is counting down. So that's why. And Moby Dick, minus minus 10. It is. Sorry. Actually, it is not clearly visible. It's a sea time documented. And after that, you have to do plus plus to the elapsed time. And you have to display and jet, you have to display. See time. So these are the actions we have to do. When Essence is equal to 10, decrement the current time intimately, I left the time and showed the current time. But you cannot decrement see underscored time when you have reached zero. So during down counting, when you reach zero, the application should automatically go to the idle mode because the countdown is over, right? So that's why, based on the value of see underscore time extended variable, we have to decide whether we have to take an internal transition or an external transition, a feat underscored time becomes zero. That would lead to external transition to an ideal state. That's why now we have to make a decision based on. An external variable for making decisions in the Umstead machine, you can use choice pseudo state. So here it is. That is the chief pseudo state. This is a choice to the state. Just draw that here. So now this is to make a choice. The choice illustrated will have two sections. One is incoming transition and outgoing transitions. So now let's first draw the outgoing transition. I'll just write something like this, or this is the outgoing transition. So outgoing transition is guarded, OK, so I will come to that in a moment, and I'll write one more outgoing transition. So like this. And let me now draw the incoming transition to the pseudo state. This is the incoming transition for now. First, let's define the incoming transition that is this one. I'm going to address this, OK? This is not actually required here. So this is how we can implement this in the incoming transition to the tri state. So the trigger for this is time. Take the guard. Of subsequent is equal to 10. Now, let me put that here. Look at this diagram. So whenever an event happens and if the subsequent field is equal to 10. So this double is equal to, then the control goes to the tri state child. 2.8. So here something is evaluating the evaluation is actually you can write something inside the studio state, but the software is not letting me to write anything inside this pseudo state. That's OK. Let's write the evaluation here itself. What is the evaluation? The Amobi of The time is equal to zero. You see, the user time tick happens and if the three time variable is zero, then the countdown is over. So that's why the outgoing transition goes to the ideal state. So this guard is as. Yes. All right, so here, if she underscored time is not equal to zero, then it would take this part. That means there is no external transition, so this is an external transition. This is not an external transition, OK? This is actually an internal one. This part doesn't mean that it has exited from the countdown state and reentered. It's not like that. Basically, this trigger is actually going to the Child Zero state and the child pseudo state implements one two or more external transitions. So it can implement any number of external transitions, but there is only one external transition which is guarded by this, so otherwise it just signifies it will be given a countdown state. That's why I want to clarify that this is not existing and reentry. Now let's define some action for this transition here.

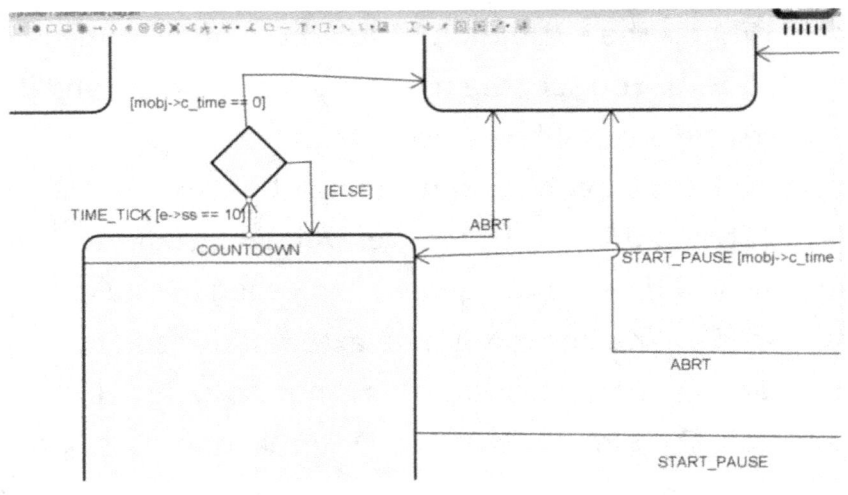

So triggered a time tick guard. Is this what action is? You have to document the three things. Difficult time. And you have to increment the elapsed time M or B K increment the ET time, and then you have to update the display right for display time. The underscored time. So these are the actions here. You can see this belongs to this trigger. If this guard is true, then Ammo BJC Time is dick cemented elapsed, the time is implemented and the time is displayed. And then so the feed time is evaluated at time is equal to zero. That means the countdown is over. Then there is an external transition to idle mode. Now let's explore Cheye State. A choice state is a pseudo state. So it is represented in a state machine diagram umph state machine diagram as a diamond shaped symbol. It has got a single incoming transition and to our more outgoing transitions, basically, we use this to evaluate which extended transition should be taken based on the evaluation of an extended state variable. For example, consider this case based on the value of it. It is a variable R. It's an extended state variable based on the evaluation of this variable. Either this external transition can be taken or this one. You can write the God condition like this.

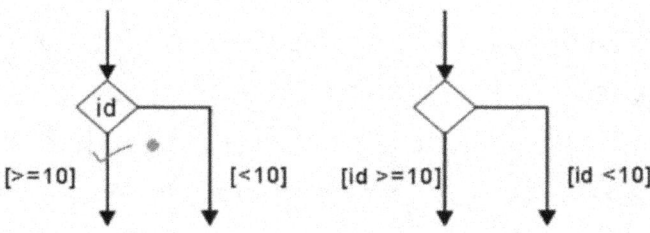

It has a single incoming transition and two or more outgoing transitions

So if the value of its variable is good too, and is equal to 10, then this transition is taken. Otherwise, this transition is something like that. Or you can. Instead of writing inside of it, you can also write something like this. But the software doesn't allow you to write that variable inside of that diamond symbol. So you can also write like this what the specification says about the pseudo state. The choice is used to realize the dynamic conditional branch, so it allows splitting off compound transitions into multiple alternative path attacks. The decision on which path to take may depend on the result of behavior execution performed in the same compound transition prior to reaching the choice point. For example, in this case, that is one behavior, execution or an action prior to reaching this, try a pseudo state. So then the variable is evaluated here. And after that, the variable is evaluated here. So there are different evaluations on different outgoing transitions. Okay? And whichever is true, and that park is taken, if none of the guards that you listed are true, then the model is considered ill formed. They should not put this child through a state in such a condition that none of the guards evaluates to true, then that is not correct. They are using that child to the state. So that's why what you can do is it is recommended to define one outgoing transition with a free defined as guard for every child. State. It's a recommendation that you use the health outgoing transition with each child to the state that you use in your state machine data.

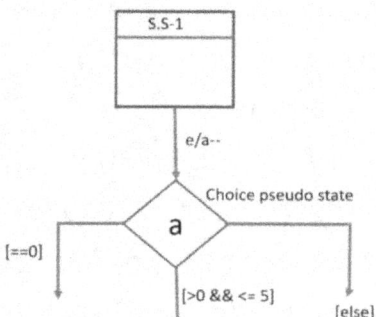

[OMG® UML 2.5.1]

choice is used to realize a dynamic conditional branch. It allows splitting of compound transitions into multiple alternative paths such that the decision on which path to take may depend on the results of Behavior executions performed in the same compound transition prior to reaching the choice point

If none of the guards evaluates to true, then the model is considered ill formed

If more than one guard evaluates to true, one of the corresponding Transitions is selected

it is recommended to define one outgoing Transition with the predefined "else" guard for every choice Pseudostate

If more than one guard evaluates to true one up, the corresponding transition is selected based on your application. Logic that is no priority is the specification doesn't define which outgoing transition should be taken if more than one guard evaluates to true for that depends on you. All right, though, we have not defined any entry action for this threat, I think the interaction is not required for this state. So now what could be the exit action? You know, the exit action, it should be that for the state. Let me tell you why you see her. In this application, we are tracking the productive time at the right time. So whenever the countdown is over. It has to update the Pete time. And that should happen when this state is left. So when the state is left, it could be either due to the completion of conduct or it could be due to pressing the start or pause button or it could be due to the application received. But even so, that's why let's define the exit action for this bag. That action will be Amobi J. Pete Time should be updated. Plus is equipped to add more B.J. elapsed time. Please add the elapsed time to the productive time. After that MLB got elapsed. The time is equal to zero. You are to make that zero because you are leaving that state. So that's why my lapse of time must be reset to zero. That is the action for this state, so that it fits about this state and in the next project, we've called for this state to start in the next project.

INSTALLING MICROSOFT VS CODE AND PLATFORMIO EXTENSION

So in the previous project, we have already completed this state machine diagram, part of our application. And now let's create a new project and let's start implementing this state machine using the C programming language. So for this exercise and for future exercises, I will not be using the Arduino IDE to create Arduino based projects because in this application, we use lots of structures and other things. And, you know, we need features like suggestions, autocomplete, etc. So which will obviously make code writing faster, but they are denied it lacks those features. So that's why for this exercise, as well as spiritual exercises, I will introduce a new setup and the setup is to use the Microsoft Visual

Code ID along with platform real extension. Microsoft IDs are, as you know, it's a great idea, and it supports all the OS platforms like Windows, Linux and Mac, so you'll not face any issues while installing the software. And now I'll explain how to install the platform your extension with Microsoft Visual Court, and we will create a new project on that for this application and then we'll implement this.

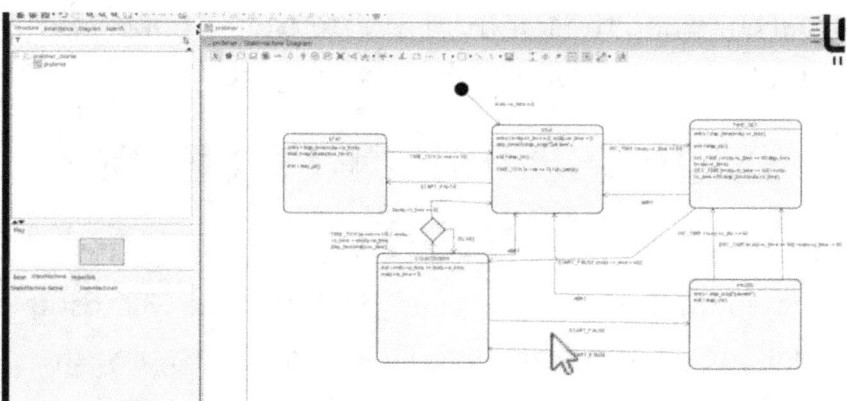

All right, so now I will show you how to install the Microsoft Visual Code. So everything is simple. Just go to this website called Dart Studio dot com. OK, and just download it for your machine and just install it and offer the installation. Just open that. OK, Visual Studio Code app. OK, so here I have some of my previous work space. No problem, OK? And once you open that, go to the extension. And here there is a third extension box, is that right? So that just right flat farm, are you OK? And click on this flat from your ID and you have to install it. OK, that fits for me to go today and start. That's why it is showing me the option. Uninstall. But for you, you should see the installed button here and just start to. After the installation just closed, Heidi, and then opened it again or restarted it. And here you see our message activating extensions. OK. And it will activate the platform extension of what you just installed. So that's how you install the visual code and the flat from IU extension. I hope you can do that and I'll see you in the next project.

EXERCISE-003 CREATE NEW PROJECT

So now I think you have already installed the Microsoft Visual Code I.D. and you should also have installed the Flash from Iyo extension on that. Now let's open the visual code I'd. So when you open this for the first time, you may see this welcome page here and it takes some time to activate the extensions. You may see some message boards here saying it is activating the extension. So once all the extensions are activated, you see the flap from the icon here. Now, what you can do is click on this icon that from you, go to Hall and click on Open. So it opens the pillow at home. And here you can either create a new project, or import any existing article project. Let's click on Create New Project. All right, so let me give you the project name. Zero zero three Pro Timer and select the board. Let's select the board, just type one off and select Arduino Uno and the framework of the Arduino and use the default location. So just check what the default location on your platform iOS settings, but we will not use this default location. I'm going to change it, and I'm going to now.

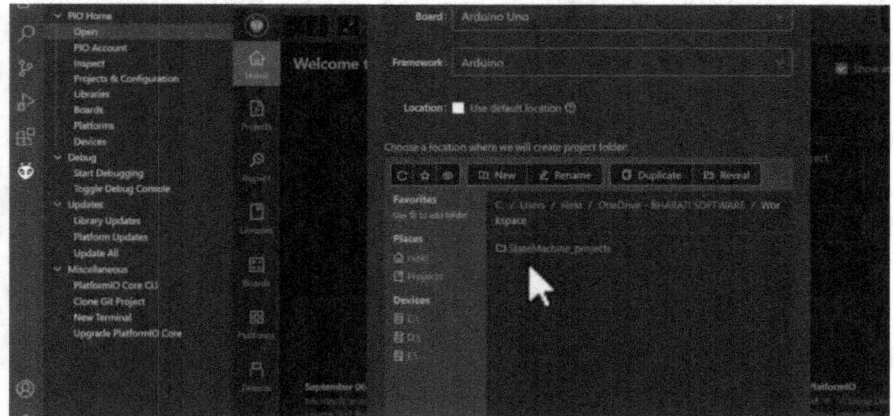

Let me say this project in the earlier directory, what I had created to save all the projects, that is this one state machine project. And here we already have two projects. And this is the third project. And I would say here that click finish. After that, just click here. I trust our turf now. Whenever you are creating a project for the first time, it may do some network activities. You have to wait until it finishes all the network activities. Since I have already created many projects with this extension, you didn't stop me from installing something. But if you are creating a new project for the first time on the platform of your extension, then it may do some network activities to install some tool chains, etc.. All right now, we have successfully created one project and. You can see that there, the source folder, and that is the main duct tape so that from my extension actually named May Main Duct Tape instead of may not and not as you might have seen in Arduino IDE. Here is the loop and set of functions. After that, let's go to trial and let's save this workspace that was your workspace. And I would say that here, I've just said it as a workspace. No problem. Save. Now, just connect the Arduino board to the computer. Now let's try uploading a small program. So just connect an Arduino board to the computer.

I have already connected it. And you can see the connected board in your home under both sections. Not Board three in the Devizes called. So now you can see that the software has already detected that the Arduino UNO is connected at the port number a Carbon-14. When you upload a program from this ID, it uses this composite. That's right, a small program to print Hello World on the feed and want, so I'll just use the trio. Print, Alan, you can see that this is displaying suggestions. This is one of the nice features of this ID, which we don't get in. Arduino is Native ID. So let me use print LAN. And let's set up the board rate. Begin at the border eight nine six zero zero. How to compile this program. So just save it, and you can see that in this panel. That is a bold option. And also there's the upload option and clean option, serial monitor option and other things. Now let's click on the build. And now the program has successfully. Let's upload. So it says that I'm not connected to the internet and it wants to do some network activities. I think I have some issues with my wife, I. So now let's try once again. And now let's upload. It is installing something here. We can see that. So now it has been applauded. And where do you see the output on the Syrian monitor? This is a Syrian monitor and you just click on that.

And you fear it is printing the text hollow word because it is in the loop, since it is in the loop function, it is printing repeatedly. Now, let me change the serial border to love and fly to zero zero. I just want to check whether the serial monitor automatically configures that border or not. Or I don't know whether we have to set it manually or not. I don't know. Let's check that. I'm just building the project. And now let. Applaud. That is a problem. Access is denied. That's because the fetal monitor is already connected to the board. What you can do is go to see it and monitor. And here you have to terminate this. It's safe to ask if it is running, so let's delay this process. Now, let's try to download. You can see that the download is successful. Now let's go to the theater monitor. So now you see, you are receiving garbage values because the field monitored by default is that border eight nine six zero zero. But your applications border, it is something different. So now we have to configure the civil monitors bordering it. So let me just kill this. Now where to configure the serial monitoring board. So what are you doing in your project? So that is Platform iRobot identifier. Go there. Here there is one threat, in fact, platform dot org. And this guy says that you have to add this line to the platform, iReport and I. Now let's try that. Taste that line here and favorite. And now you need to build and upload again. Just go for a serial monitor. Yeah, now we are getting the correct output. So try up to here and I'll see you in the next project.

EXERCISE-003 DATA STRUCTURE EXPLANATION

Hey, welcome back to the project. In the previous project, we set up this idea and in this project. Now let's start implementing. The first step is to create a few more headed files and source files for our project who have got May not CP. So the extension is CP here, which is the C++ file because the Arduino framework uses the C++ programming languages to buy the code using the C programming language syntax. Now, let's create one more file here ahead to file. Just select right click your file and let me cauterize mean dredge, which is the header file and also we are using LCD in this project, right? Let's create LCD dot copy A45 to keep LCD related code. And also one more file LCD dot h. And also, let's segregate the state machine implementation into a separate file, so I'll call it a pro timer. State machine, this file is a dark zip file that we will keep our state machine implementation, that is the state machine diagram implementation. So instead of putting all the code into Maine, dark zip, I'm just segregating this. So now we have got my daughter in the main Dr Heap just including the main daughter.

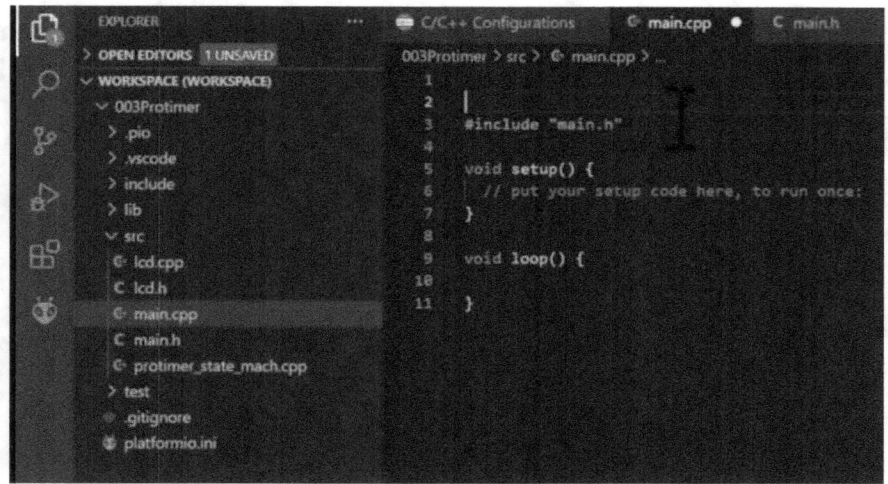

And you can put this Arduino 0.8, which is required, actually. So if you are using the flat from your extension that you just keep in mind, do. Here in the main Dot Edge platform, you include guards. If not, define main and discourage hash. Define. Man and discourage these include guard for the head file. And let's. And that. If using and if and we are also using LCD Dark, which. Here, if not defined as seed and discourage. Define healthy and discourage. And. That looks great. So now let's move forward now, let's include a couple of data structures for our application. The data structures are nothing but a couple of enemies and a couple of structures. So we have got various signal states. So that's why I define radio signals and various states of the application using the Enum. And after that, define the main application structure. Create one structure to include attributes of the main application. And after that, you have to define structures to represent events. Why structures are required to represent different things because, as you know, structure has two components right? A signal component and the associated parameter. Let's use a structure to represent an event. So here, first thing, No. 10 states, you just add all these definitions to Maine Dot.

Signals and States

- Add this to "main.h"

```
/* Signals of the application*/
typedef enum{
    INC_TIME,
    DEC_TIME,
    TIME_TICK,
    START_PAUSE,
    ABRT,
/* Internal activity signals */
    ENTRY,
    EXIT
}protimer_signal_t;
```

```
/* Various States of the application*/
typedef enum{
    IDLE,
    TIME_SET,
    COUNTDOWN,
    PAUSE,
    STAT
}protimer_state_t;
```

I have just used an enum to represent various signals of the application. Also, I have included entry and exit to enumerate if they are to represent the internal activity signals. And after that, you already know how many states we have. So just create one item definition for that. And after that main application structure, so also you should keep it in mind that these are the variables. You can also call them as the extenders state variable. So current time elapsed time, pro time, all of unsigned values and also that is one state variable. This actually holds the current active state of this main application object. Let's move forward. And for Iran. So we have got two types of events in this application. The user generated one which has got only the signal component and it doesn't have any parameter associated with it. So create one structure per a user event. And just use one variable signal as the member element to represent the signal. And after that, for ticky rent. So this is a system generated, ah, it's a synchronous event and it has got two component signals and the associated parameter for second. You start off doing this, so that is one deterrent strategy with this approach. So let's say you have a state machine function. Ah, you have got state machine implementation. And for the state mission implementation, you had to pass the event for events to be represented as structures.

Events

SM-i

```
/* For user generated events */
typedef struct{
    uint8_t sig;
}protimer_user_event_t;
```

```
/* For tick event */
typedef struct{
    uint8_t sig;
    uint8_t ss;
}protimer_tick_event_t;
```

Sometimes you have to pass this structure and sometimes you have to pass this structure. That means now there should be two receiving parameters that don't look good. So what you do is you just create one super event structure or generic event structure called event and difficulty. And you include the signal value that. And then you include this structure in your application specific rent structures. So this is also called a structure embedding R and in a or B terminology, you can also call it inheritance because the structure is derived from this structure. That means this structure includes the attributes of this structure. You know, old Pete also has card inheritance. So the advantage of this method is you can just send a pointer. This member element and then don't cost to get the patent structure address, so we see that while implementing the court, that's why I think it's better to use this method. So don't get countries here who are just using structure, embody. So keep all these structure definitions in Maine Dot. And see you in the next project.

EXERCISE-003 DEFINING INITIAL TRANSITION FUNCTION

So now in the pro time, our state machine darts will implement a state machine. So first, let's start with our initial transition. I'll just create one function here. Wide. Pro timer, let me call this as just in it, our state machine in it is to be shot. I just called the pro timer to underscore it. Here the function argument will be pointed to the main application structure for the main application structure is pro timer and of. I'll give the pointer variable name as an object. So just like what we used, this variable we used to throw out a state machine diagram. Now this structure is defined in the methodology that they include. And now here I am, will be chair of the current active state. And mortgages, so we have got associated ActionScript initial transition action that if we have to initialize, the time is equal to zero, that's it.

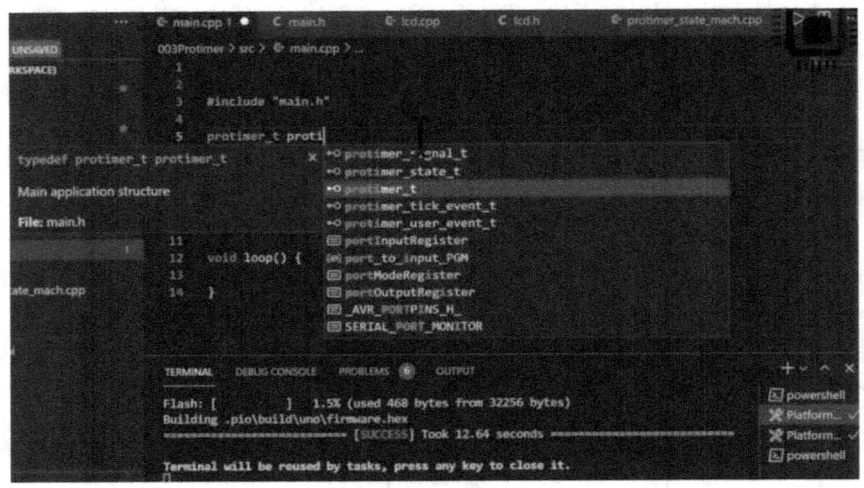

So you have to call this function from the main doorstep in the Manger Typekit Pizza just called from here. First, let's create the main application object as a global variable. Fraught time. This is the main application object. And application objects. So you can also protect this using static keyword here and send the address of this here. So now you have to get a prototype of this. This file has to share the prototype of dysfunction. For that, just copy this function declaratory and go to the main stage and give that prototype here. That looks great. Now let's try to compile this. Or actually, the completion is successful.

DIFFERENT APPROACH TO IMPLEMENT STATE MACHINE

So now let's begin with the implementation of the state machine. There are different approaches. The first one is a very easy one, a straightforward one that is the master switch approach. So this approach will also explode in the previous exercise. And the second one is the state table approach, and that is one more approach that is very efficient and this is an excellent approach.

Implementation of state machine

- Nested switch approach
- State table approach
- State handler approach [1]

And this approach is mentioned in the book Practical You Must State, charged in C and C++ written by mirror stomach state handler approach actually based on a function that points the point as to the state handler.

Each state will have its own handler, and that handler itself is considered as a state. The state handler approach is actually based on the usage of function pointers. Tool also can learn the use of function pointers in the state handler approach and will exploit that later to explore Nestor's switch approach and then will exploit the state handler approach with the same application. And then we'll explore the state table approach.

EXERCISE-003 NESTED SWITCH IMPLEMENTATION OF AN FSM PART 1

So now let's continue the coding. Let's write one function to implement this state machine. Just go to this file and timer state machine, participate and let's create one function. The function is protein. I just called the state machine. So this state machine is for the application object. This one, the state machine, will receive four times under Scotty, the made application object or each year, and the state machine also receives the event and the generalized event structure is event and Scotty pointer to the event structure. And here we are using Napster to switch that fused switch case to switch between different states, so switch and maybe get. Active state. Just remove all these things. Now, let's implement the different cases. Case back back state is that, say, the first act is state aid if the case is idle. Then let's call one function here. I'll call that function as a state handler for all timers. And for this, you have to send mortgages and eat the received event like that. You have to implement different cases. So one case for each state of the state machine.

```
003Protimer > src > C+ protimer_state_mach.cpp > ⊕ protimer_state_machine(protimer_t *, event_t *)
 8
 9     void protimer_state_machine(protimer_t *mobj, event_t *e){
10         switch (mobj->active_state){
11             case IDLE:{
12                 protimer_state_handler_INIT(mobj,e);
13             }
14         }
15
16     }
```

```
TERMINAL   DEBUG CONSOLE   PROBLEMS 1   OUTPUT

Checking size .pio\build\uno\firmware.elf
Advanced Memory Usage is available via "PlatformIO Home > Project Inspect"
RAM:    [          ]   1.1% (used 23 bytes from 2048 bytes)
Flash:  [          ]   1.5% (used 468 bytes from 32256 bytes)
Building .pio\build\uno\firmware.hex
========================== [SUCCESS] Took 13.27 seconds ==========================

Terminal will be reused by tasks, press any key to close it.
```

And in fact, this function, you have to implement one more switch kick, which switches between different events to take different actions. And we'll use this return type to return to the status of the event, handling the status could be whether the event is really handled or it is ignored or the event caused any transition. So that's why instead of White Alicia's event status here. And each event handler, these are individual event handlers also should return the event status. Like this, you implement different cases for different states. This is a part time fit for the time of day to handle our call first time set. So I hope you can complete this for other states. And now let's implement these individual state handlers. So I'll just copy this and paste it here. These are individual state handlers. There is the pointer to the main application object. And pointed to the event. And this individual state handler returns that you went to state to. I'm sorry this is not in it, so this is me. This is me. Now, this is a state handler product idea state. So I'd state prosthesis, radio signals, increment time, time, take etc and start pause. It also has internal activities.

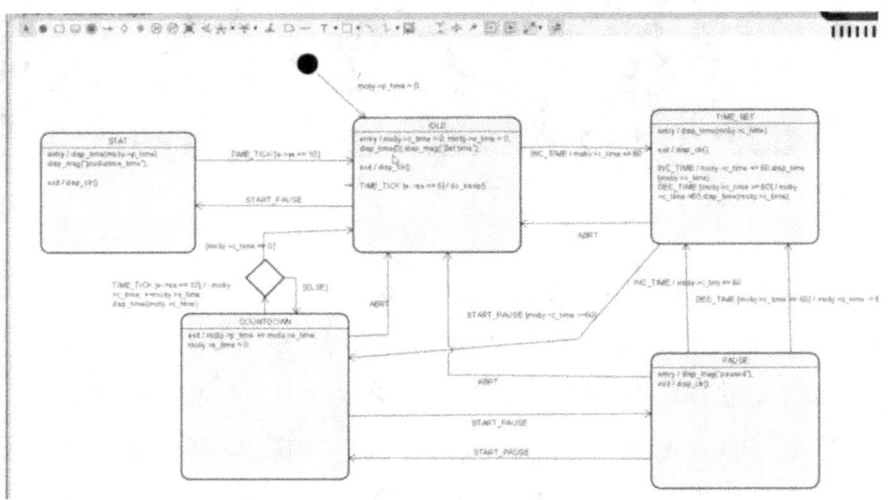

Entry and exit will also treat them as signals for the implementation purpose and will call it entry event activity exactly right. So now you have to implement another case to switch between these different signals to take appropriate actions. Let's use one more switch case. That's why it's quite unnecessary. The upper switch, that is this switch, is to switch between different states of the state machine, and the inner switch is to switch between different signals. The state processes. All right, switch the off signal. First kiss, I mean, now we have to implement one case for each signal the state processes. Let's start with an entry. Like that, we are not using break statements, though, because we have to return the status of the U.S.A. now. Let me use one more kiss kiss exit. And one more case for increment time. One more case for a tart pause. One more case for. Time to. So like that, you have to complete other state handlers implementation. I hope you can complete that. Leave that as an assignment. And now let's define this event status. Let's go to the main stage and create. TypeDef Enum, So just called this has an even state of difficulty. So the status is whether the event is handled or whether it is ignored. So here I use events. Handled. Even. Ignored an event. Sean Fisher. This actually indicates the status of the event handling. But feels about here, so this is even status under 40. So now what is the reaction? As for our diagram, Sophie, time is equal to zero. And each time is equal to zero. We have to make that happen. Let's do that and maybe get it. Current time is equal to zero, and we'll be. A lot of the time is equal to zero. And after that display time. So you've one helper function called display time. Will implement this later and after that display a message that time. Display. Message. That time. So that's the end reaction after completing the entry actually should return. Return. Event standard. It has to pretend the status. And it reaches here and here also, you should give a return. Now, let's implement the exit case. What is the exit just to display clear? Let's do that display. And it should return.

```
mobj->curr_time = 0;
mobj->elapsed_time = 0;
display_time(0);
display_message("Set time");
return EVENT_HANDLED;
}

case EXIT:{
    display_clear();
    return EVENT_HANDLED
```

Even standard. And after that increment time. Increment time, it has to take one action here, so it has to add 60 seconds to see time. Let's do that. And mobile. Current time is equal to 60. Return. Event Handout. Right, so if you are wondering why the state returning is required, this is required for the event dispatcher. We will implement that. You ran the dispatcher later. So even the dispatcher actually dispatches the state machine implementation or the state machine function. So we'll talk about that later. So the increment time causes the transition, right? So we didn't implement that. That is the transition. And mobile. Active state is equal to. That is a transition. So the new state is assigned to active state stockpiles for stockpiles. There is no action. So just a transition. Let's do that. And mobile active state is required to start. Here, since there is a transition, there is a transition, right? So we should not use the event handle rather, will youth event transition? So return the status of the event transition. So we will understand later how that status is being used. When the event is handled, just handle, you just write the event handler when the event is handled. But that event, if it causes that transition to another state, then you returned the status and event transition, but here also. Event transition. Four times tick. What is time tick? Actually, the time tick is the internal transition so that it'll guard how to implement this here.

You have to access the second feed of the event. So what should we do now? Now you have to downcast this point to this structure type. Because the fifth member element in this structure for time or event, the pointer, what we have is. We have to get to the point where only we can access this member element. So that's why if. Four timer, Typekit event star. So you have to typecast this pointer. Then you have to access the airfield. It is equal to. Then you have to call a beep. Then you have to return. Event. Handled. Suppose if this condition fails, then you just return. Return event ignored. So this is the end of the case. If this state is any other event that it is ignored, so that's why at the end you just return. Event ignored by default. That's it, so that's the implementation of the handle of the state I the likewise you have to implement similar functions for other states that compile this. But before that, let's fix some compilation editor for let's pick these red lines. First of all, these are helpful functions to implement. Our actions will implement that at the end. For the first helper function is display time. And after that display a message. So this is basically a string value string, which is a string, which the user defined data type provided by the Arduino framework to represent string value. I would just use string. To be. So now you give the prototype of this function. So just provided the prototypes of those functions here. And after that, do you have to provide a prototype of these functions as well? So let's make them static. Because these are private. This file, so all functions, you can make it static. No problem. And as a good practice, so here this point, her content can be modified. You have modified that. But this pointer cannot be modified. That's why you can use your contact and object is a contact pointer pointing to variable data. Data can be modified. You did that here, but this pointer cannot be modified. That's why, as a best practice, you can use Konst here. Similarly, you can use Konst here and here. You should not modify that you want a pointer as well as you should not modify the content pointed by that you run pointer. That's right. You can also use content here. So how to interpret this E! Is a cost pointer pointing to conf data of this type data as pointers are constant here. The hand should not modify that. I just used it. But here the data can be modified. So that's why a mortgage is a cost pointer pointing to variable data. There's change here as well. So now you have modified the function declarative. That's why these functional prototypes also have to be modified. Life changes here as well. Now, let's try to compile this, let's see whether we have any errors or not. That we built this. Florida showed a couple of warnings here. So what is the thing in this function? These enumerators are not handled. That's fine so that I will leave you as an assignment. I hope you understood the way I implemented the state handler function. Similarly, you implement for the rest and I fear in the next election.

EXERCISE-003 NESTED SWITCH IMPLEMENTATION OF AN FSM PART 2

So let's continue with these handlers implemented in the previous project. I actually asked you to implement these handlers, and I believe you have completed that. Please note that in the diagram, whenever you see a God condition, that means you have to use the if statement while implementing that in the court so God conditions are converted into decision making statements of any programming language, like a statement. We have got all these handlers. Let me explain the implementation of this here. This is actually an internal transition, which can be an external transition, sometimes on the evaluation of this guard here. That is a choice. Not. Let's see how that is implemented in the code. You see your case. Take. And this is the guard condition, which is converted into an if statement, if it is equal to 10. The higher you receive a generic point of that is that it must not cost it to this type. So I would guess segregating it like this. You can feel this is a point to which it doesn't cost it to this type after that, use one more parenthesis here and you just access the member element of this structure that fits. If SS is equal to 10, then you have to take the action. So the actions are taken here. Current time victim entered a lapse of time incremented, then displayed a time display and a difficult time. And after that, this is evaluated by the underscored time and the condition. So if it is really zero, then this will be true.

```cpp
003Protimer > src > G protimer_state_mach.cpp > ⊕ protimer_state_handler_COUNTDOWN(protime
130              case EXIT:{
131                  mobj->pro_time += mobj->elapsed_time;
132                  mobj->elapsed_time = 0;
133                  return EVENT_HANDLED;
134              }
135
136              case TIME_TICK:{
137                  if(((protimer_tick_event_t*)(e))->ss == 10){
138                      --mobj->curr_time;
139                      ++mobj->elapsed_time;
140                      display_time(mobj->curr_time);
141                      if(!mobj->curr_time){
142                          mobj->active_state = IDLE;
143                          return EVENT_TRANSITION;
144                      }
145                      return EVENT_HANDLED;
146                  }
147                  return EVENT_IGNORED;
148              }
149              case START_PAUSE:{
150                  mobj->active state = PAUSE;
```

If it is true, then that's actually an external transition to the ideal state. If this is not true, that remains as an internal transition. So I just return events handled here, if this is not true, that we just return events ignored here. So you have to implement the rest of the code here. In fact I have not implemented this in the fact and reaction exit action and after that time is an external transition. So this is one guard. How to implement this if. You take the E down COVID, because of how to access the SS member element. Short timer underscored tick, underscored event. And then put this in one parenthesis. Access the effort, if it is equal to 10, then you have to make a transition. Active state is equal to. And her return event underscored transition. Otherwise you have to return. He went undiscovered, ignoring that fit. We have completed the implementation of all the state handlers and now let's implement the U.N. dispatcher. The event dispatcher dispatches events to the state machine implementation unit dispatcher that says malfunction we will write in may not see. And also how to implement other Halpert functions which are pending. We have used many helper functions and also how to implement other patrol specific functions like entity functions and other things will implement that later. Now let's implement the event dispatcher.

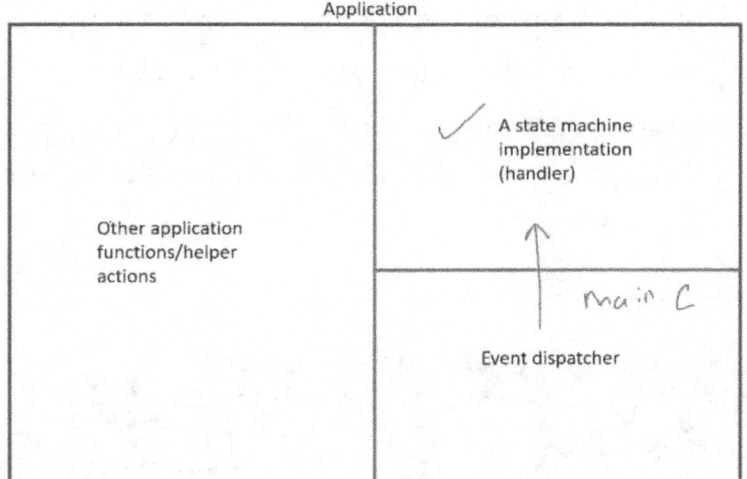

Let's go back to the code. And let's try to compare this to the fact that boots are not. Below are successful. No problem. And now let's go to the main dark copy here. Let's implement the event dispatcher. I will call this to ask for a timer underscore event, underscore dispatcher. This also raises a pointer to the application object pro timeout and difficulty. Main object and event and difficulty story. This is an event dispatcher, so let's make this as a contest. This is also contact. This is also a concert. That's the gear type of dysfunction right here at the top. We can also make this static. No problem. It's received that you rent your and it dispatches to the state machine implementation. So what we do is we will just straight away call this function for a machine. You have to now copy this function decorator and go to Maine Dot Edge and get a prototype of that here because this is being called from the Maine Dot CP. So let's use that function here and just dispatch the event Ammo LBJ. And the event that captured the state wanted to be written, I'll call it status equal to let's create the status variable event and discuss status status.

```
static protimer_t protimer;

void setup() {
    // put your setup code here, to run once:
    protimer_init(&protimer);
}

void loop() {

}

static void protimer_event_dispatcher(protimer_t *const mobj, event_t const *const e){
    event_s
        event_status_t    typedef event_status_t event_status_t
    event   EVENT_TRANSITION
    status  protimer_event_dispatcher
```

If status is equal to even transition. That indicates there was a transition if there was a transition. First, you have to run the exit action. Then we have to run the entry action. And reaction for the new state. Or rather, I would call this run the entry action for the target state. Ran the exit action for the source state. Ran the entry action for the target will do one thing, we will create one variable here, even under Scotty E. First, we will write this random entry action for the target state e dark figure is equal to entry. And you have to call this function once again. And Moby Jay, we will call this as an event or activity event, double E. And send out just that for here. E dot figure is equal to exit. When the transition happens here, this is a received event. This is a received event. The event, which was received here. You fund that event to the state machine. But before that, you had to make a note of the fourth state. That's why I will create one dummy variable for timer state. And in this variable, we will make a note of the source state or the current state, and we'll be J Active state. So this is just to remember the whole state that will get executed only if status is equal to event underscore transition. If there was a transition, if there was a transition, then only you have to call the exit and enter action. If there was really a transition, then the active state which was inside the structure has definitely been updated, right? So that's why we will call the entry action for that.

```cpp
static void protimer_event_dispatcher(protimer_t *const mobj,event_t const *const e){
    event_status_t status;
    protimer_state_t source;

    source = mobj->active_state;

    status = protimer_state_machine(mobj,e);
    if(status == EVENT_TRANSITION){
        event_t ee;
        //1. run the exit action for the source state
        ee.sig = EXIT;

        //2. run the entry action for the target state
        ee.sig = ENTRY;
        protimer_state_machine(mobj,&ee);
    }
```

But we also should call the exit action for the Old State or for the source state, which was favored here. That's why what you need to do now is what you have to do. Active state is equal to sort. And then you have to call this once again here as an exit action. I hope that makes sense. So let me explain once again. Plus, the fresh rent is received here, and the first event is sent to the state machine. But before that, we take a note of what is the active state in a temporary variable. The year round is sent to the state machine. If there was no transition, then nothing to process. It's over thought that event was handled or ignored or don't kick back. If this status is even an underscored transition, that means there was a transition and the active state of this object has already been updated. As per the specification, we have to first call exit action and then the transition action. But here we have slightly modified that first, that transition action is already executed here inside the state machine function. After that, we run the exit action for the source state, which we saved here. And for the entry action. Here you have to update the state really about at least equal to the target. So the target variable we have not created. So let me create one target variable here, and I have to initialize that here. Target is equal to an object of active state. Or I would just enjoy life here. If there was really a transition, then the new state is the 40th state is saved in that target, really. And that is used to execute the entry action. But the source state, which you settled here before processing the event or before sending that government to the state machine that was used to render exit action. Now we have completed the pro time or even dispatched the court, and this event dispatch , called from the loop function in the low function, will be doing three important tasks. The first one is how to read the button pad status. So we have got three buttons. We will call it a button pad. We have to read the status of that and then make an event. Convert that button pad status to an instance of an event structure, that is, make an event and then send that event to the event dispatcher. So now to implement the first task reader button pad status, we have to understand how the button is connected to the Arduino, and we also have to discuss the software button bouncing in the next project. We will explore the hardware connection, like the connections of the button pad, and I would also discuss connections of the LCD to the arm in a board. And then we will call the rest of the program. I'll see you in the next project.

EXERCISE-003 HARDWARE CONNECTIONS

So now let's talk about hardwired connections. There are three buttons, but on one, two , three and the first button increment time, second button is dictum and time and third button start pause button. And these are connected to these pin numbers. The Arduino board and that is also one buzzer. You can either use it or act on a passive buzzer. The buzzer is connected to the PIN number 12, and also the project is a 16 across two LCD, and these are the connections between LCD pins and the Arduino pin. Now let's do the connection. I'll show you the connection and go to the Tinker card and let's grab Breadboard. And let me also grab the one on board. So I'll just rotate this. And let me use a few buttons. A push button. I'll just keep that here. I will use three buttons. So the hardware connections, do you have to do exactly like this that will help you to troubleshoot basis? Three buttons, and I will interface the buttons to the Arduino board in pull down configuration. What I do here is so I will use these tools to connect to the board. This goes to the FCC.

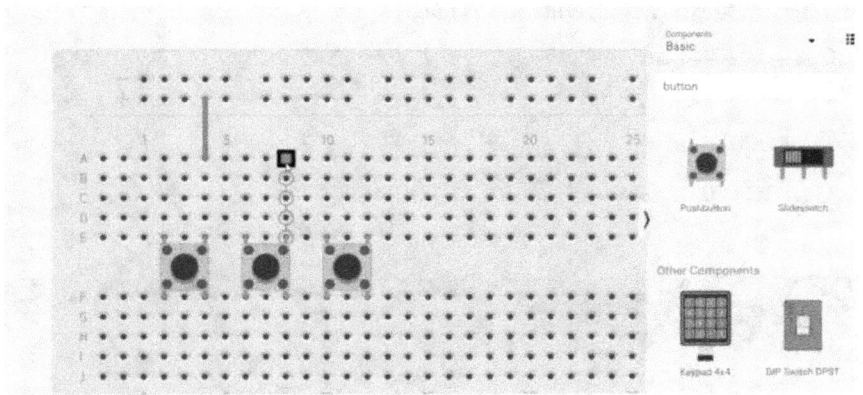

That's connecting these leaves of the button to the BBC. And these levels you use are 10 all pulldown resistors. So this is a 10kg pulldown resistor. And just copy that. After that, you connect these three buttons to the Arduino board, according to this table, the button one should go to the Arduino pin number two. This is a button one from here. He'll connect it to the number two. So this is still three. And from here to. PIN number for. This will make it as red colored wire, so this indicates that we see connections. Fine, and we also have to take one healthy. So to get the LCD. I will place that here. What are the city connections LCD artists should go to be number five? RF is right here in number five. Or just make this as a green color. This is to fix. This is too far when the enable pin up the LCD should go to Savannah and never to seven, correct. After that, we will be using LCD data communication in portrait mode.

Arduino and 16x2 LCD connection

LCD pins	Arduino pin number
LCD_RS	5
LCD_RW	6
LCD_EN	7
LCD_D4	8
LCD_D5	9
LCD_D6	10
LCD_D7	11

So that's why in the portrait mode you cannot use the data lines did not D1, D2, D3. So they are not used before you have to use D4 too. Eight. D, four, two, eight, nine, 10, 11, eight. Nine. Ten. And then 11. This is actually the anode of the backlight energy of the LCD anode should go to the VXI. Actually, it has to be through a fixture folder. Take our sister.

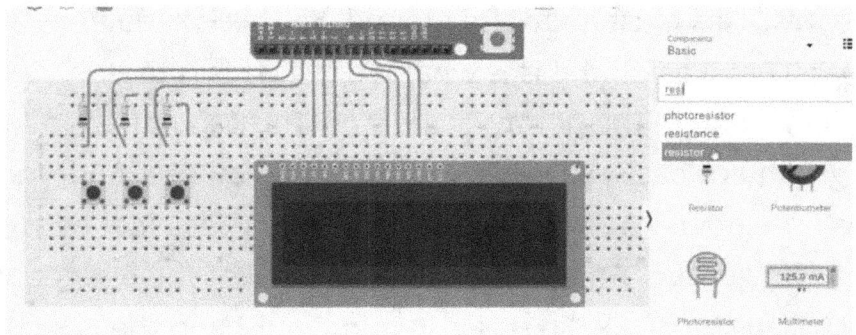

Because it is connected to the internet and the right, the power to the entity should go through. Our sister connected to the A.. And make this as Tom, oh, that's sufficient. Nobody's connected here. And the cathode of the elderly, that's a negative terminal of the energy that is the backlit energy should go to the. Ground, this is ground connection. And after that, you also need one potential meter. So just take part. And the party's around 100 kilograms. So just make it up to 50 or 100 kms. This is for the contract setting of the LCD. So just keep that here, or I'll just keep that here. And we also need one buzzer. Please observe. Just keep that. Some here. This is a positive. This is the negative. So whether we will intervene later. I'll do one thing, I'll just keep the potential mystery here. I'll just keep the peace over here. This is the wiper of the potential meteor. The white board must be connected to the contrast, being up to the LCD. So just do like this. This must go to the ground. So this is ground. This is. Contrast and this is what we see. This is the terminal one of the potential meteor. This can either go to ground or basis, so just give it to me if you see. And this time now, if Terminal one is you. Then Terminal two must be ground. And the positive terminal of the budget, we will give it to 12. So this is in number 12 and the negative should go to the ground. That said, those are the connections you ought to make. So after that, finally, you have to connect the ground up the Arduino board to ground up the breadboard. And if I were to. 500 the breadboard. So this section of the power is really not connected to this section of the breadboard on the real bread, but here it is showing that it is a continuous connection, but it may not be the case. That's why it is better to chart. These sections of the power that. Or I'll just show this with a different color. So that's the connection you need to do. OK. The court so far you have written you can just paste it or here in the. Tech section, and you can simulate that. So I'll leave you that as an assignment to you, but I will test this on the real heart because on the ticker card application, I cannot upload the multiple files in the project. We have multiple files, isn't it? So all those files you have to convert into a single ayano file, then you have to paste all that code here because this doesn't have provision for maintaining multiple forced files. So that's the drawback. Optus. If you don't have these components, then don't worry, just convert this project to a single ayano file and then paste all the code here to simulate that. So in the next project, I will talk about reading the button, perhaps take two outs in the next project.

EXERCISE-003 IMPLEMENTING EVENT PRODUCER CODE

Hey, welcome back to the project. Now let's implement the new function, and now let's implement the first task. Read the button part status. So for this, let me create a couple of variables here. Eight Underscore B1, B2, B3 These three variables are used to hold the individual button status. And how to reach the button status. We know that to be one is equal to how to use digital read because the button is connected to the digital pin after Arduino. There is no analog thing in the world here, so just a digital read, so we will provide a couple of macros for the pins. We haven't given that let's do that at the top here.

Arduino and Button connections

Component	Arduino Pin number
Button 1 (INC_TIME)	2
Button 2 (DEC_TIME)	3
Button 3 (START/PAUSE)	4
Buzzer	12

Button pad truth table

B1	B2	B3	Value	Signal
0	0	1	1	START_PAUSE
0	1	0	2	DEC_TIME
1	0	0	4	INC_TIME
1	1	0	6	ABRT
Other values				XX

 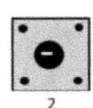 

1   2   3

Define 10 by 10 one, which is two like that, so button three to Arduino pin number four. And then puts up 12 and four LCD connections. Define pain, health. First, let's give the macro for RF RF stands for Register Select. And the top table of the button part is like this. So if button one status is zero button to status zero and if button three is pressed, it seems that we are using the pulldown configuration in button interfacing. Here we have used the pull down configuration, right? So that's up, we're down register going to the ground when the button is not pressed. So this is ground that you can see that this is grounded. The pin is grounded when the button is not pressed to. When the button is pressed, the button is actually connected to the ABC. That means when the button is pressed. The pin status will be high. When the button is pressed, the pin status will be high. Suppose a

B3 is high, that means that the start pause button is pressed. That means if the button pad status sees one, then that is start pause. If the button pad status two, then that is deployment time. If the button pad status statuses for this is binary for then it is increment time. If it is six, then it is apart. The other values don't count. Let's define those values here. I'll just call this button pad value or button pad increment time is for. I discovered, in fact, the value for increment time is for. Then Barton had. Value for decrement time.

```
WORKSPACE (WORKSPACE)       12
v 003Protimer           •   13    //lcd connections
  > .pio                    14    #define PIN_LCD_RS   5
  > .vscode                 15    #define PIN_LCD_RW   6
  > include                 16    #define PIN_LCD_EN   7
  > lib                     17    #define PIN_LCD_D4   8
  v src                 •   18    #define PIN_LCD_D5   9
    C+ lcd.cpp              19    #define PIN_LCD_D6   10
    C  lcd.h                20    #define PIN_LCD_D7   11
    C+ main.cpp        3    21
    C  main.h               22    #define BTN_PAD_VALUE_INC_TIME   4
    C+ protimer_state_ma…   23    #define BTN_PAD_VALUE_DEC_TIME   2
  > test                    24    #define BTN_PAD_VALUE_ABRT       6
  ● .gitignore              25    #define BTN_PAD_VALUE_SP         1
  ⊕ platformio.ini          26
                            27
                            28    /* Signals of the application*/

TERMINAL    DEBUG CONSOLE    PROBLEMS  3     OUTP

Checking size .pio\build\uno\firmware.elf
Advanced Memory Usage is available via "Plat
RAM:   [         ]  1.1% (used 23 bytes fr
Flash: [         ]  1.5% (used 468 bytes f
=================================== [SUCCESS]
```

Let's use this in the program. So digital read. PIN button, one that reads the status of button one in B one. I'll just remove this. After that two is equal to. Read the button to status to be to. And after that. Likewise for Button three. Now, she has one more variable here. But 10 had. Value. Now, button pad value is equal to so he can write something like this, be one shipped and write to be twice are. The one shifted by one Budweiser B three. So you have to merge all these states to form a value. So you just use Bitwise or for that. After that, though, we got the button part value here, but that needs to be a protest against the button, balancing how to process the button, bouncing in the software to see that later. But for the time being, let's give one function for that. What I would call this process. But 10 had value. You have to process means it has to be processed far from button bouncing. So we'll do that in the function process, but in pad value, you just send the value here. This rally here. So think about implementing this function later. And receive a protest around you here. So this is part, but an Indiebound thing. The deep bonds do value what we get here. But on pat value and then you just have to compare that value. Button pad value. So now this function returns a non-zero value. If there is something president on the button pad to lead this function, return a non-zero value if the button pad has been pressed or if any buttons up the button pad have pressed if this function returned zero, that means there is no activity on the button pat, so no button has been pressed.

```
003Protimer > src > C++ main.cpp > ⓧ loop()
19        //1. read the button pad status
20        b1 = digitalRead(PIN_BUTTON1);
21        b2 = digitalRead(PIN_BUTTON2);
22        b3 = digitalRead(PIN_BUTTON3);
23
24        btn_pad_value = (b1<<2)|(b1<<1)|b3;
25
26        uint8_t btn_pad_value uncing
27        btn_pad_value = process_button_pad_value(btn_pad_value);
28        if(btn_pad_value){
29
30        }
31
32        //2. make an event
33        //3. send it to event dispatcher
34
35
```

If nobody pressed, then the value is zero. So that's why we will process the button pad value only if it is non-zero. Here, if the button 's paid value is equal to Barton's value. Abbott, ah, let's start with increment time. That means we have to now send the increment time event, so will create one event variable here. Four times the timer. User event, I quote it as a U.S. user event. User event. Super thing is equal to increment time, have to populate the signal parameter. That's it. So that's the only thing you need to do. Alpha. But 10 had a value equal to. But Button, add value, Dick Freeman time. Then you have to populate the signal variable with decrement time and numerator and. That's how you make the event. This is the second task. Make an event. Next, elusive, next, elusive, this is for the balls. This is for. A BRT. And then here you just turned that event to the dispatcher for a timer dispatcher. We have. You have to find the address of the more B.J.. Sorry, not what is that man application object fraud timer? And the address ws that he went. So it says that the argument of time here, you should not stand like this. You should send a pointer to this UN type. That's right. Our resolve. You eat super. And implement this now. Let's implement this here. So we'll implement this in the next project. You returned a difficulty. But, Pat, well, value. And the prototype last returned zero for a time being. They felt so you can keep it as static. So find it to the Iran dispatch, this is the third task. Now we completed defending the user event. Now again, we have to implement some code to send the ticket rent, so we haven't implemented the call to dispatch the ticket rent. We'll see that data. So this completes a sending off user event.

EXERCISE-003 DISPATCHING TIME TICK EVENT

In the previous project, we implemented the call to dispatch the user event, and we had to implement this function. I will do that later. Let's write a small code to dispatch their time to the event that will make use of the millis function provided by the Arduino framework. Now, let's see. What does it do? It returns the number of milliseconds passed since the Arduino board began running the current program. Basically, it returns the milliseconds past, so this number will all flow up to approximately 50 days because the data type is unsigned long, and that is the way it is for Byte. You can see here one example code. Here they have used a Middle East, and in this code statement, they are storing the current time into this variable. Current time is not the clock time. It's not the clock time. It is the number of milliseconds passed since the Arduino board began running the program.

Example Code

This example code prints on the serial port the number of milliseconds passed since th the code itself.

```
unsigned long myTime;

void setup() {
  Serial.begin(9600);
}
void loop() {
  Serial.print("Time: ");
  myTime = millis();

  Serial.println(myTime); // prints time since program started
  delay(1000);            // wait a second so as not to send massive amounts of data
}
```

So that means the number of milliseconds passed before executing. This statement here, so that value is stored here, and we will make use of this function. Now let's get back to our project and here this is one function. What we wrote earlier. So what we will implement here. Dispatch the time tick event for every hundred milliseconds, because that's what we decided to do, that our state machine, this is the time to give and for every 100 milliseconds. So I will create one local static variable here. This is just for the current time, it's up to Typekit U.S. territory in difficulty. And initially, I was told the current time using the military function. So just enjoy life. This with this function since there's a static variable. So the first time when the controlled reach of this loop, only one time this variable will be initialized to the current time is in terms of the number of milliseconds after that. Here I will write one small logic if. Monies for this returns the actual current time. This becomes the fear at the current time. So this is the actual running current time, minus the third current time. If this difference is equal to or if it grows bigger than 100 milliseconds, then that means 100 milliseconds has passed.

```
}else if(btn_pad_value == BTN_PAD_VALUE_SP){
    ue.super.sig = START_PAUSE;
}else if(btn_pad_value == BTN_PAD_VALUE_ABRT){
    ue.super.sig = ABRT;
}
//3. send it to event dispatcher
protimer_event_dispatcher(&protimer,&ue.super);

}

//4. dispatch the time tick event for every 100ms
if(millis() - current_time >= 100){
    //100ms has passed
}
```

In that case, what we should do, we should first reset this time because for the next generation, we have to reset this with me. I'm just resetting this variable with the current time. Because this court will not execute for every look, because it is a static variable. That's why I am against initializing it. And after that, let's create one variable. From time to time to give rent, I call Dusty. And you can even make the RSS feed here that is equal to zero because we have to use the second print. Then what do I do now is we have to make an event death Hooper think is equal to time tick. T if we are to implement this. Whenever 100 milliseconds have passed, we have to implement this. Its value varies from one to 10. That's why here TFF grows bigger than 10 and we have to reset TFF to one. So can you do something like this? That means it has to be the static variable, right, because it can't be a local variable, otherwise for every loop, this will be new life to zero. You had to make this as static, then this initialization may not be quite because the static variables are by default initialized to zero. That looks good when this becomes 11. It refers to one after that we have to. Call the event dispatcher Pete Super, that's about dispatching the time to the event to the state machine. And you can also do this using a timer interrupt for every 100 milliseconds you can generate a timer interrupt and that also you can do that. Now let's try to compile this. There are no errors, but a couple of warnings. The compiler doesn't recognize this type of initialization. It says unimplemented, no problem will remove that. The next project, let's understand the button bouncing thing, and I will try to implement this, I've in the next project.

BUTTON BOUNCING EXPLANATION

In this project, let's discuss button bouncing and also discuss later how to debunk it using software. This is how we interface the push button to the Arduino board. We actually interface the push button using a pulldown resistor so you can even do it using the palabra system. Here this is our interfacing and looks like a switch. And this is a pulldown resistor of 10 K going to ground. This is actually the picture of the push button. Its internal structure is something like this. When the switch is not pushed, that is when the switch is open. You can see that this pin is connected to the ground while this pulldown resistor.

Push button interfacing to Arduino using Pull down resistor

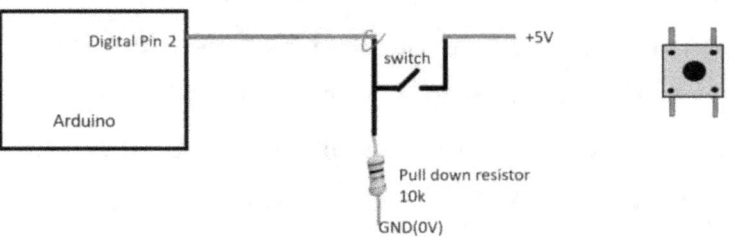

That means that we are at the end point of the input voltage we are in. This is us. That is actually zero. It looks something like this if you measure the wattage at the endpoint, that much emitter actually shows zero. This is actually the plus firework. Suppose if you close the switch, then what happens is we in point are actually connected to fire. It looks something like this to be connected to the pirate. This point, if you measure the old age at this point now it shows you quite well. So the circuit looks something like this.

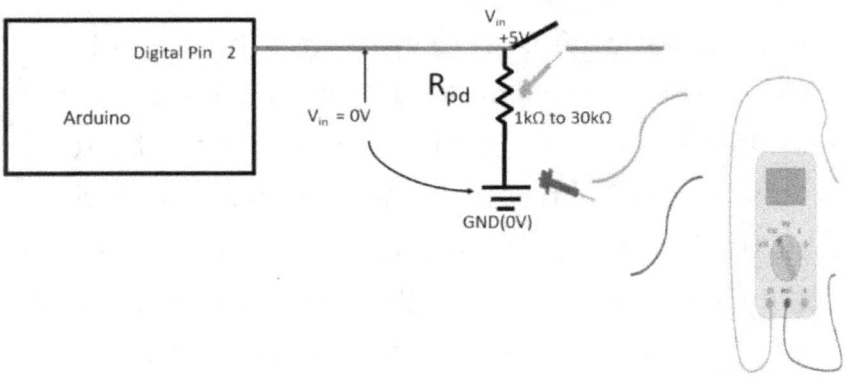

There is a pulldown resistor. Going to ground and that is a battery of firewood. And this point is going to the pin we in this is the in. When the digital pen of the microcontroller is in input mode, its input impedance is very high in terms of Mega Ohms. That's why when you close this switch, there is no abrupt increase of current. The current will not move inside this microcontroller pen because its input imprudent that pins the input impedance is very high. So no current flows actually, except some leakage current. That's why you need not to worry about a lot of current thinking into the pin. It doesn't happen because of the input impedance up to paint, but if you are cord mistakenly, if it configures this digital pin more as output than the input input impedance suddenly drops and large current may flow into the pin and it may damage your pin. That's why it's better to introduce one more resistor here that is the current limiting resistor in this pot. Maybe around 220 or something. This is our interfacing. And then the button is not pressed, the Penn State is the right word. And when the button is pressed, Penn State goes to Firewalled. But in reality, the transition is not this mode. In reality, that transition from zero to fired or fired to zero would underpin look something like this. This is called button bouncing that is bouncing between zero or and five. What a couple of times before settling for either five 2.0 or why this bouncing happens. It happens because of mechanical contact. What is actually a switch switch is nothing but mechanical contacts. So this is a mechanical contact or metal contact. These are metal contacts when you push one metal contact on other metal contact, one metal contact tends to bounce upon the other metal contact. That is a slight disengagement when you touch this metal contact to this metal contact, so they bounce off of each other. I mean, that is a slight disengagement and engagement for a couple of times that results in bouncing off all stages between zero firewalls.

Button Bouncing

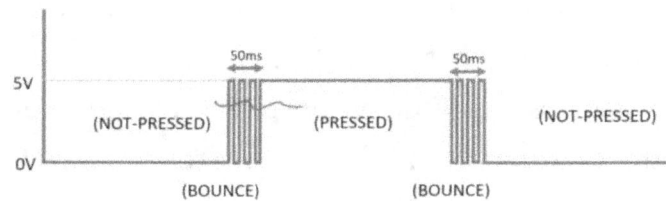

Because of that disengagement, for a small period of time, that time is very small. It could be in terms of microseconds or in some switches. It could be intense up milliseconds, different switches. They have different bounce times. And for this application, we're to crudely take it at 50 milliseconds. Strictly speaking, you have to check the bounce PDA or bounce time in the oscilloscope.

You have to verify that in the oscilloscope for your switch or what exactly the bounce PDA does. You have to check that then you can use it in your application, but will clearly take it as 50 milliseconds for our application. This is how the activity on the PIN looks like. You can name the different situations of the pin like this, not state bound state. Press the state like that. This is actually button push. This is actually the button release. Now, through software, you have to get rid of this problem. Will your software be a bouncing technique? There is also hardware, the bouncing technique to get the clean transition, something like this. For that, you have to attach the deep bouncing circuitry between your switch and the digital pin. But for this exercise, you'll go for software debunking. And how to do that, I'll show you in the next project.

EXERCISE-003 BUTTON SOFTWARE DE-BOUNCING IMPLEMENTATION

Hey, welcome back to the project. This project will implement Soft Fat Button debunks the previous project. You saw that these are the activities on the pin when the pin is pushed and when the PIN is released, so you can visualize this as different situations. And then those situations you can also target have different states of a pin. So that's why whenever a switch is pressed or relieved, the PIN undergoes these various states. So that's why pins of different states can be represented by a state machine diagram. Here I have written a small state machine diagram for our button bouncing. You can't create as many models you want here, just right click on this and go to create diagram and state mission diagram. You can do that. So it will not implement the standard, um, specification based state machine. We'll just implement this as a normal function. But I just wanted to let you know about the pindi. Bouncing also can be represented in terms of state merchandiser. Here I have got three states not pressed, pressed both of them that this is implemented as a function and the function receives button pad value. First, the pain will be in a non craft state. And then the button pad value is non-zero. That means someone has pressed the buttons, so that will be a transition to a bounce state. And the action is set at the current time, so we'll discuss that later. What exactly sets the current time? But the key point here is when the pin is then not crafted. And if the button pad value becomes non-zero, then the state machine must balance state and in the bound state, it has to wait for 50 milliseconds so that the bounce period 50 milliseconds is spent here. The beginning of that 50 millisecond is marked by the set current time, so we can do this using Millis. I would say that later. So while the state machine is in a bound state after 50 milliseconds, it has to rewrite the button pad value once again, the fresh button pad value. If it is zero, that means no one has pressed the button. So that's why it goes to a not pressed state. But if the button pad value is non-zero after 50 milliseconds, then it goes to the press of state. So that indicates someone has really pressed the button. And while it is in the press state, it just stays that until the button pad value returns to zero, when someone releases the button, then the button pad value becomes zero. So that's the indication that someone has released the button. That's why the transition will come to the bound state again, because you have to debunk the release date also. And the beginning of the time is marked by a fat current time function. It happens like that. So now we will implement this as a small function. Let's go back to the court here. So we have already defined a function process button pad value inside. This will do that. First, I will take a static variable called. But on the state machine. Initially, it is equal to doing one thing, we will create another enemy here. TypeDef. In. But 10 State and Scotty.

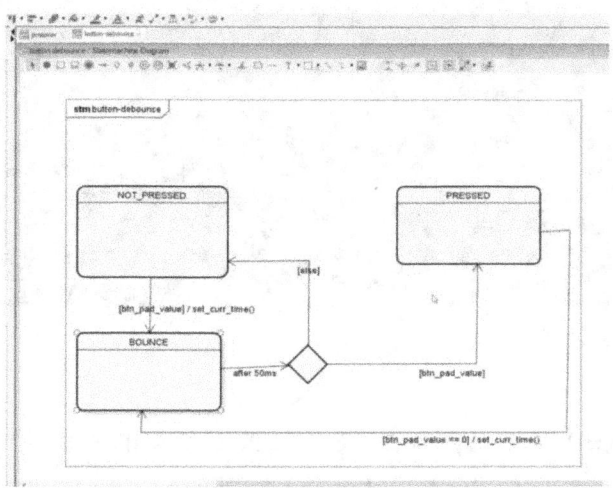

Button State is initially not pressed. So now let's use the Switch case. But Penn State. Right. Different cases for not theft. So, right. Different cases here. When it is not pressed. The state machine says if the button pad value is non-zero, then there is a transition. And we'll take one more variable here, just for the current time required to initialize this with this.

Here current time you have to set the current time. That will be used in the bound state to timeout after 15 milliseconds. After that, you have to put a brake statement here. When it comes to the bones, it should not do anything until the 50 milliseconds passes. That's why. That's do nothing until 50 milliseconds passes. Now here, recheck, that had value, so if. Barton had value. If it is fat, then go to préfere state. But Penn State is required to. But Penn State is required to not trust. And then. Break. So while it is in the press state. So if button pad value is zero. Then it has to go to the bound state. And. Since it is going to bounce that you have to re-initialize the current time because this marks the starting point, the 50 milliseconds will be recalculated. Put a brake statement. That looks good. And also, this function returns something Wright wanted a chance to hear Theia if it is really pressed if the function decides that up to 50 milliseconds something has really pressed, then it has to return here. Return the button pad value. Because this button pad value is a value after the software debunks that is after rating for 50 milliseconds. So let's wait, let's pretend that value back to the caller. And dysfunction. By default, returns zero here. So that's implementation, this is a kind of small state machine, but this will help us to visualize how to debunks the pin, which is connected to the push button. So we just completed this function. And when it returns, the button pad value here and then if it's a valid button pad value, I mean, if it returns zero, then that is not processed and if it returns something non-zero value and if it's a valid value, an event will be formed and it will be sent to the dispatcher.

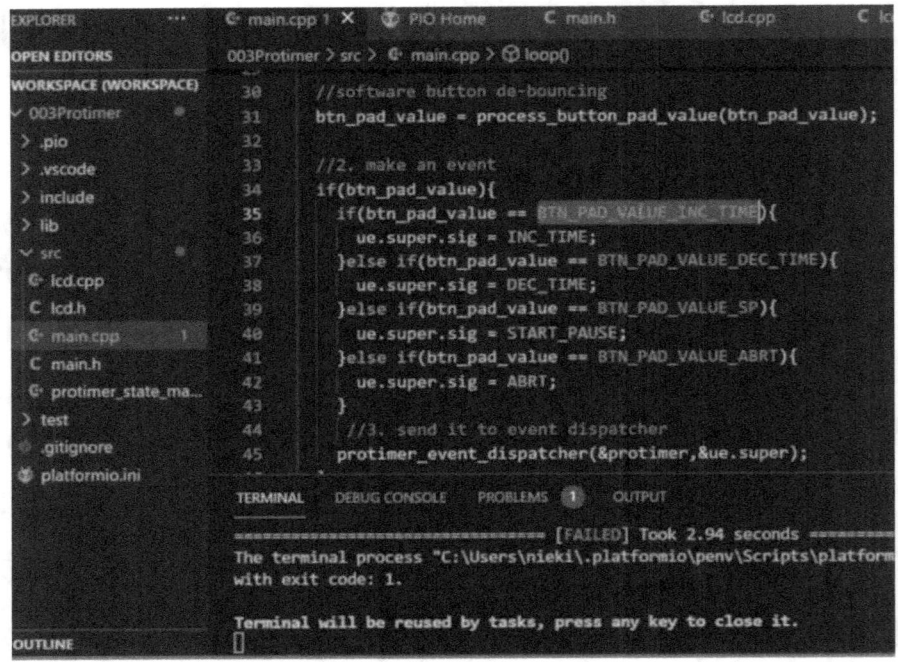

So I hope you can follow this. So now let's give our attention to implementing the LCD darkened LCD dark trials that will be our last implementation, and after that, we can test it. So first of all, we were right. The setup function in the setup function, we have to do various setup set up LCD, the serial monitor. If we use the fetal monitor setting up the digital pin mode, we have not done that. So we will do that here. I would just write a function display in it. This initializes the LCD display. We will implement this later and also. Theories begin. Nine six. On one one five two zero zero. So if you are printing anything on Cyril one chair, then it is required. And after that, we were able to print something here. After that, we will use the pin more function of the Arduino to configure the mod for the buttons. All right. So about the pin more function for the PIN, more function as you know you are to provide the pin and more modestly nothing about any of this value. Input output with Pull-Up input with pull up option is already available, so that means that you need not to use the external pull up register. But using external pull up resistors are usually generic methods because sometimes we don't know whether a microcontroller pin supports the internal pull up or not. So you have to do more investigation on that pin. But if you don't want to use those transistors, take it all, then you can use the option input with pull up. And now let's use this.

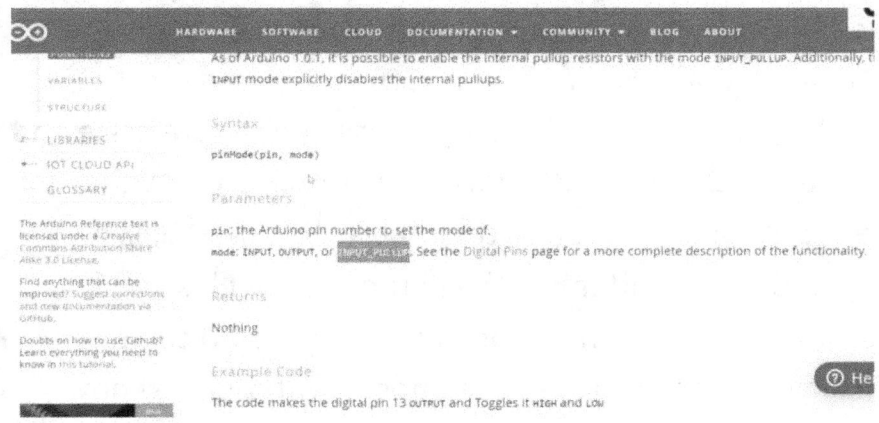

So just go back to the code, and here it is. PIN underscored button one. And the motive is put. So you have to copy and paste it three times. And after that, do you call this function? Now let me just compile this function. So that is one warning. Let's see that there will be two effects, but not used. This is not one, this is B too. So please make that change. And now let's compile. The competition is fine, and in the next project, we will explode the Arduino LCD library and we will try to use the Arduino LCD library method in our project to drive over 16 cross to LCD. And after that, we will have this project in our heart. I've seen the next project.

ADDING ARDUINO LIBRARY TO PROJECT IN PLATFORMIO

Hey, welcome back to the project. So in this project, let's explore Arduino is the official LCD library, and for that, you have to go to the documentation, go to reference and reference. Do you find libraries? Just click on that and here click on displays and the official libraries. Click on Liquid Crystal. And this is the library where I lost communication with alcohol, numerical liquid crystal displays. Just click on read the documentation to know more about this library. This is for liquid crystal displays. Based on that you've HD four four seven eight zero or compatible chipsets. And we are using the same chipset based 16 across two LCDs. And you can understand more about this library here. There are various examples of code they have given and at the right hand side, what you see, these are the matters, different matters or functions of their liquid crystal libraries. In our project scenes, we are using our platform Iyo extension. We have to first install this library.

```
case ENTRY:{
    display_message("Paused");
    return EVENT_HANDLED;
}
case EXIT:{
    display_clear();
    return EVENT_HANDLED;
}
case INC_TIME:{
    mobj->curr_time += 60;
    mobj->active_state = TIME_SET;
    return EVENT_TRANSITION;
}
case DEC_TIME:{
    if(mobj->curr_time >= 60){
        mobj->curr_time -= 60;
        mobj->active_state = TIME_SET;
```

```
Flash: [=        ] 13.8% (used 4460 bytes from 32256 bytes)
Building .pio\build\uno\firmware.hex
================== [SUCCESS] Took 2.57 seconds ==================
Terminal will be reused by tasks, press any key to close it.
```

I will just show you how to install that library. Very simple. Go home. So if you don't know how to access this home, then that is the home button here or you go here. Platform and that is a home button. Quick access home open and here go to libraries. And in the library, searching for this name suggests Karpeles name and searches for you. This should be by Arduino, because that's the official one. Right here. After that, you just click over that and add to the project. Like that, you just packed a project and set up your project. So this is my project, I have just selected that. And add. So this is a project wise library attic, so you can either add project wise or workspace wise. You can also do that. So we'll just do a project twice. We'll just add this to our project. Then add. And once you add that. You can see that in the platform, ipod Dot I and II. So you can see that that is added here. Library dependency. So with this LCD, you can do all this functionality if you want to print a text, then you can make use of the print method if you want to know how to use this print method. Then just open that documentation. It explains to you how to use that. So if you want to print Hello World on the outside, then you have to first create the outside object. This is an LCD object. This is a cloth. So the liquid crystal cloth. So this is the object we created. And these are the pin numbers up the Arduino board. You used to connect the LCD to the Arduino board, so you have to carefully mention the documentation expense. What order do you have to mention these pins? You can see that here. You can go to this liquid crystal function. It says that you have to create the object or you have to supply the argument to the object in this order. First artist Annabelle before de 67. If you use RW, that is to read the right pin. So if you use the lead right pin of the LCD, then the read right pin must come second. Like that? These two are not used in our application, so this is for eight bit communication, so we will use this one. I'll show you how to use that while recording. If you are confused? Don't worry. Now, we don't think so.

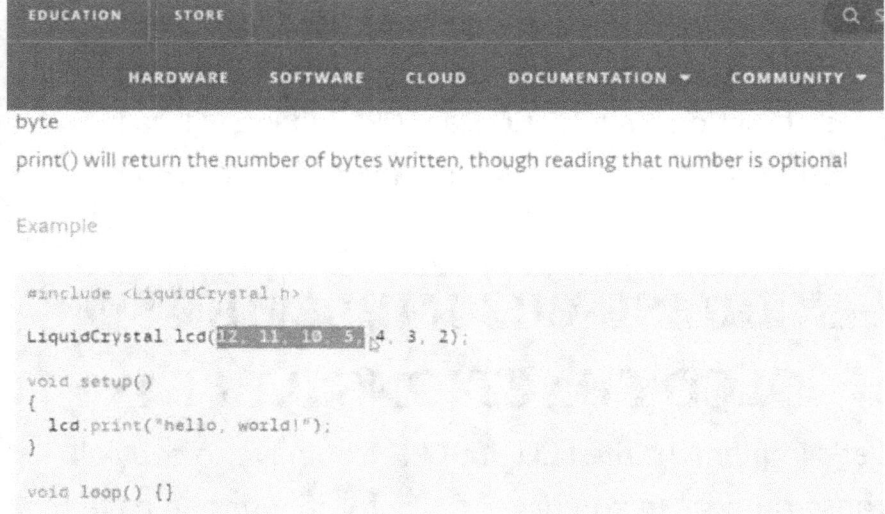

We'll go to the LCD dark file of our project and we will add all of these raptor functions, though we will support all these functions to deal with the LCD, LCD, clear LCD. If you want to print a character on the LCD, then you use this function. This is to scroll the LCD display to scroll left to scroll right. OK. This is to set the cursor at a different position of the display, like setting the curves that are given row number and column number. And this is to stop the auto scrolling. This is the LCD initialization. So like this, we will give various wrapper functions. So if you are wondering, how did I arrive at fixing this function? Just go to the method. So these are the different methods. These are nothing but some wrapper functions for these methods. So in the next project, we will implement all these functions in the LCD Dark CP, and we will call these functions from our main source file out to the next project.

EXERCISE-003 IMPLEMENTING LCD FUNCTIONS PART 1

Let's implement the LCD dot CPP. You have to copy all these things and you have to pay for it and then have to implement the functions one by one. In Dale City, Dot CP suggested LCD dotage. And here is the top. You create the LCD object for the liquid crystal library of Arduino. Or you can just look at one usage example. Here first, you have to create the LCD object. Let's do that. Death type, liquid crystal and object name. This is a class name and the object lesson name LCD. And then you had to pass the pin details Arduino pin details per week. You have connected the LCD pins for today's artists. How macro and TRF. This is not acceptable here, but let's do one thing, let's also include the main data here. LCD that is pin LCD artist Karma. Next one is Annabelle PIN LCD, Annabelle. We also have connected and a read right print that is RW pin. That's why. We also have to use that.

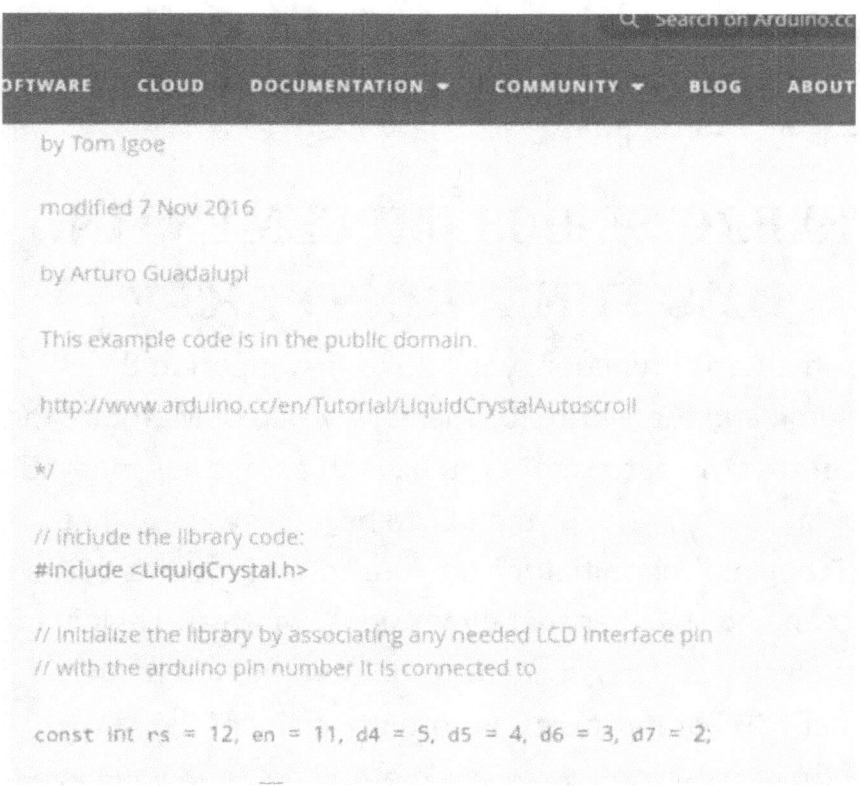

That position is second read, right? That's right. The second argument is pin LCD, RW, then pin LCD and vote, then deport Defy. 63. We just created the object, this actually caused the constructor of this class and the library initializes the. Since you have used this class, you have to add it's hard to file. The header file is liquid crystal dotage. And now you use this object to access its various methods for LCD clear. You can just go here and call LCD clear that fits the LCD print cap. You can use LCD print, you can pass the character for LCD scroll left. You can use LCD just to LCD scroll display left like that. Complete all these functions, and I will see you in the next project.

EXERCISE-003 IMPLEMENTING LCD FUNCTIONS PART 2

For the Carter function, you had to first mention the column and then write for the library said of Method. And after that, no auto scroll. You have to access this method, no auto scroll. And for the LTT to begin. Let's see what LCD begins. This initializes the interface of today 's LCD screen and specifies that dimensions, width and height of the display and begin needs to be covered before any other LCD library comes. Before using any of the methods, you should use this method first and you have to pass to argument number of columns and number of rows. Your LCD has slightly modified this highly. As you enter and discover eight columns and rows, you have to mention columns, comma, Roth and then more cursor right to left whenever you print a character to the display.

The cards are more from right to left. If you call this function, the configuration function, you can make the cursor move from left to right instead, which is also by default. Then you can call this function. If you don't want to see the cursor on the display, call this function. Cut it off. This calls for nor cut off the method of the LCD object and not blink if you don't want to blink the cursor. Then go for this. If you want to put into any number, you can use the LCD print with the argument type, integer or rather, I would call this as LCD print number and print string. It doesn't matter whether you want to print a character or a string or a number. There is only one method that is printed on the LCD. Let me make this 3D print number. And this is not white Rose. And let's include FTD in the Rich List compiled, see whether or not.

```c
#ifndef LCD_H
#define LCD_H
#include<stdint.h>

void lcd_clear(void);
void lcd_print_char(char c);
void lcd_scroll_left(void);
void lcd_scroll_right(void);
void lcd_set_cursor(int r, int c);
void lcd_no_auto_scroll(void);
void lcd_begin(uint8_t cols, uint8_t rows);
void lcd_move_cursor_R_to_L(void);
void lcd_move_cursor_L_to_R(void);
void lcd_cursor_off(void);
void lcd_cursor_blinkoff(void);
void lcd_print_number(int num);
void lcd_print_string(String s);
```

Healthily for intrigue, there is one problem. The string is not recognized here. You also have to add our known dotage. Let's build. This fine, just remote, this is strange, it's not required if you're out this one. We have implemented LCD, Dark Cap and LCD, Dark Age. Now what we do is we go to our main dark sleep and complete dysfunction first display in it. Let me implement this at the bottom. Display in it before calling any matters of their city first, you have to initialize the city. There are a lot of initialization commands that need to be sent to the LCD before using other functionalities of the LCD, like sending commands or sending text to display. All those things can be done using LCD begin map of the library just you have to call the LCD. Begin will call that first. Here we have our LCD data. Let's include that data. And let's try to access all the wrapper functions. LCD begins. You have to power 16. Mark two. That's our LCD. And after this line, you can send whatever. Come on, you want. I would like to go for these settings for my LCD. After beginning, I clear the LCD and the cursor is set for left or right. Swipe left or right because select faces are LCD 16 across two LCD and this is left. This is right. Let's be clear here. Whenever you write the first character, let's say if the cards are more to write, it comes over here that the default nature of the LCD. But you can also configure it using this function. That is a function. More cards are left to right because of this method of the LCD object and setting the cursor to the zero zero location. This actually configured the coordinates of the LCD, which internally used a set cursor. For example, if you want to set the color here, then according to the functional L1 column, I'll just modify this. I first mentioned the column and then drew because the library actually takes that in that fashion column.

```
129
130         return 0;
131     }
132
133     static void display_init(void)
134     {
135         lcd_begin(16,2);
136         lcd_clear();
137         lcd_move_cursor_L_to_R();
138         lcd_set_cursor(0,0);
139         lcd_no_auto_scroll();
140         lcd_cursor_off();
141     }
```

First, Rifkind's first argument is column number, and then it is a draw and it turns up the scrolling of the display. And this actually turns off the visibility of the Carter. Carter wound up here on the display. That is actually the display in it. And now our final tough case to implement the helper functions are help for action functions like you have to display the time display. The message display is very simple. You just call LCD and display clear. Here it is not accessible. We'll do one thing. We will add LCD data here. And called and said clear here and display time now how to display the time on the LCD. Let's discuss that. Here it is. The time has to be displayed in minute and second fashion. That is no field for art information. This is the m m m. This is yes. If there is one column, the time must appear in the road zero and it should start at column five and that column 10. Here you have to display that. And when it is in the idle state, let's say the application is an idea state it should show at that time that fact time must appear at these coordinates on the display here, the timer is set 400 minutes, the second whenever it enters the Portal state, the post state a message should appear yet parsed at these coordinates and whenever the application is in fact state, the message should appear at these coordinates of that city.

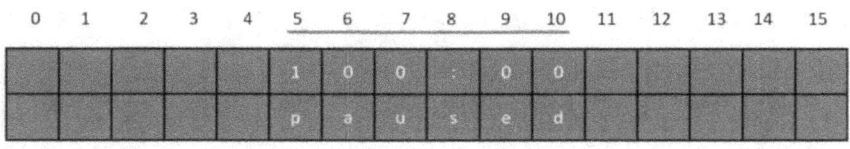

16x2 LCD

So now how to display the time, how to convert the current time variable to minutes, then second. Very simple. Let's assume the current time is equal to, let's say, one two five. Then minute is equal to current time modulus of 60, which gives you five. Sorry, this is not two minutes seconds. Second is equal to current time. Martella, 60, which gives you fight and minute, is equal to current time, divided by 60. The integer division gives you two 125 mins two minutes five seconds. It should be displayed like this. Zero zero two column zero quite like that. Zero zero two column zero five. That's how you convert current time to seconds and minutes while displaying in that display time function. I believe that I am an assignment to you. And after that display message for the display, a message that is one information we have to provide in the application. The messages are getting printed on different coordinates. For example, this message is getting printed at these coordinates. And this message and this coordinate and this message is that this coordinate? That's what I will do. One thing. We will also receive the coordinates for this function because the messages are coordinate dependent. I will just take column numbers here and row numbers here. It will modify this function. Like this display message? Wherever you have you, the display message, for example, I have used the display message here. You also should send the coordinates of the first column Vendrell, for example. You can see here for the first time, first you are to send it. First, you have to send that first column veto and a role that is zero. And again, you have to call this display message this time, the message is time Harlem is zero, raw is one. He has paths. The fifth column is five rows. I hope you can modify that and just implement that function here and these functions, and for the beep, you can use that tone function of the Arduino, that is the tone function. And the reference is a cartoon tone function. And you can use this tone function, and you just have to mention the pin, which is connected to the bazaar frequency and the duration, the frequency of the square where it is fed to this pin, which drives the buzzer and the duration, how long that beep should come out. And I hope you can do that. And in the next measure, I will show you the implementation. But before that, you just tried to call this function and I'll see in the next election.

EXERCISE-003 HELPER FUNCTION IMPLEMENTATION

Here is the implementation. First, let me show you a very simple display message. You just have to call first and see the third quarter and then you have to call LCD print, a string that fits and for the beep, you have to call the tone function with the pin of the buzzer. This is the duration of 25 milliseconds. I mean, the beep will come for twenty five milliseconds. I Chartbeat, and this is a square wave generated and it's the frequency of the square wave generator which is fed to the buzzer foreclosures. And after that, let's go to the display tying function. Here you receive the current time and that current time is divided by 60 to get the minutes. And then modulus with 60 to get two seconds. And then we convert this into a string. The minute and second information for that will use the sprint function, and we will store that string in the buffer, a character buffer. These are the former to specify if used.

```
203          return EVENT_IGNORED;               > display_message
204      }
205
206      //////////////////////////helper functions//////////////
207      static void display_time(uint32_t time){
208          char buf[7];
209          String time_msg;
210
211          uint16_t m = time / 60;
212          uint8_t s = ti (const char [10])"%03d:%02d"
213          sprintf(buf,"%03d:%02d",m,s);
214
215          time_msg = (String)buf;
216          lcd_set_cursor();
217          lcd_print_string(time_msg);
218      }
```

TERMINAL   DEBUG CONSOLE   PROBLEMS 2   OUTPUT

RAM: [==   ] 17.8% (used 364 bytes from 2048 bytes)
Flash: [==   ] 16.8% (used 5408 bytes from 32256 bytes)
========================== [SUCCESS] Took 4.71 seconds =====

Terminal will be reused by tasks, press any key to close it.

This will convert these numbers to a string format and that string will be stored here in the buffer. Here I have used a percentage zero three D for a minute because I need a minute with three characters. This actually generates an integer of three characters. The unused character will be filled with zero. And the same is true with this and that buffer, I just convert it into a string format. This is provided with our framework. Just type that and set the code up before printing the time information that occurs. The first column is five and row is zero five zero. And then call and print a string that fits that compiled this. There are some issues I had to make some changes here. Here for this message. Columnist one draw is one. Let's compile once again. The competition is fine, and I think we have completed almost all the code required for this application and in the next project. Let's test this on the real hard fact and I have also given you that I am no fan of this project. A single file. And using that, you can test it right away on the Tinker card application.

EXERCISE-003 IMPLEMENTING INITIAL TRANSITION ACTIONS

Last test this application before testing that, let's take a look into our full timeout init function once again here. This is the initial transition. It is making a transition to idle state, but idle state has its entry action for entry activities that's why whenever you set the state as idle here, you have to call it into action.

```
13   static event_status_t protimer_state_ > display_message
14   static event_status_t protimer_state_handler_TIME_SET(protimer_t *const mobj, event_t
15   static event_status_t protimer_state_handler_COUNTDOWN(protimer_t *const mobj, event_t
16   static event_status_t protimer_state_handler_PAUSE(protimer_t *const mobj, event_t cons
17   static event_status_t protimer_state_handler_STAT(protimer_t *const mobj, event_t cons
18
19   void protimer_init(protimer_t *mobj){
20       mobj->active_state = IDLE;
21       mobj->pro_time = 0;
22   }
23
24   event_status_t protimer_state_machine(protimer_t *const mobj, event_t const *const e){
25       switch (mobj->active_state){
26           case IDLE:
27               return protimer_state_handler_IDLE(mobj,e);
28           case TIME_SET:
```

TERMINAL   DEBUG CONSOLE   PROBLEMS   OUTPUT
avrdude done. Thank you.

============================ [SUCCESS] Took 6.29 seconds ============================
Terminal will be reused by tasks, press any key to close it.

We actually forgot to do that. Let's not. I would just create one temporary variable event and reaction, which he thinks is equal to entry, and you have to call this from here for time on the state machine because you have to execute that interaction because you have to send the entry event to the island state and LBJ and send the address of this variable. This function is used only one time. Let's test this.

EXERCISE-003 TESTING ON HARDWARE

All right, so now let's test this application on the real hardware. So I have the setup here. Now here, as you can see, I have the LCD. This is about the. The potential meter to set the contrast button pad, and these are the pull down resistors and these connections are made exactly like the way I explained in my Tinker card reader. So no changes, you have to connect exactly like that. And now let's launch our application. This is our application. So it compiled well, let's compile once again. So the compilation is fine, and now let's upload. So it is getting uploaded to the board. Here you can see that we are actually seeing the output so you can use the potentiometer to adjust the contrast. It is in Iowa State now, it's behaving exactly like the way we expected voters showing the time display that time, and that is a buzzer, which is beeping for every five hundred milliseconds. So now let's test the functionality first, let me check implementation time. You can see that whenever I. Press this button. The minute is incrementing and this is decrement time, and you can also observe that the button presses the bounds.

So you can see that. Right. This is a decrepit time. Yeah, it is behaving as expected. It can go all the way to zero. And now let me start the countdown. It doesn't start because it is zero. Now let's start the countdown. You can see that. It is counting down. And you can't cause it, so I just paused it. When it is positive you can decrement it, you can increment it and start. And after that. You can abort this countdown if you want. You have to press these two buttons together, so it is about right now. Now it is indeed a state. So now let's start. The countdown once again. And. Now, let's pause. Decrement starts. OK, aboard. And now let's check stat. When it denied the more you had to press the start button to get into the stock. So as you can see, when I press this, it goes to the state state and it comes back to the idle state after being medically checked. Up to one second. So what's the implementation? Who doesn't look like one second? It stays there for one second. Let me do one thing. So here there is a small bug in the fact function compacting the assessed value to 10 doesn't look good because when the application comes to the start handler and when it receives the time tick for the first time, the assessed value could be anything. It need not be zero. It could be anything.

```
188        switch(e->sig){
189            case ENTRY:{
190                display_time(mobj->pro_time);
191                display_message("Productive time",1,1);
192                return EVENT_HANDLED;
193            }
194            case EXIT:{
195                display_clear();
196                return EVENT_HANDLED;
197            }
198            case TIME_TICK:{
199                if(((protimer_tick_event_t*)(e))->ss == 10){
200                    mobj->active_state = IDLE;
201                    return EVENT_TRANSITION;
202                }
203                return EVENT_IGNORED;
204            }
```

TERMINAL   DEBUG CONSOLE   PROBLEMS   OUTPUT

avrdude done. Thank you.

================================ [SUCCESS] Took 5.97 seconds ================================
Terminal will be reused by tasks, press any key to close it.

It may not be one, right? It could be 10. So in that case, what happens here? You know, it immediately returns to the idea of state. But our requirement is that the standard must be shown, at least for one second. So that's why this doesn't look good. I'm going to remove this logic. Instead of that, I'm going to add one variable to count. If this is equal to 10, if two events are received for ten times, then I would make the count equal to zero. I already set that. This is a static function, actually a static extended variable. So let's define that here. Static you in and difficulty to count. You can modify it like this. So same logic you can use wherever you have processed time to. He also said you can use the same logic. So because it's the very first time, this could be anything, right? So now with this change, let's again test this court. So let's do one thing. Let's make this as 20 or 30 instead of 10. Let it stay for three seconds in the stacked state. Let's compile. Let's download Discord. Let me start the countdown. And let me know about this. Let me press the Start button, and you can see that it stays for three seconds. Try to reproduce this application, and if you find any bugs now, you should be able to fix that and also you can try to give more features to this application. You may introduce new events or you can introduce a new stage to introduce different features to the application. So one change that I would like to see here is you hear if I want to set that time to 30, for example, I have to press the button for 30 times, so that is not user-friendly. You can modify that supposedly by pressing and holding this button. Then for every second, at least, it should increase by four. You can implement such logic here. I have to press every time. And fame for decrement time, but. All right, with that note, I would like to end this project, and in the next project onwards, we will explore the function pointers and we'll also redo this exercise using the state handler approach. I'll see you in the next project.

FUNCTION POINTERS IN C

Hey, welcome back to the project. In the previous project, we explored the Nestor Switch approach to implement the state machine. And in this project, let us understand the state handling. After that, we can explore the state table approach. So the state table approach and standard approach, they all use the function to point to a concept. That's why. First, let's explore the function point fee. So afterwards I continue with that approach. First of all, what is a function point to now, let me explain that with an example. Let's say you have some variable definitions, so let's say in P. This is a variable definition. Or you can also call it a declaration. He r p. He's really able to hold. In the data. So now this is very simple. You already know four things. Now if I were in the top kill set. What is this? This is also a variable definition. This is also a video by definition here. Cue is a pointer variable. To hold an address. The address points. To that data of TIE. In the queue is a pointer variable to hold an address which points to the data of type INT. Now, let's say I have a function called Bar. Function. It doesn't take any argument, doesn't return anything. Now, let's say I have a function and the function is doing some operation. So obviously, when you load this programme into a microcontroller, obviously this function will get stored in memory, right? Strictly speaking. So this function? I mean, the code generated to represent the function will be stored in the core memory, which is nothing but a flash memory. So that means this function will have its own address. Functions I trust you can represent in a program by using its name. So here I can write something like this, cue is equal to ampersand. This represents the address of this radio, and cue is created to hold the idea for that's why I am starting something like this. So similarly, you can use Ampersand before a function name to represent its address, or you can just use the function name as an address. So can I write like this? Cue is equal to ampersand bar. Can I write like this? This actually gives Ara that fee. Or perhaps a warning, it's not an error either. First effort to remove this compiler warning about another variable, let me write like this. Let's build.

```
24 }
25
26
27 int main()
28 {
29      int p; // this is a variable definition(declaration) ;
30      //'p' is a variable to hold 'int' type data
31
32      int *q;//this is also a variable definition
33      //'q' is a pointer variable to hold an address
34      //the address points to the data of type 'int'
35
36      q = &bar; //error
37
38      (void)p;
39      (void)q;
40
41
```

```
Problems  Tasks  Console  Properties
CDT Build Console [p1]
Info: Internal Builder is used for build
gcc -std=c11 -O0 -g3 -Wall -Wextra -c -fmessage-length=0 -o "src\\p1.o" "..\\sr
..\src\p1.c: In function 'main':
..\src\p1.c:36:4: warning: assignment from incompatible pointer type [-Wincompa
    q = &bar; //error
      ^
gcc -o p1.exe "src\\p1.o"

10:38:38 Build Finished. 0 errors, 1 warnings. (took 715ms)
```

What's the warning for assignment from incompatible point to type? Here it says incompatible to type. Why? Because you see, Q is used to hold the address, which points to the data. Remember that? But this is an address entity which doesn't point to a data point to the code. So that's why what you are doing here and address which points to the code, you are storing it into a pointer variable, which is created to hold the address, which points to the data. That's why this doesn't make any sense. Writing like this doesn't make any sense. And this is wrong. So in Thi, you can create a special point variable, which you can use to hold the idea of a function. Let's create that. Let's see how to create that. So here also you need a point to really appoint a variable that is created by an asterisk. And that says F and what you do here is you put that inside the parentheses like this. So create a point variable, a pointer variable, and put that inside the parentheses. Since this is, use it to hold the address, which points to the code and code that doesn't have any type data have different types like in cab unsigned finding long floor double code doesn't have different types. So that's why this doesn't have any type, but this is used to hold the address of a function. So you have to mention it here. The function, parameter, type and function return Typekit like this and then end this variable definition with a semicolon. So this is also a variable definition. So F is. Function pointer variable to hold the address of a function which. Doesn't take any input arguments. That's why White. Doesn't return. Any data or any value? Jen Typekit is also white. Like a bar function here, a bar function. It doesn't take any input arguments and it doesn't return anything. Now, if can be used to store the address of this function, let's say a physical 10 percent bar. Or simply, you can use the Power Bar. No problem. But it's better to use an Ampersand Bar because it gives you the notion that you are storing an address. So that's why it's always better to use it like this. Here, after it's called a function point, because it's the function, this is a function point or variable. So now after initialization, you can call this at a function pointer because it points to the function. Since it points to the function, you can reference that function and you can jump to that function by using parentheses like this. This is. Jump to the function. Pointed, right? This is like a function call, so you have to direct that pointer and put that in one parenthesis and use one more parenthesis to send arguments to the targeted function. So since this point, the definition tells that there are no input arguments. So that's why you can use an empty parenthesis here. So instead of using this, you can also do something like this. You can just do this. This is the same as ever, so this is allowed, but this gives you the impression that you are calling a function whose name is F.. So this doesn't give you the impression that you are using a function pointer to call a function. That's why it is better to use this method instead of this one. That is just a recommendation. Some people use it like this. Some people use it like this. What could be the output here, what happens whenever the program control comes here? I have faith insulated to this address and the code jumps to this function. And it executes this. Let's see what happens. That's the build of this. And let's run this.

```
26
27  int main()
28  {
29      int p; // this is a variable definition(declaration) ;
30      //'p' is a variable to hold 'int' type data
31
32      int *q;//this is also a variable definition
33      //'q' is a pointer variable to hold an address
34      //the address points to the data of type 'int'
35
36      void(*f)(void);//this is also a variable definition
37      //'f' is a function pointer variable to hold the address of a function
38      //which doesn't take any input arguments (void), and doesn't return
39      //any value(void)
40
41      f = &bar;
42
43      (*f)(); //jump to the function pointed by 'f'
```

```
Problems  Tasks  Console  Properties
CDT Build Console [p1]
Info: Internal Builder is used for build
gcc -std=c11 -O0 -g3 -Wall -Wextra -c -fmessage-length=0 -o "src\\p1.o" "..\\sr
..\src\p1.c: In function 'main':
..\src\p1.c:36:4: warning: assignment from incompatible pointer type [-Wincompa
    q = &bar; //error
    ^
gcc -o p1.exe "src\\p1.o"

10:38:38 Build Finished. 0 errors, 1 warnings. (took 715ms)
```

Now, let's say this function takes some argument, let's say, in entire. And now let's see what happens. So now there's a problem. This function actually returns, right, but its input parameter list is not white. It takes one argument. Now this alignment is incompatible. Why? Because this pointer variable is created to hold the function, which doesn't take anything and it doesn't return anything. But the function bar actually takes one argument. That's why let's change this variable definition to end. So now it is fine. Now, it doesn't let you call this function without mentioning the argument. So you can mention that argument in their head. Separated by commas. Let's say Britain's. Something. And. Let's see what happens now, also says it's an incompatible pointer type. Because here this is defined that changes to no. And now it is fine. You can create variables. To catch the return value. So that's why whenever you want to make a function point to variable definition, make sure that you have to create a pointed variable, but you need to keep that inside the parentheses. So only that you have to remember, and since you do the function pointer, it doesn't point to the data. So hence the pointer definition doesn't have any data type. You have to mention the return type and input parameters, type up the function, whose address you are planning to store in this variable. So now let's say I want to create one more variable of this type, so then there is no provision. I have to rewrite this and I have to change the variable like this. Let's say I want to create one more variable called F1. I cannot write Karma Story F1 here or I cannot write something like this story F1 like that. There is no such provision. So a pretty variable definition, then I can easily write P one p to something like this, right? So you have to write this once again, and you can give a different name for the variable. But instead of that, what you can do is you can use the Typekit portion of this. So I'll show you that what you do is so you just copy this. And you just create a Typekit type. Like this for, yes, use of Typekit of key words and right to our function point to variable definition. So if you write like this, then you can use this name as an alias name for this definition. Now what you can do is you can create something like this. You can create more variables by using this alias name, so I just use this as F underscore T to market as it typed up name. What you can do is you can just use this type alias name and you can create as many. Function point and variables you want. So all these are function pointer variables of this type. So, which is actually an alien name for? And after that, let me just be modest. And after that, you can use this if you want to. This is a function point. You can use this to store the address of this function. And then you can reference that either like this or. These are legal usages. So now in the next project, we will learn how to pass a punch and pointer as an argument to another function.

PASSING FUNCTION POINTERS AS FUNCTION ARGUMENTS

In this project, let's see how to pass a function pointer as an argument to another function. So we'll do a small exercise. Now let's say you have a command variable. And based on this, come on the radio, you have to take some action or you have to execute some code that they command, value is zero, you have to execute a Plan B. If command values one, that is a minor feat. If the command value is two, then a multiplication now, how do you implement this? Let's say you have two variables and. Let's say a is equal to 10, B is equal to 15. And come on values, let's say two. What do you do? You either use a Switch statement on this variable to implement various factions. Are you mad that you fell flat? What if I tell you you should not use any statements like this, which are if? Then how do you implement based on the value of the command, you have to take this action without using if or switch statements here. This problem can be solved using function pointers. Let me show you how to convert all these actions. Different actions are coded into separate functions. I'll give three functions here. In a in B. It returns a plus b Timberlake for subtraction and multiplication. Now, what you can do is let us create one generic function. Operation, what this function does is it takes a function pointer as an argument, first of all, let me create a typed up version of function pointer variable definition.

```
19 #include <stdio.h>
20
21 int add(int a , int b){
22     return a+b;
23 }
24
25 int sub(int a , int b){
26     return a-b;
27 }
28
29 int mul(int a,int b){
30     return a*b;
31 }
32
```

Result = 100

I'll use typedef in a star or PR and difficulty and argument least stock type and call my ENT. So this function takes the function point off as an argument of this type. All PR and difficulty, one variable. I'll just speak. And it also takes an integer value after that is operation, what it does is it's a generic function. It just jumps to that function, point it by this point and it uses the arguments and B or you can also simply kind of like this as a night shift. What is the same? Please note that P is a function pointer variable of this type, which is typed after this definition. Now here in the main Let's Create Function pointer area to store these function addresses. So again, use this and it is difficult to create a function point array variable support If you want to create a cat pointer, what would you do? This is a cat pointer. Now, if you want to convert this into a cat pointer, what would you do with the array of cat pointers? P is an array of pointers. Similarly, so here you just use this. Type, type name here and create a variable that cards or PR. And initialize this to. Function pointers add subtraction, multiplication. You can use something like this. Here this is the function pointer area, which is initialized to these function addresses. Now you can. Doing something like this results in a cartel operation. Call this generic function operation. Any of these agencies appointed by this command value we can use to command value here and a bit. Here's what's happening.

This generic function is called with three arguments. These are integer values and this is a function pointing to that function. Pointer is received here at P. That's how you can pass. Function pointer from one address to another address.

```
40 int main()
41 {
42      oper_t oper[] = {add,sub,mul};
43
44      int cmd,a,b;
45      //0 -> a+b
46      //1 --> a-b
47      //2 --> a*b
48
49      a = 10;
50      b = 15;
51      cmd = 2;
52      int res = operation(oper[cmd],a,b);
53      printf("Result = %d\n",res);
54
55 }
56
```

<terminated> (exit value: 0) p1.exe [C/C++ Application] D:\GOAL-21-23\002EmbeddedC++\embc+
Result = 100

Thought a hair into a into B. He had just returned the result. The function pointers could be helpful in our state mission implementation because, you know, if it was an

211

implementation, we have different handlers, state handlers and the state handler function is switch case statement. It represents a unique set of instructions. All these different cases can be segregated as different functions here. Different functions like this. You can think of this as an event based on the event risk, or you can pass eight associated event handling functions. To the January dispatch at code, you can think of this as a dispatcher code. Each of the event handlers address here and it executes the event handler function. You can think of this as a table consisting of various function pointers. Those are nothing but addresses of different event handling functions. We actually use in the state machine implementation card, state table approach, the state table approach that is a table which is full of function points, and each address of that table is nothing but address off the event handling function. So we'll see that when we cover the state table approach, it doesn't matter whether you use the state table approach or the state handler approach to the function point. Knowledge is must. That's why I just covered the basics of function pointers in C and the next project. Let's explore the standard approach.

EXERCISE-004 IMPLEMENTATION USING STATE HANDLER APPROACH

Hey, welcome back to the project, let us understand the state handler approach. This is almost similar to the previous one, but the important difference is if you remember, we use an activated variable in the main application structure to switch between different states. Active state actually reveals what exactly the current active state in the state cannot approach. This variable will be a function pointer, and by using this variable, we can directly switch between different state handler upward projects.

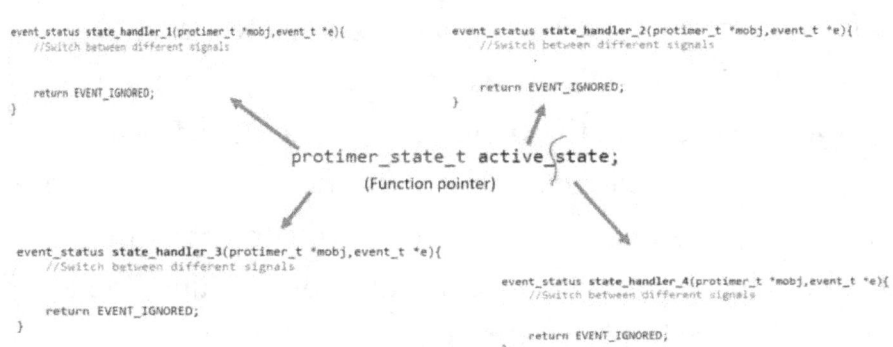

And in the state handler, you actually use a switch case statement to switch between different signals that want a job. This method allows you to get rid of the outer switch statement. What was happening in our project? The current project is there are two Switch statements in our project that is one Switch statement inside this state handler function, every state handler function and this outer switch statement. What's happening here is you are decoding this variable to decide what exactly is the current value of this variable. And based on that, you are executing different state handlers in the state handler approach. You need not to do this because it contains the pointer to the state handler function itself. That's why, instead of doing this, you can directly reference this variable and you directly call the current state handler function. And in the state function, of course, you have to use a switch statement to switch between different signals. So that's why in this method, these state handlers will not get affected. They will remain as they are. The only thing is we can get rid of this function and our dispatching code in the main Dart CP slightly changes don't really explain what are the changes we have to do here. First of all, let's create a new project. Let's not change this project because it is already working fine as the necessary implementation. Now let's create a new project to create a new project, go to Platform Io. Got a whole new project. I'll call this as zero zero for. Floor timer, state handler and select the board. After that, And after that finished the project. We'll create a new project here. Go to that project folder, just right click here and go to reveal in File Explorer. And go to the previous project. Copy all this code. Come back to the new project and delete this, paste those files. And go back to the record in 04, you see all those piles. Now let's compile. Before compiling, if you go to the LCD, it shows a red line here because we have to add the LCD library because in the previous project, we added that, but it was product specific. Go here and click on open libraries. Just type liquid crystal.

```
#include "lcd.h"
#include "main.h"
#include<LiquidCrystal.h>

LiquidCrystal lcd(PIN_LCD_RS,PIN_LCD_RW,PIN_LCD_EN,PIN_LCD_D4,PIN_LCD_D5,PIN_LCD

void lcd_clear(void){
    lcd.clear();
}
void lcd_print_char(char c){
    lcd.print(c);
}

void lcd_scroll_left(void){
    lcd.scrollDisplayLeft();
```

```
Copyright (C) Microsoft Corporation. All rights reserved.

Try the new cross-platform PowerShell https://aka.ms/pscore6

PS C:\Users\nieki\OneDrive - BHARATI SOFTWARE\Workspace\StateMachine_projects\003Protimer>
```

Yeah, this one by Arduino. Click on that add to project the project. Now, let's go to the project that is already highlighted because this is the current working project. And now let's compile. So now we are in our new project. Now let's do some changes to this project. First, let's put the main dredge in the main draw here. This is not required, so how to remove it? Because now we are not using these values to store it into a variable, then decode using a switch statement to find out which handler to call. That's why I'm going to remove this. So instead of that, we will use a function point. OK. So what you do is go to your main application structure. Now, this has to be a function point to really this function quantum variable. It will hold the address of a state handler and the state handlers prototype is something like this. It returns the UN status and it takes these things. So that's how to convert this to a function pointer variable. As I explained, it is to take the variable name, give us to. This is a point to really put that in the parenthesis. And give it a parameter list and that it is involved. How does our functional state handle a prototype, looks like it returns in this one event status and difficulty? That's right and type. And it takes an input parameter list, which is this form. So here you need not to mention this variable name. This is sufficient.

Now this is a function pointing to video instead of using. Here we can use a typedef version. So what you do is just copy this and paste Apple and make it as Typekit. He had used the name for time, our state and difficulty. And create the variable of this type. Act two states. This Typekit type of definition is an alias name. This is a function point variable. That's the first change you have to make. And after that, now let's go to the pro timer in it. In the time in which you have to initialize this active state variable right now directly initialized with the address of the idle handler, decide land. So just use that. That's it. Or you can also do something like this. You can use a couple of macros here. And you use this macro to represent this handler address. And here, instead of this, you can use I. So you just directly store the address of the handler. Now, this is not required, so I'm going to remove this. And here now we remove this function, right, Ethereum or this. So directly referenced this and called that handler initially. So how do you do this? Parentheses. To directly call this. What's the first argument and will we get? Second argument is the address of the event. Jump to. Idle is harder to execute than to react. That is the second change you have to note. And after that, there is no change as far as these handlers are concerned. It will remain positive. Now we have to modify it. DISPATCHER called, by the way, the logic, whatever you had implemented in the low function it remains as it is. That is no change at all. So now in the dispatch record, what happens? So now these are function points of thought and target. Now these are function pointers.

```cpp
static void protimer_event_dispatcher(protimer_t *con
{
    event_status_t status;
    protimer_state_t source, target;

    source = mobj->active_state;
    status = protimer_state_machine(mobj,e);

    if(status == EVENT_TRANSITION){
        target = mobj->active_state;
        event_t ee;
        //1. run the exit action for the source state
        ee.sig = EXIT;
        mobj->active_state = source;
        protimer_state_machine(mobj,&ee);

        //2. run the entry action for the target state
        ee.sig = ENTRY;
        mobj->active_state = target;
        protimer_state_machine(mobj,&ee);
```

So here first, the active state value is stored here. That's fine. And after that, now this is the remote. I was very modest. Call the current active state handle. Just that. Thought of him or B.J.. So with a more picture and eat. After that, if the event transitions, then. Save the target. That's correct. Now we have to first execute the exit action, so you copy thought to the extent that's correct after that here, this function is to do more or less, remove it and call the state handler represented by the act of state. And after that, you prepare the entry signal. Now change this value to target and again call. This one. Or instead of doing all these things, what you can do is you can simply do this. So just be this. And I just removed this as well. So here, anyway, if the state of the country, when transition is a target, first, you have to call thought so I'll just write thoughts here. This also you can do and then target here. So that's the change we have to make. So there is no change in this function. Now, let's try to compile this. There are a couple of areas. First of all, Events, data, thunder, Scotties and initialization. So now we have a problem. Function for type definition here, what's happening? So here, as you can see, event and of course, do defender Scotty, which is a type of structure which comes after this line.

```
004Protimer_SH > src > C main.h > +0 protimer_state_t
42          ENTRY,
43          EXIT
44      }protimer_signal_t;
45
46
47      typedef event_status_t (*protimer_state_t)(protimer_t *const , event_t const *const);
48
49
50      /* Main application structure */
51      typedef struct {
52          uint32_t curr_time;
53          uint32_t elapsed_time;
```

```
TERMINAL   DEBUG CONSOLE   PROBLEMS 29   OUTPUT

typedef event_status_t (*protimer_state_t)(protimer_t *const , event_t const *const);

src\main.h:47:25: error: typedef 'event_status_t' is initialized (use decltype instead)
src\main.h:47:25: error: typedef 'event_status_t' is initialized (use decltype instead)
src\main.h:47:27: error: 'protimer_state_t' was not declared in this scope
typedef event_status_t (*protimer_state_t)(protimer_t *const , event_t const *const);
src\main.h:47:22: error: 'protimer_state_t' was not declared in this scope
typedef event_status_t (*protimer_state_t)(protimer_t *const , event_t const *const);
src\main.h:47:27: note: suggested alternative: 'protimer_signal_t'
```

So which actually comes here? So what you can do is you can just cut this court from here and maybe put it at the top. And now let's compare. There are more areas. In the main dot h. So now here again, there's a problem, you see, we have used this typedef function pointer definition before these Typekit structures. So that way to get rid of this error. What we can do is we can give our declaration to this function point of definition. For that, what you need to do is go to your main application structure and give a tag for this structure a tag name. I'll just call this astro timer under the Scott tag. I used this to give a four-hour declaration. Right here. This is a far declaration and use this here. Same thing you do for. Even tag. Here is the event you tag name. And. Use this structure Typekit. And I'll see what happens. So now it is fine. There's one more warning in function white even dispatcher aesthetic, but not used. To see that. So here it is. And percent eat. So that's Comput. Now it is fine. So now I think we completed this exercise.

```
82          ee.sig = EXIT;
83          (*source)(mobj,&ee);
84
85          //2. run the entry action for the target state
86          ee.sig = ENTRY;
87          (*target)(mobj,&ee);
88      }
89
90  }
91
92
93  static uint8_t process_button_pad_value(uint8_t btn_pad_value)
```

```
Building in release mode
Compiling .pio\build\uno\src\lcd.cpp.o
Compiling .pio\build\uno\src\main.cpp.o
Compiling .pio\build\uno\src\protimer_state_mach.cpp.o
src\main.cpp: In function 'void protimer_event_dispatcher(protimer_t*, const event_t*)':
src\main.cpp:80:13: warning: variable 'ee' set but not used [-Wunused-but-set-variable]
      event_t ee;
      ^~
Linking .pio\build\uno\firmware.elf
Checking size .pio\build\uno\firmware.elf
Advanced Memory Usage is available via "PlatformIO Home > Project Inspect"
```

So just recheck this code by executing on the hard that are simulating this. So and as I said in the state handler, you need not to do any changes because whenever you want to change the state, you change the function pointer, for example, in the eye, adjust it in the increment time. That is a transition. This is a transition. You change the active state. You change this with a new pointer. So this is a pointer. So these are pointers. So that's why if you use these macros, then you need not touch the state handler function. So if you don't use these macros, then you have to change every rat. So you have to replace this with the function point of the handler. So with that note, I would like to end this, let's just please test this on the hardware to see whether everything works or not, or you can even simulate this on the Tinker Cat or any simulator software. I've seen the next.

EXERCISE-004 STATE TABLE APPROACH FOR IMPLEMENTATION OF AN FSM PART-1

So now in this project, the story is about the state table approach and in previous projects we had discussed the standard approach and an ostrich approach. Now in the state table approach, we are going to use a state table for hence the name state table approach. Now let me explain this with an example. In the previous two methods in the state handled method or in the method which mattered, so we had used lots of comparisons. The comparison is implemented by using the Switch statement. Were fish, it read. A couple of cases, a lot of competitions. Now in this method, there will be no competition whenever an event occurs. The function related to that event is executed and we can achieve this by means of function. Point at the state table is nothing, but it's a table contained in our various handlers. It's a table of handlers, actually, or you can call it a table of event handlers. For example, let's say in your application, if a stark path event happens when the application is in, let's say, countdown state, then this handler is called. Which takes care of handling this event when the state is condo, so like that you have to make one table and for each event you have to write it to an event handler.

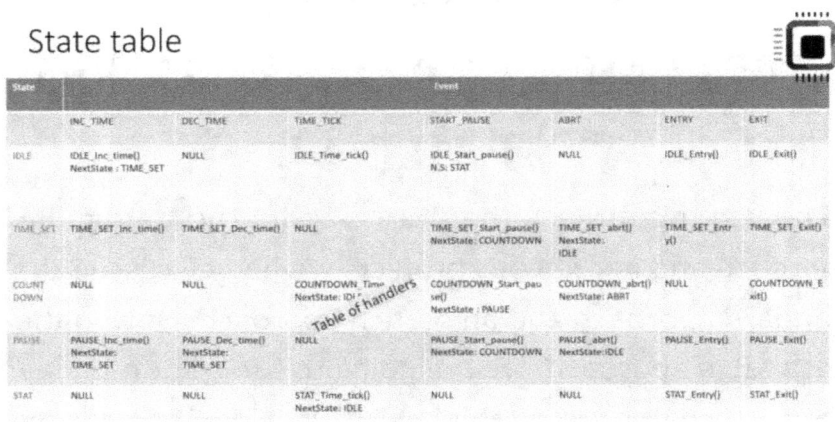

State table

Considering the state, that's by far our application. There will be a table which consists of five Roth furrows indicating the number of states. We have got five states, so Phil Roth and Event indicate the column. And in our case, the table will have seven columns because they have got an even. After that, you cannot disable it to some data structure in your program. You can't use a two dimensional array to save this information. And after that, you can use that two dimensional array to execute different event handlers. So I'll show you that later. Now what we do is we create a new project and we will remove all the switch statements and we will convert each case into different event handling functions. Let's go back to the project. Now let's implement the state table method. Create a new project. So I have just created a new project with two zero zero five timer underscores. And after that, just go to the project folder, go into this zero zero three project and reuse the files of this project. So just copy all these things. And go to the City here and pay for it, replacing the fight in the destination. Let's go to Heidi. And now let's go to their pro timer state machine Dart CP. It was our ancestors whose implementation now there will be no switch case statements. First of all, what you need to do now is just remove this function. This is not required. So we now have only state handlers. Now what you're to do is for each case, you have to create one function and the function prototype remains the same as this one. So let me create one function to handle the entry case of idle state. So I would write like this, I would stand for the state and escort entry outright like this and treat. This recounts the theme of dysfunction. And after that. These are the two input parameters. So this is a non static function, you need not to put the static function because you have to share this with main darts TPP to include it in the state table.

```
 C· protimer_state_mach.cpp ●
 005Protimer_ST > src > C· protimer_state_mach.cpp > ⊕ IDLE_Entry(protimer_t * const, event_t const * const)
 21        ee.sig = ENTRY;
 22        mobj->active_state = IDLE;
 23        mobj->pro_time = 0;
 24        protimer_state_machine(mobj,&ee);
 25  }
 26
 27
 28  event_status_t IDLE_Entry(protimer_t *const mobj, event_t const *const e){
 29
 30  }
 31
 32  static event_status_t protimer_state_handler_IDLE(protimer_t *const mobj, event_t const *con
 33       switch(e->sig){
 34           case ENTRY:{
 35               mobj->curr_time = 0;
 36               mobj->elapsed_time = 0;
 37               display_time(0);
 38               display_message("Set",0,0);
 39               display_message("time",0,1);
 40               return EVENT_HANDLED;
```

So that's why this can't be the static function. Now what you do. Just copy all this instruction from this case and just paste here. That's all you need to do. Like that? And let's create one more function. The next case is for exit to create one function, exit and copy whatever that in the. A good case and faith to you. Similarly, you have to do it for all the states covering all the events after death, you go to the time set handler and create a similar function. For example, here you may have to create time, underscores that underscore entry and include these courts or that. I hope you can do that. And after that, you just delete this state. These are not really quiet. That's why I'm also going to delete these function protests. These are not required because we are going to remove that. Complete this and I'll see you in the next election.

EXERCISE-004 STATE TABLE APPROACH FOR IMPLEMENTATION OF AN FSM PART-2

Hey, welcome back to the project. I just created different event handlers for different states. And you can see that we have got a lot of functions here and now the addresses of these handlers should be stored in the state table. That's why you have to share the name of these functions with the main Darts CP, right? We are going to implement the state table. What you do is create prototypes of all this function and include it in main data. In the main party, you have to include their prototypes. Let's go to the main edge, and here you paste the prototypes. And after that, you have to create this table in the table. You have to mention two important details for the first of all, which event that we are going to call that you are to mention and what is the next state when that event happens that you need to mention? After that, we have to convert the state table into a two dimensional array.

State table

State	Event						
	INC_TIME	DEC_TIME	TIME_TICK	START_PAUSE	ABRT	ENTRY	EXIT
IDLE	IDLE_Inc_time() NextState: TIME_SET	NULL	IDLE_Time_tick()	IDLE_Start_pause() N.S: STAT	NULL	IDLE_Entry()	IDLE_
TIME_SET	TIME_SET_Inc_time()	TIME_SET_Dec_time()	NULL	TIME_SET_Start_pause() NextState: COUNTDOWN	TIME_SET_abrt() NextState: IDLE	TIME_SET_Entr y()	TIME
COUNT DOWN	NULL	NULL	COUNTDOWN_Time NextState: IDL*	COUNTDOWN_Start_pau se() NextState : PAUSE	COUNTDOWN_abrt() NextState: ABRT	NULL	COUN xit()
PAUSE	PAUSE_Inc_time() NextState: TIME_SET	PAUSE_Dec_time() NextState: TIME_SET	NULL	PAUSE_Start_pause() NextState: COUNTDOWN	PAUSE_abrt() NextState:IDLE	PAUSE_Entry()	PAUS
STAT	NULL	NULL	STAT_Time_tick() NextState: IDLE	NULL	NULL	STAT_Entry()	STAT

Table of handlers

In the next project, I'm going to cover exactly what the two dimensional array is and how to access the different elements of a two dimensional array and how the memory organization looks like that two-dimensional array. If you are already familiar with two dimensional arrays, then you need not to watch the next video. This is just for beginners who are near to seeing programming languages. I didn't cover the two dimensional in the previous course, though I just covered it in the next video. You're aware of that. Then you can simply skip the next video I see in the next project.

2D ARRAYS IN C

So two dimensional arrays and see you already know about the one dimensional area, right? For example, if you consider this statement here, this is that one dimensional array of three elements of type you indicate that is one by top data. So the array of three elements and each element is size one bite. And this indicates the name of the area, its type is actually a point to type. But here this is the name of the array and this is the initialization. You already know this and we call this a one dimensional array because you can't index this array in only one dimension. You call it X Dimension. For example, here you can index something like this. So this is the direct element, the first element. The Second Amendment making scored four zero will give you the value 10. Making scores of one actually gives you the value 20. We call this indexing. The indexing can only be done in one dimension. So that's why it's called one dimensional. So that's about the one dimensional you already know. What is a two dimensional array? So the two dimensional array is a data structure in C, which is used, which is helpful while representing a set of data which is in the form of a table, for example. What is a table? A table is something which has a number of growth and number of columns. For example, We call this a table which has. Three rorth. And three columns. And in this arrangement, you can say a couple of. Data here, actually, you can say nine data here to represent this kind of data. That is one provision in Thi that is to use that two dimensional logic in a two dimensional array representation. There are two index points, or you can do the indexing of the array in two dimensions. Consider this example here, of course, is actually a name of the two dimensional array. And this indicates a number of roles in the table. And this indicates the number of columns off the table table is nothing but some data arrangement. And this is how you can initialize it. Two north, zero and one. And the number of columns is three. So you don't want to. And here the value 10 is stored, 20 stored here, 30 stored here. 33 is stored here. 22 is stored here. Fortify stored here.

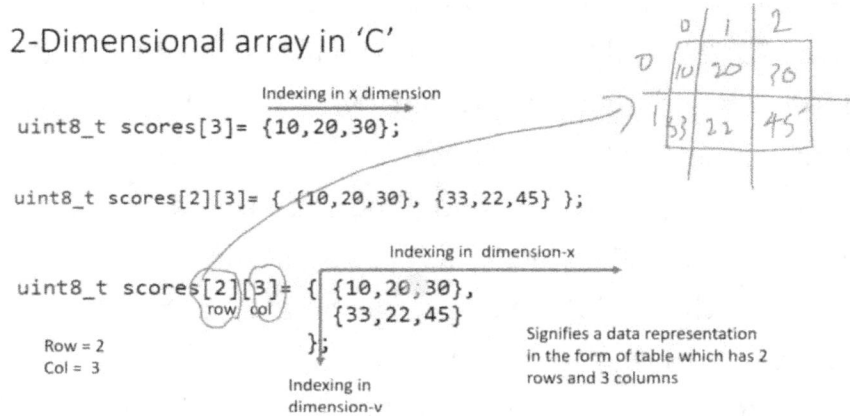

And by using this field, you can switch between different roles by switching between different roles. And by. Using this field, you can switch between different columns. Panthers call it the Two-Dimensional idea, because there are two switching points: you can switch in the right direction or you can switch in the X direction. The two day missionaries are initialized like this cluster, you initialize the pastoral, give a comma and initialize the second rule. These data values of the first row have to be inside the breath of. Now, suppose if I do something like this, if court of zero and one, if I write like this. Then I get the data off the right row first column. This is the right row, first column, so I get 20. Just like that. If I make a raw one, this is two, then it means row one. Column two zero one two. So the value that it provides is 45. It's like that, so you can do the indexing, which is why it is helpful. Consider this example. Let's say you have a mock shoot off test of one of your clothes as per the raw Lambert. Let's say there are four students. Raw numbers are from zero to three and there are four subjects. Consider this is a subject with cord zero, its cord is zero physics chemistry, according to Economics College three. These are the first to read role numbers, and these are the mark cords by the student. Now you want to store this in your program, then how do you do it? You may think of using an array of one dimension, you can do that.

Marksheet of Test-1 as per roll numbers

Roll No. \ Subject	Math(0)	Physics(1)	Chemistry(2)	Economics(3)
0	34	56	77	99
1	67	34	89	44
2	78	33	30	67
3	98	45	21	43

```
uint8_t marksheet_of_test1[16] = {34,56,77,99,67,34,89.......21,43};
```

What's the mark scored by roll number 1 in Chemistry ?

```
uint8_t mark = marksheet_of_test1[1 * 4 + 2];
```

There are 16. DataStore. That's right. You create one area of 16, right, and you just start storing the values like this feistiest or 34 or 56 aren't like that up to all the way to the last numbers. You can do something like this. The result of this method is when you want to fetch some values. For example, what's the mark scored by rule number one in chemistry? Now, how do you find out if you use one dimensionality? It is possible, but it is tricky. This is how you are going to calculate that. So you have to work it out. First of all, mock court by rule number one. That means first you have to arrive here. How do you arrive here so you can arrive here by the road in question, is the row in question? That is rule number one. Multiplied by the total number of columns, so you have to multiply that. For example, here one multiplied by the total number of columns for this is zero. If again, the indices for this. Zero one two three. This is four. So you arrive here. And then add the subject called so you want for chemistry demonstrates that you had to do it. This is +1 and +1. Then you arrive at that point like that, for example, I want to know the mark scored by rule number three in physics. The number three in physics. How do you arrive at this place? First, you have to arrive here. How did you get here? The row in Question three multiplied by. Total number of columns for that is 12. That is already off 12. What is your day off? Well, zero one two three four five six seven eight nine 10 11 12. So you arrive here and then add the subject call. Let's say you want to know physics. That is one. Plus one. Quantify like that. So that means our table can also be represented in the formal one dimensional. No problem, but you have to struggle a little bit to find out the required coordinate. For exactly that purpose, the C programming language has given you our data structure called two-dimensional order in two dimensional. You just define our two dimensional area as four rows and four columns and initialize the values here. This table of math, this is the first row. This is the initialization of the second row and third row for Trump. Exactly like in the table. It is very easy, let's say, if I want to obtain a mock score by rule number two in chemistry. Here to do very but just mention the wrong number and the column number. So rule number two problems are two. And here the column number is also too. Which gives me this value. It is very easy for you to damage it. You need not struggle with how to obtain those coordinates. Now, let's understand, how does the two dimensional array get stored in the memory, so it's exactly like how the one dimensional array gets stored. What happens in the case of one dimensional array in the individual array, the memory allocated for the one dimensional array is contiguous in nature. For example, here there are three data elements in this array, and three bytes of memory will be allocated adjacent to each other. And these will be the memory addresses, for example. And here they are in name calls. The address of the first element of the array.

Storage of 2D array in memory

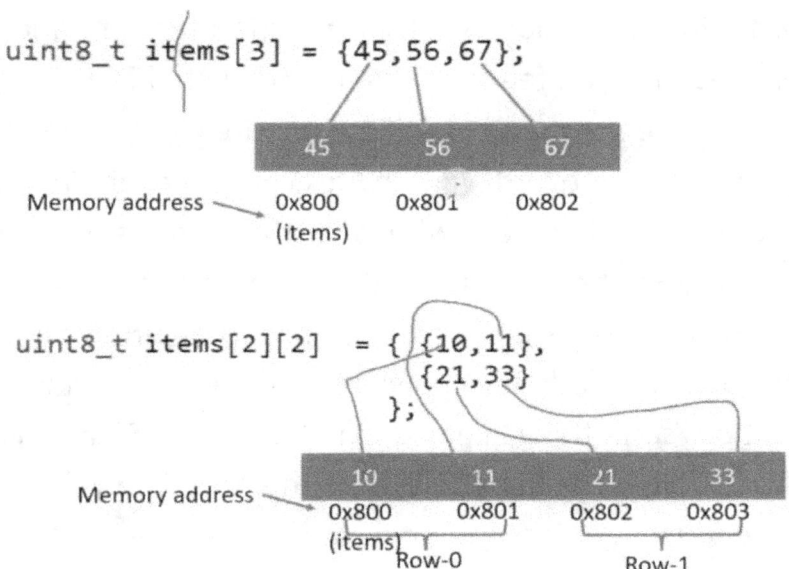

So you know this fact right now, if you consider the two arrays, the memory allocation is exactly the same. For example, in this case is that two dimensional array having two rows, two columns. That means there are four data elements, as you can see here in the memory. The data are stored in a row wife. First, Raw is laid out here. The second drum and the memories are contiguous in nature. If that is any Roar three, then it would come here like that memory is laid out in the royal fashion that it's very simple to understand. For this reason, whenever you are equalizing the Two-Dimensional array, actually, you need not to mention this information. The raw information you need not to mention it could be optional, but the column information is mandatory. This is mandatory to mention. Why? Because you fear I can even write like this. I can keep this as empty, and I can't even write like this and equate it to whatever I want in life. You can even do what the compiler will do here whenever the compiler sees this statement. So the compiler understands that there are two growths. That's why you need not to mention this information. So let's say I have a two dimensional audio definition, something like this, and I enjoy life. They still want to. This is the initialization of the first. And you can do the initial additional second row, something like this. Or you can also do like this. This is also fine. When a competitor sees this definition, the compiler should understand it has got to draw on it, I've got two columns. So then you may think that there is no need to mention this. So that seems logical, but that is not the case. If you compare this, it will throw an error. And what error says this, you must provide the column information. The column information, the outer bound, you can see it, the bounce you have to mention. Let's say I type two years and compile this is OK. This doesn't produce any errors. Why when the compiler sees this, it understands that there are two rules. That's why it will feel this information itself. No problem. But you have to mention the column information because here there are two entries in the road doesn't mean that it has two columns. This is also correct. For example, I can make this into four, and this also compiles well. What does this mean? This means there are two laws that are fixed, but there are four columns out of which two orange and red stars are initialized to zero. That's the meaning of this. This is outbound. So remember that while initializing are two-dimensional, it's mandatory to mention column information and raw information can be optional. The column information helps the compiler to decide each row boundary during the memory allocation for that two dimensional array. OK.

EXERCISE-004 STATE TABLE APPROACH FOR IMPLEMENTATION OF AN FSM PART-3

Let's go back to the project. And get inside the main dark copy here in the setup function, let's call a function called Timer State Table in it. Let's create one function here. Let's implement that below this event dispatcher. And it receives. The pointer to the main object. Static function and returns, nothing. Now we have to create a two dimensional array. I will call this astro timer state table of max states and max events are signals. Let's go to the main data. Here we have a state. Just add one entry here,

Max states. And here you can add one more entry max signals come back to the program. This is actually a two dimensional array of type function pointers. What we do now is we will go to the main stage and we will create one type of function point of definition.

```
uint8_t ss;
}protimer_tick_event_t;

typedef enum{
    EVENT_HANDLED,
    EVENT_IGNORED,
    EVENT_TRANSITION
}event_status_t;


typedef event_status_t (*e_handl)
                        EVENT_HANDLED           enum event_status_t::EVENT_HANDLED = 0

void protimer_init(protimer_t *mobj);
event_status_t protimer_state_machine(protimer_t *const mobj, event_t const *const e);

//prototypes of event handlers
event_status_t IDLE_Inc_time(protimer_t *const mobj, event_t const *const e);
event_status_t IDLE_Time_tick(protimer_t *const mobj, event_t const *const e);
```

How to do that here, and that is typedef event status, function pointer and start our card as E handler and difficulty. And this actually takes the parameters of these types. TypeDef, this is a function pointer type for event handlers and will use this type for the array. What we're going to create an array of function pointers of this type and after that, let's initialize this table. Now you have to initialize this two dimensional arrangement. The point is you have to initialize this exactly like this table. The first row is for idle state and the first event is this one second event. Is this one like that exactly like this table while doing two dimensional array initialization? You can also do something like this, let's say that there are two rows, two columns, and you can also do something like this. First, you write the wrong number. This signifies that you are initializing row number zero is equal to and then use the basis to initialize that role. You can also do something like this. This is also valid initialization. Let me compile this. This signifies that you are initializing Rose zero. This signifies that you are initializing low number one.

```
sketch_sep16a
1
2 #include <Arduino.h>
3 void setup() {
4     // put your setup code here, to run once:
5     Serial.begin(9600);
6
7     uint8_t items[2][2] = {
8         [0]= {1,2},
9         [1] = {3,4}
10    };
11
12    Serial.println(items[0][1]);
```

Sketch uses 1492 bytes (4%) of program storage
Global variables use 188 bytes (9%) of dynamic

So I'll use a similar approach that will provide more clarity. Let's go back here first. Let me enjoy life for rose zero, which is far higher to the state, is the quarter. That's the first law initialization next for half. For the table, it is four times set times that is equipped to next for Countdown. Next, Four Paws come up. Next for STAT. That's it. These are five growths. And after that, each row should have seven entries. Some are null because this indicates that the event is not handled by that state for that event. First, here you have to mention the event handler part implementing time while in the idle state and percent. You have to mention that I thought that I'd increment time karma next to find out next for tick time or just off idle time tick. After that, I'd start to pulse. For that now.

Protimer State table

State	Event						
	INC_TIME	DEC_TIME	TIME_TICK	START_PAUSE	ABRT	ENTRY	EXIT
IDLE	IDLE_Inc_time() NextState: TIME_SET	NULL	IDLE_Time_tick()	IDLE_Start_pause() N.S: STAT	NULL	IDLE_Entry()	IDLE
TIME_SET	TIME_SET_Inc_time()	TIME_SET_Dec_time()	NULL	TIME_SET_Start_pause() NextState: COUNTDOWN	TIME_SET_abrt() NextState: IDLE	TIME_SET_Entry()	TIME
COUNTDOWN	NULL	NULL	COUNTDOWN_Time NextState: ID: (Table of handlers)	COUNTDOWN_Start_pause() NextState : PAUSE	COUNTDOWN_abrt() NextState: ABRT	NULL	COU xit()
PAUSE	PAUSE_Inc_time() NextState: TIME_SET	PAUSE_Dec_time() NextState: TIME_SET	NULL	PAUSE_Start_pause() NextState: COUNTDOWN	PAUSE_abrt() NextState:IDLE	PAUSE_Entry()	PAUS
STAT	NULL	NULL	STAT_Time_tick() NextState: IDLE	NULL	NULL	STAT_Entry()	STAT

After that address of idle entry and other staff, I exit. Max Signal Value seven. That should be seven into a thin year. Similarly, you do it four times that countdown and pause and start. Once you complete this initialization, then what you do is you store this state table pointer in our main application object because we need it later in the dispatch function. We have to access this state table to get the appropriate handle address. That's right. Let's go to the main application structure, and here it will create a pointer to a state table. What should be the pointer type? If you ever get that doubt, then no problem. Just type your PR and select you into BTR underscore key. And let's create one variable state table, which is a pointer variable just to hold the address up that array. Let's go back and in this function, let's make that static because it can't be a local variable, so it should be a static local variable because the address of this variable has to be persistent after that in the main object. Get the pointer state turbo and start it here. Address up this table. Zero zero. Lester, the base address off this table are both addressed. It's nothing but the first element that is zero zero. You just use them percent. The point is our type this one. That's why you may have to typecast this you into Peter. And. I hope you can complete these roles. I have attached the state table file and you can just download that. And according to that, you can initialize this. That seems to be one error. This system, for now, is fine. With that note, I would like to end this project and I'll see you in the next project.

EXERCISE-004 STATE TABLE APPROACH FOR IMPLEMENTATION OF AN FSM PART-4

Now, let's continue with this recording. We just completed this function. Now let's give the prototype of this function in the main dart sip. Maybe here. Whenever the control cost comes to the set of functions, it calls the state table and it with, ah, just off the main application structure. So this one now we did this. So now our state table is ready in the state table variable Pam OPG. Let's go back now, let's fix this function plus for timeout in it. Let's go. Showtime is now. We don't have this function for time on the state machine that removed that. First of all, what we do here. We set up an event Act two state is made as I do approach time variable is set to zero, that you have to call the entry function of idle state and you had to get that from the Amobi state table point to how to get that. Let's create one variable. EA handler and quality test event handler, event handler is a function point or variable of this type.

```
 7   static void do_beep(void);
 8   static void display_clear(void);
 9   static void display_message(String s,uint8_t c , uint8_t r);
10   static void display_time(uint32_t time);
11
12
13   void protimer_init(protimer_t *mobj){
14       event_t ee;
15       ee.sig = ENTRY;
16       mobj->active_state = IDLE;
17       mobj->pro_time = 0;
18       e_handler_t ehandler;
19   }
20
21   ////////////////////////////Event handlers////////////////////////////
22
23   event_status_t IDLE_Inc_time(protimer_t *const mobj, event_t const *const e){
24       mobj->curr_time += 60;
25       mobj->active_state = TIME_SET;
26       return EVENT_TRANSITION;
```

This we actually defined in the main data say, I hope you remember this. Now, each handler, I would just create this. At the top here. Each handler. It quotes to you how to get the address from the Mobike state table pointer. Remember, this is a pointer variable. All type into this has to be treated as a pointer to the one dimensional how to fetch idle state entry address that is this value. How to fetch that? First of all, you have to arrive at this place. So how to arrive at this place? The raw number in question is that I multiplied by Max. Signals. AMAX Max columns. Is zero two values, zero zero multiplied by seven zero? You arrive here. And for this, you have to add its value. So there you go. Entry, you have to add entries. Plus, one plus one plus one plus one plus one one two, three, four five you arrived at. Like this, you had referenced this point.

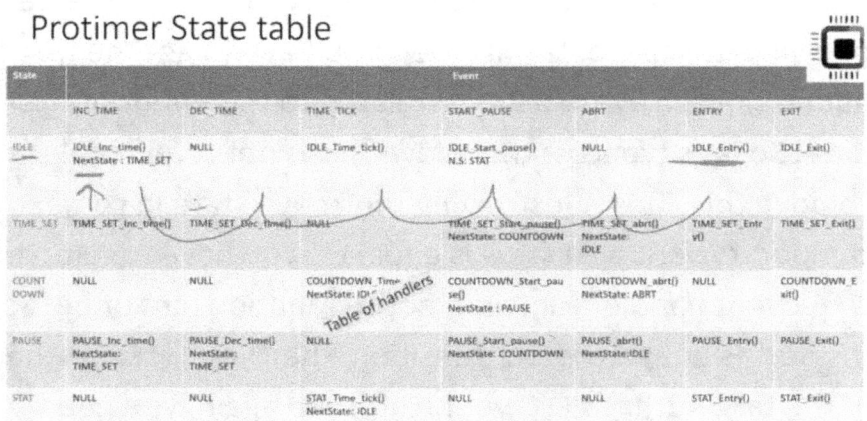

Protimer State table

Now if you do this, what happens? The value which is stored here will be fetched and it will be assigned to death, which is nothing but a function point or address of a function. And each type is this one. We may have to typecast this. That's it. And after that, just jump to this function pointer, you know how to do that. His handler. And you have to pass and Moby yet. And at the. Now we fixed the innate function, and now let's go back to the main Dart C.P. and we've called for the event dispatcher. Let's go to the event dispatcher. Here we have got status. This is OK. And target. This is OK. An active state variable that is OK, now here, what's happening, you are calling the state machine with this event. We have to do something like this status is equipped to a mobile. Get the state table. Active state. Act two states multiplied by Max. Signals. The signal name that we can get from your signal. Let's do one thing. Sorry. Here you have to create one variable called. His handler. You have to get the first address of the event handler related to this event of this date. So let's typecast this. Now, this is not required, let's remove this. This is just saving the active state in some temporary variable status is equal to. You have to jump to that event handler function, not to mention him or be. So if status is equal to even transition, then you just fear that in the target, that's OK, your exit. Here again, you need not to do all these things. Just remove this. So you have to run the exit action for the fourth state. Just remove this exit action coastal state. Get the handler in the courtroom and maybe get. State table ran the exit action for the state. So thought. Multiplied by Mach signals. Plus exit. Then again, you have to call like this. Similarly, you have to copy and paste that here. This is an entry. And this is a target. Here it is not easy. It is one percent eaten. Now we may encounter null entries, so that's why I think it's better to check for null here. That is why you have to put one condition beforehand. Whatever you reference that point to that function pointer, you have to put the condition. Let's compare.

```cpp
if(status == EVENT_TRANSITION){
    target = mobj->active_state;
    event_t ee;
    //1. run the exit action for the source state
    ee.sig = EXIT;
    ehandler =(e_handler_t) mobj->state_table[source*MAX_SIGNALS + EXIT];
    if(ehandler)
        (*ehandler)(mobj,&ee);

    //2. run the entry action for the target state
    ee.sig = ENTRY;
    ehandler =(e_handler_t) mobj->state_table[target * MAX_SIGNALS + ENTRY];
    if(ehandler)
        (*ehandler)(mobj,&ee);
```

You can see that it is building the current project, a current project which is open. And sometimes if you want to select a different project to build, I would show you how to do that. Currently it is building, you can see it. It shows this is the current project. This is successful. Now, let's say I want to build a different project in this workspace. I want to build this project now. What you need to do is just select the project here. I would select digital for SRH. Then it changes to this one when you build. It actually builds that project. So like that, you can switch between different projects. I'll go back. Since our project is compiled fine, we will check it on the hardware to see whether the output is the same as before. I'm just. Loading this project to the board. So the project is behaving fine exactly like before. Try to reproduce this at your desk and re verify it. And on that note, I would like to end this project on implementing a state machine using a state table.

HIERARCHICAL STATE MACHINES(HSMS)

Hey, welcome back to the project from this project, onward will explore at just them the stands for high tech, it goes straight machine. In the previous exercise, we used the flat state machine approach for our product to correct the flat state machine to mean there are no composite states. You don't see any data embedded within and at the state. The state machine diagram had a couple of states which are interconnected by a couple of arrows here. So those are nothing but external transitions. And as you can see, this state machine diagram looks messy for this exercise that read just five states, so it was quite manageable. But when you want to introduce more features to an application, you could be introducing more states and when you introduce more states, obviously there will be many transitions among the states' more guard condition. So driving your state machine gets complicated when the complexity of the state machine diagram increases as it becomes too tedious to maintain, visualize and to troubleshoot. That's why it would be better if we explore hierarchical state machines, which are to use to tackle this problem.

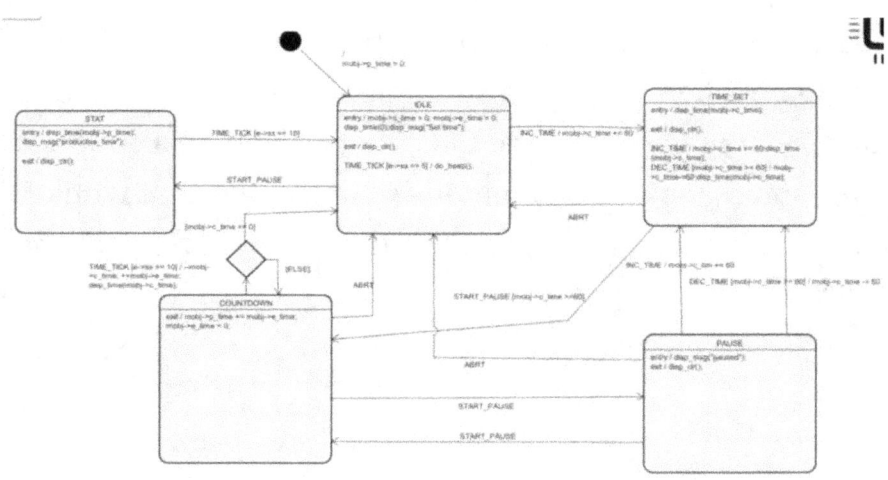

Each of them will greatly reduce the complexity introduced by the flat state machine approach. What are the disadvantages of using a flat state machine? So as the number of states increases, the number of transitions tends to increase, which increases the complexity. Flat state machines are hard to visualize how to draw trees and troubleshoot chances of committing more mistakes by missing transitions. When you have more states than you have to draw more transitions, that would be a risk of waiting, drawing some transitions. So which will surely add books into our application and code repetitions in flat state machines across? You have less chance for poor visibility. So what is a hierarchical state machine? Actually, the word hierarchy we observe in our day to day life. For example, consider the hierarchy what you find in the corporate world, in the company that a strict hierarchy under which all the employees work and the company operates with a strict hierarchy that will be CEO of the company under the CEO, there could be a couple of VIPs and managers and under each manager that would be a team of engineers, etc. But this is a hierarchy for the state.

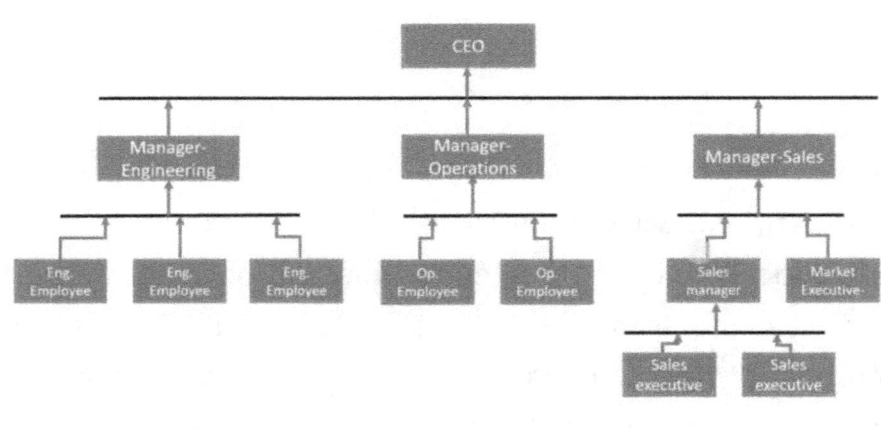

Corporate hierarchy

Also, you can draw such a hierarchy. For example, consider this picture. So here these are. States are such a substate or child state of this super state, which can be introduced like this that the state F1 and underage, that could be a couple of sub states like that. So here you can't see multiple levels of hierarchy here. This can be called as a direct substrate of F1 or F1 can be called as a direct super state of these substates. S1 also can be called as a simple composite state, and F1, S2 and S3 are direct states of the super state. If not, and like that here F1 underscores zero is not a direct substrate of if not, you can call it as an indirect state off. If not, here there are three levels of hierarchy. One two three. Hierarchies can be of any level. Now, consider this example here. There are three states S1, S2 and S3, and all of these have a common behavior. And the common behavior is whenever the trigger T one happens, the applications date most from one state to another. For example, let's say currently the application date as to when the trigger T one happens. The application states most from f 2.2, if not that of an external transition and this behavior is common among all these three states. That's why it could be a hint that we can transform this state machine diagram into this one using a hierarchical approach. Your SS one is a computer state or a super state, which consists of three sub states S1, S2, NFC.

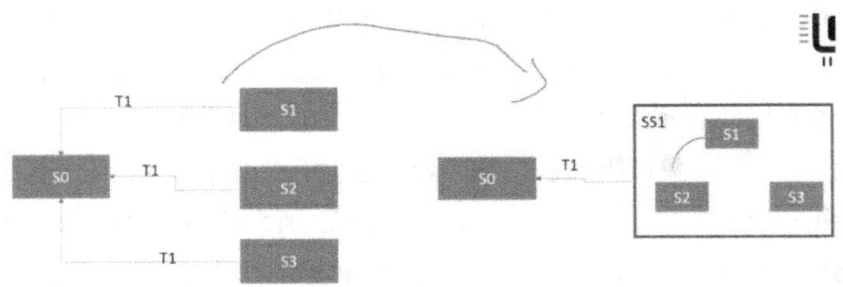

And it actually inherits the common behavior of the three states itself. So what is the common behavior when it happens to you and happens? The state must change too, if not that far. You just draw only one transition from this super state to, if not now. Like this diagram? Let's say that application stages swamp current treaties as one and then trigger two even happens when the application is in the state. So the meaning of this diagram is if one doesn't handle Taiwan, it doesn't handle Hanratty one. That's why the trigger actually propagates to its superstate. That is the SS one and SS one handles it, and that the transition to is not. That's the meaning of this tape machine diagram. Same thing applies to these states as well. When the application started in S2 and when that event happened after it didn't have one hand. It propagates to a super state and says one handles it and the state most two does not. So for any reader of this diagram, it should look something like this. This is a hierarchical state machine. This is a flat admission when you redraw this hierarchical state machine to FSM, it should be converted to this diagram and here was the sequence of execution 21 happens. Let's say the application is in state one and two. What happens when the execution sequence asks for the UMS Spec. First bag. The doctrine of this will be executed, the exact action of this one and then that transition action will be executed. And lastly. And reaction of, if not, will be executed in that four sequence. Same thing should apply here as well. Now, when the state is three and when Taiwan happens, the Taiwan propagates to their superstate and super state handles that trigger T one, and that will be an external transition when that transition happens. First, the exit action of three will be executed. And then exit action of this super state would be executed if it is defined, because in this case, when Taiwan triggers the super state, f one one is also excited, right? In this case, aspartame imports vacation. When the super state is exited, the exit actions must be executed from the innermost leaving state toward the outermost state. And after that, that transition action will be executed. And then and to action off new state, if not, will be executed. But the advantage is in each of them, definitely the complexity that is used. And also, you can control code reputations in the flat-footed machine, for example, the transition action has to be mentioned at three places, but here that is only one place where you have to mention that transition action. So one place means there is only one point of control. At only one place, you have to modify something if you wish to do so. But do you have to take care of three places? That's why it just helps you to reduce code reputation. We will learn more about SFM with, for example, in the subsequent projects.

RUN-TO-COMPLETION AND QP™ FRAMEWORK

Here in this application, you can see that this is the code that generates that U.N. is that you can't produce a code, and the U.N. producer sent the U.N. to the U.N. dispatcher, dispatcher function and then dispatcher function post that event to the state machine. And the state machine executes the behavioral action of that event. And then the state machine returned back to the event dispatcher and then even the dispatcher returned back to the super loop. So that is about the Arduino loop function, so we can summarize the whole step like this. First, the code checks whether the event is available or not, and then if the event is available, then post that you went to the state machine. State machine executes the actions associated with that event, then the state machine returns back to the Super Loop. This is actually the run to completion. RTC paid to what is ROTC, which transfers and to complete a processing of the current event must finish faster before processing the next event.

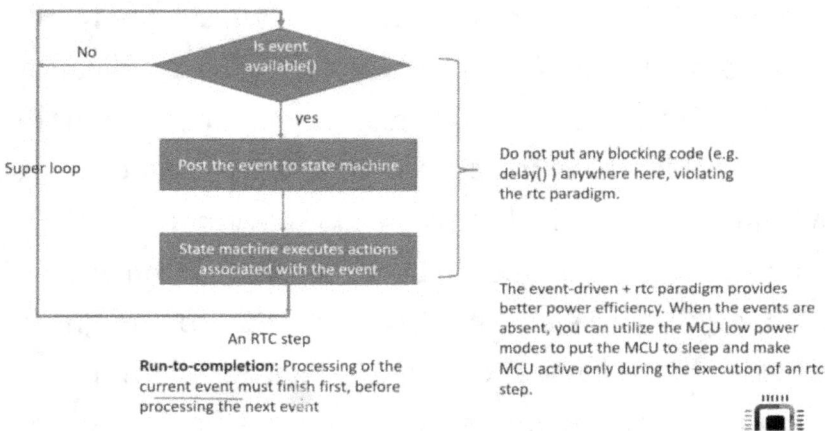

That is what we call a run to completion paradigm. Please note that if you are using the run to completion paradigm, then you should not put any blocking code like the Arduino delay function anywhere. In these steps, so which was the RTC paradigm? Please note that the use of state machines, the implementation of Umstead state machines follow the Ranta completion paradigm. So this is what the specification faith ran to. Completion means that in the absence of exceptions or asynchronous destruction of the state, machine execution pending event occurrence is dispatched only after the processing of the previous occurrence is completed and a stable state configuration has been reached. So this is to say processing of the current event must finish first before processing the next direct. That is, an event occurrence will never be dispatched while the state machine execution is busy processing the PBS, which is why this behavioral paradigm was chosen to avoid complications arising from currency conflicts that may arise when the state machine tries to respond to multiple, concurrent or overlapping events. That's why please remember that the you must machines should be implemented in run to completion. And even the driven plus RTC paradigm provides better power efficiency because when the events are absent, you can make yourself empty or low power mode to put the microcontroller to sleep more to save some power. In this, you went to architecture. The microcontroller will be active only during the execution of an artist. This is an artist's step when the art you step is completed. The microcontroller can sleep until it is woken up by the end of that event. Now, to solve hierarchical state machines is to implement the high tech machines we need and even press that code. The event processor actually sources traversal of nested hierarchical state machines. I mean, it traverses through various stages which are nested inside of the High State machine, and it causes the appropriate state handler. It takes care of executing various transition sequences as per the utmost specification for all this. We need a background event process set in the previous exercises. We used a flat state machine and we didn't use any event processor generic code, which processes calling off various state handlers and solving various state transitions as per the specification. But when you start using the nested hierarchical state machines, it would become tedious to implement various state policies and maintain execution of transition sequences. Everything by yourself. That's why you have to go for some framework, or you have to use some generic event processor code, which can help you to implement the high technical state machines in your project. That is why, in this course, I'll be introducing the kewpie real time embedded framework and a new tool by Quantum Leaps LLC.

HSM event processor

[1]QP™ real-time embedded frameworks (RTEFs) and QM™ modeling tool by Quantum Leaps, LLC

Explore more:
https://www.state-machine.com/
https://www.state-machine.com/products/qp
https://www.state-machine.com/licensing

Miro Samek
Founder and CEO, Quantum Leaps, LLC
https://www.state-machine.com/

And this is a famous framework, and it also comes with a graphical modeling tool called Quilpie Modeler. And this is quite famous in the field of model number system programming using event driven architecture, and you can explore more about this with these links. And finally, importantly, we would like to thank Mr Samak, the founder and the CEO of Quantum Leaps LLC, for giving us permission to use the kewpie framework and its associated components. In this course, you will be using the Cupich Framework Kewpie model to queue at Jassem Event Processor and Kewpie Nano Arduino Library to implement that event driven hierarchical state machine project. Some of the features of the kewpie framework are that it runs to completion and even does an architecture, and it supports the implementation of nested hierarchical state machines using your mistake charts and by using a tool called kewpie modeler also called I've come to it. You can graphically model your application. That's actually a graphical modeling tool. So we are going to use that tool in this section, and you can generate the code automatically that is converting your state charts into traceable C and C++ code. So we'll see that later. And it also supports the act of object design pattern paradigm. And in this section, I will not be coding at two objects, but the framework supports the act to object to our active design pattern, then two objects are used in an application to schedule various two objects of your application. You may need the current various lightweight kernels provided by Kill me. Q Okay. Q Okay. Q Which means it's a simple cooperative kernel which is available in the framework itself, though you need not to pull any other part of this. Q K is a preemptive run to completion kernel, which is non blocking and Q F K is a preemptive dual mode that is either you can use it as a run to completion or a blocking out of kernel actor object. Also have other features like they come with that or even Q and various data encapsulation techniques. So you can explore more going through the act to object to the documentation provided by the quantum ledger. And the framework also supports a tracing tool called Q Spy. Realtime tracing is possible using Q Spy, and that is also one more tool called Q Test. This tool is to carry out the unit testing, and the licensing is very friendly. It comes under dual licensing. Both open and closed licensing are provided. Please explore this link to understand different licensing schemes, and the framework is Mr. C and Mr RC ++ Coding Standard compliant. For more information, please visit this link. After that, the kewpie framework comes in three flavors. One is cute, pithy, and stands for quantum platform in Thi. The framework supports YAML based FSM and nested XM implementation in C language and Kewpie C++, which stands for content platform in C++. So if you are using C++ in your project, then you can use kewpie C++ and that is one more flavor called Kewpie Nano, which stands for quantum platform Nano, which is a lightweight package or framework of your PC. This is actually intended for low end eight or 16 bit microcontrollers such as Aviad MFP for theoretical refinement, which I regard as very limited ram and rom size.

 QP™ Real-Time Embedded Frameworks (RTEFs)

QP framework type	Note
QP/C™	Quantum Platform in C. The framework supports UML based FSM and nested HSM implementation in 'C'
QP/C++™	Quantum Platform in C++. The framework supports UML based FSM and nested HSM implementation in 'C++'
QP-nano™	Quantum Platform Nano. The framework is also based on 'C' and it is intended for low-end 8/16-bit microcontrollers such as AVRmega, MSP430, or 8051 with very limited RAM on board (less then 1KB).

And this is a block diagram of this framework. So this picture I have taken from the state machine. This is a picture of the whole framework in this section will be using this hierarchical event process in. And please note that the kewpie framework is also available in the former Arduino Library so that libraries can just copy paste into the Arduino Library folder and you can start using this framework.

AVR based Arduinos
QP-Nano Arduino library
QP-nano framework support will be discontinued

ARM based arduinos
QP/C++ Arduino library

Explore more : https://www.state-machine.com/arduino

So far, we are based Arduino, such as Uno and Nano. The kewpie nano Arduino libraries are already available. You just have to download it and you can start using that. And for arm based Arduino, such as Arduino Duo, which is based on ARM Cortex architecture, the Kewpie C++ Arduino Library is already on the book, so you can use that with these ports. Or you can also use CU PC framework on these boards. So, but for Arduino, UNO board or nano board, we have to use Kewpie Nano Framework, which is actually a lightweight watch, an Occupy seat and you can get more information about Kewpie in a library at this link. In difficult scenes we are using, Arduino will not work, so we'll be using Kewpie Nano Arduino Lab, but it is not recommended for new design because the kewpie nano framework is discontinued, as mentioned in this web page for newer designs. So you have to upgrade your hardware to newer, advanced hardware such as Arduino do AR Arduino zero, which are based on arm based, already knows. In that case, you can either use the kewpie C++ framework or cubic framework. Let's move forward now we have to download a couple of things. First of all, we need the kewpie framework that you can download from here and also the Q graphical modeling tool. Everything comes with one download, I would show you that. And also we have to download be Arduino Library. And we also have to add effort to some of the API for Kewpie Nano Framework to use that framework. So I'll show you that later. Now, let's download these two things. So in the state machine dot.com website, go to product and queue model based design to just click on that. And use this option, download cu.m as a part of Kewpie bundle. And here you download the Kewpie bundle as per your machine. So I go for Kewpie Bundle for Windows.

DOWNLOAD QP™ NANO ARDUINO LIBRARY

All right, so now let's download Cupid Nano Arduino Library for that to go to resources and go to Arduino. And after that, download kewpie Arduino for your machine and go to windows. Now, first, let's install the kewpie framework. So just double click on this. And select the directory by default, it will get installed in C. That's fine. So here you can select things that you don't require. For example, we are not using an arm processor here, so you may dislike these options. And we're also not using Kewpie C++, so you can dislike that too. But I'll keep everything because I have enough space. Just click next and next. Install. It is taking some time. Now, let's click finish. So the installation is over, and now let's install Kewpie Arduino Library. Let's go back to the download and let's extract this. And now you have to copy all these things and you have to paste it into the Arduino Sketchbook location for that. Just open the Orange ID. Let's hope they are denied. Here, go to file. And chances. Copy this location. And go to File Explorer and open that location. So this is my guest book location here, you have to paste it, what you do is go to kewpie library. Just copy this. And in the sketch book location just pasted. That fit. So I have already done this. That's why I was asking to replace some facts. I'll just go to replace the file in the definition. Now you see the files are copied here. And if you go in the library, you can see there are two libraries for arm based Arduino boards and coupon, which is a kewpie nano framework for a wired based Arduino board. And so this has all the framework related thought fights.

Transition execution sequence and Event propagation

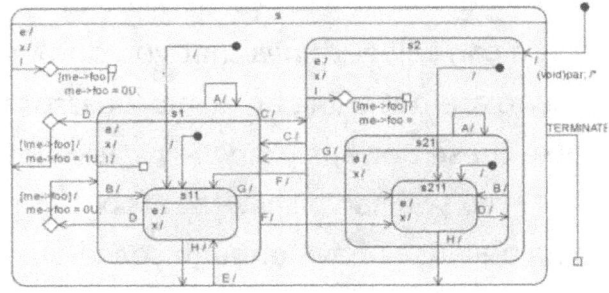

Location : <installation drive>\ qp\qpc\examples\workstation\qhsmtst

So we successfully integrated the Arduino Library. And in the next project, we are going to test our transition execution sequence and event propagation on an Arduino board. This is actually an example to understand various transition execution sequences and even propagation in a nested hierarchical state machine diagram. And this example is already available in the kewpie framework that you have downloaded and installed. It is at this location so you can test this application directly on your machine. You need not to use any part that is doing the hard part or any other board trick and test it on the machine. But in the next project we will test it on the Arduino board and so that we learn how to use this tool along with visual code and platform IU extension. So I'll cover this in the next project.

HSM TRANSITION EXECUTION SEQUENCE TESTING

Hey, welcome back to the project. In the previous project, we installed the kewpie framework, which also installed the QM two graphical modeling tools. And we also installed the Kewpie Nano Arduino Library. Now, in this project, we will understand various transition execution sequences in nested hierarchical state machines. And we also understand event propagation. So when the events are sent to the nested high technical state machine, I mean how the transition happens from one state to another state and what the order of execution of various behavioral actions. So to understand this, that is already an example code available at this location. And you can straightaway launch that application and it was your studio and you can test it. I'll show you that fast, so that you don't need any board connected to the computer for that.

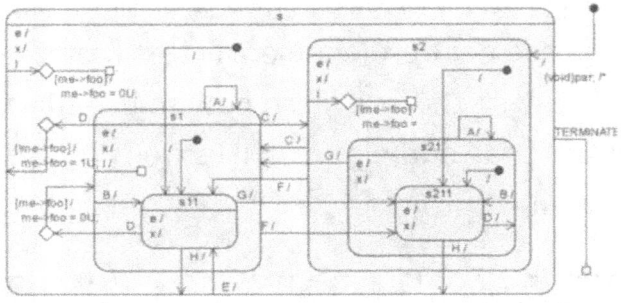

Location : <installation drive>\ qp\qpc\examples\workstation\qhsmtst

What you need to do is you just have to go to the kewpie installation folder. Let go that this is in starting C drive kewpie and go under, let's say kewpie c and that good example workstation. And here just open the Q HSM test. Here you can launch this project and just launch this video through your phone, you should buy this, you have to install a visual studio, so I have already installed that. Let's open that. The project is open. And let's go back to that. And this is a QM artifact. This you have to open using the cu.m tool. What you had installed in the previous project. In the previous project, you installed the kewpie framework that also installed the two tools. So now let's launch that. And after that, by using that cu.m tool, open this model file. Oh, just copy this part and go here. File open model. Just open this. And after that, expand this package. Double click on this, so that opens the state machine of this class, so we'll understand later how to create all these things by scratch, like creating a class, adding attributes, adding operations, adding state machine and those things will understand it. So this is actually a nested, hierarchical state machine of this project. And as you can see, it receives various events so that events are named like, you know, ABC up to I. There are various events which are sent to this project to observe various transitions. So now to test this on the machine, you already had opened this on the Visual Studio. So just compare this outfit. Compile and run. And daughter, they started running. Now you can send various events. For example, you can see that the court is currently in the state.

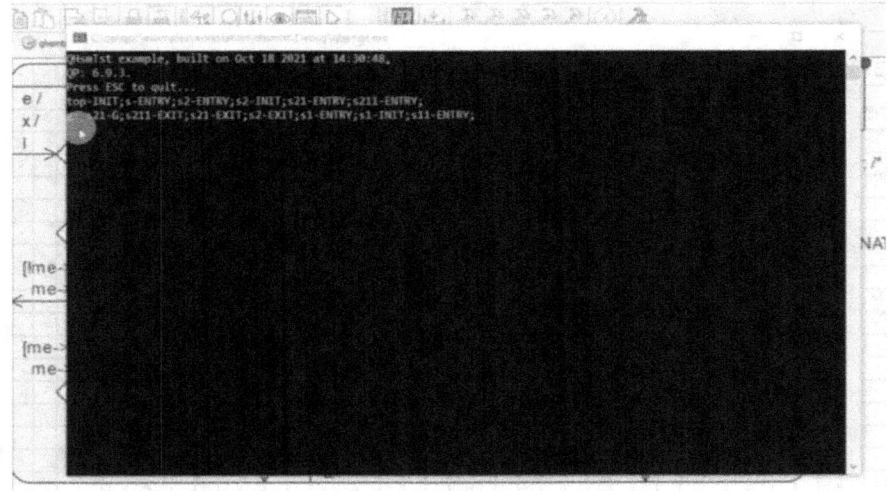

If two one one that is after one one is this one less than one event. For example, let's say I will send that event. I'll send. So let's see what happens. Defend the event. Gee, I'm going to type the letter T. When you do that, this is a transition execution sequence for the event, which is reviewed when the state machine's state was asked to one more. Now the state machine is in yes, one one the state. That means the state machine transitioned from Earth to one one two one one. And in between, this is the order of execution of various factions. So we understand this one by one. But before that, we will understand how to integrate this project with Arduino and we will understand how to create the file like this. And we learn how to use Kewpie Framework Accord Generation Directive to generate various function declarations and function definitions, etc. But if you don't want to try with Arduino, then you can just try with the computer, as I just explained. So that fits with this project and you can find various events to this program you can fear. To the transition execution sequence.

EXERCISE-006 TEST HSM TRANSITION EXECUTION SEQUENCE ON ARDUINO

Hey, welcome back to the project. So in this project, we will create a new Arduino project to test this model. Q At just some Test DXM, which is already provided in the kewpie framework, and the goal of this exercise is to understand various transition sequences in a nested hierarchical state machine by sending various events. First of all, let's create a new Arduino project. I just closed this. This was actually Visual Studio and I closed this too. First, let's open the Visual Court I.D.. Now, to create a new project, I go to a flat made from iron ore pun and here is a new project. Project name for Typekit zero zero six Q HSM test. And select the board or not. Framework is Arduino, and the location really is the previous location.

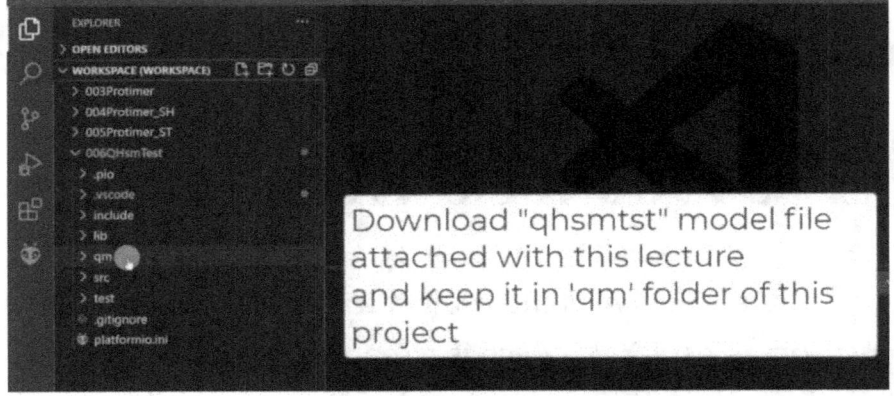

This was our location and click finish. So we just created a new project. At home test and here create a new folder Cardiff QM. So this folder will be used to keep the queue and model. OK, now it's very important. Download the Cu.m model file attached with this project and keep that in this cu.m folder. OK. I would just paste the model file in this directory. QM. OK. I can't pay that here. No problem, let's open this in the File Explorer. QM, so just paste that. That's it.

ADDING FILES IN QM TOOL

Now what you do is just open the QM Martin file using the QM tool that opened the QM tool. Let's open the model. Fine. Please note, when you open that QM model file, it should show a coupon here. OK? In the project, it is showing UPC. Yes, ignore that because I was working with QVC for some other reason. OK. But for you, it must show a coupon. So now you have to auto generate the cord. For this model, the cord can be generated into five. You can mention the file names here under which you want to generate the cord when you load this project. The project already has two five years. And here this is how he had to file. And this is a Nazi file. These files actually contain code generation directives of the kewpie framework to generate the code so you can use the direct truth, you can control what kind of code you want to generate.

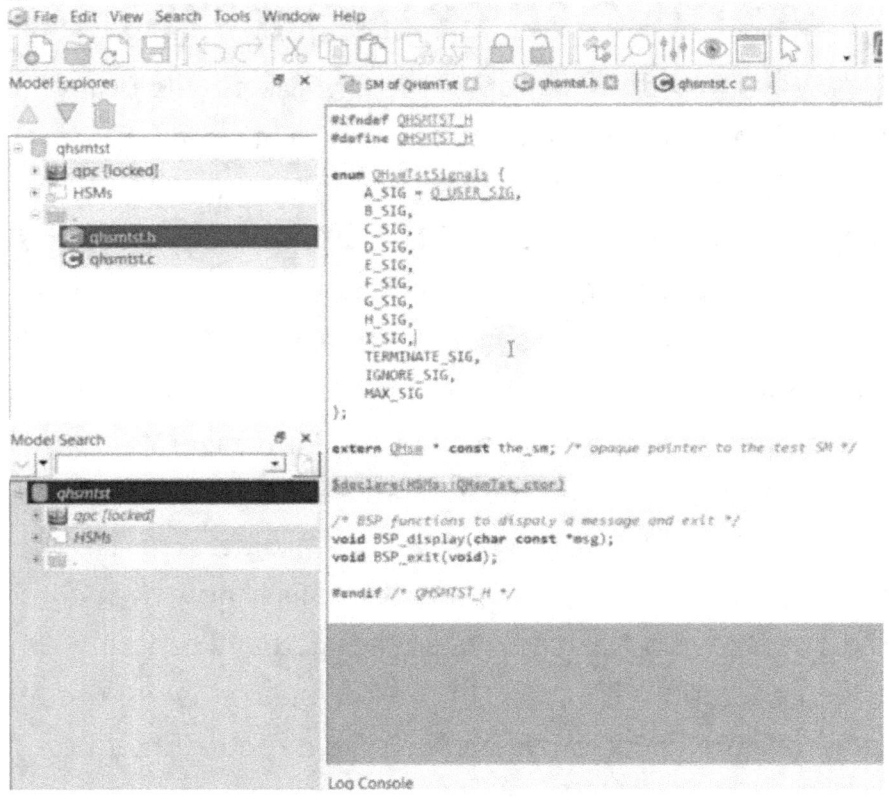

Even if you just want to generate the function declarations, then you can use the declared directive if you want to generate the function definitions you can use. Define a directive like that. I will do one thing. We were just delayed. And we will create that once again so that we can understand the usage of the code generation director's off the framework. Not what you do is that click on this. And create a directory that's select add victory. And here you can mention the part of the electorate. If you just mentioned the dot here, then that signifies the directory in which this model file is present. That means if you just mentioned DOT here, it refers to Q and folder because under cue unfolded. We have the model file. That's why these poppies are to the directory in which the Model five is present, and to this directory we can add files that add a file. Let me give the name Alexei Wild-Card CPP. You just created one file. Filed our tip in the current directory. So if you want to see that file, then you have to. Generally, the court, let's click on generate court. And you can see that one family generated and that file you can see under this photo here, it is created so it doesn't contain any court because to include code, we have to use the Code Generation Directive, but I don't want to create any files here, but rather I want to create under sort. And the thoughts I have already got made are TPP, and I am going to create two five here. I'm going to create two files. One is to queue at some test underscore feminazi that is state machine Darcy and state machine data. Each state machine Darcy contains all the state machine implementations. That means state handler function definitions, usually state handler functions, will be prior to a fire. That's why you can keep them as static to a fire, and you can also keep state handler function declarations in feminazi. And you can also use this fire to keep any private variables related to the state machine. Quote our project will create this upstart. You can also create one state machine that got its head right here. You keep everything which you want to share with other files like function declarations of exported functions, event definitions like enum for events, etc. any details you want to share with other five you can keep in a state machine dart each.

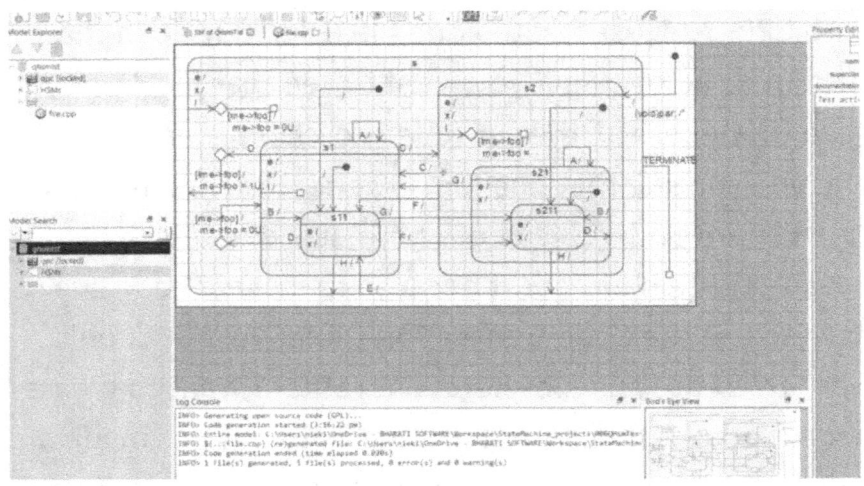

Now I'm going to create two files for this model. One is a queue at some test and of course, FM dart ship and dart each flight. And I want to keep those two five under this fast report that can be done here. So I'll do this. Now you point this part to a different electorate. What you can do is you can come out of the current directory using Dot Dot Flash, so you actually came out of Cu.m Directory. And then point to the FARC directly. I'll just write FARC here. After that, let's create two files here at file. I'll call this

RFQ SFM. Dart CP. And another file. Q HSM underscore. Test dot edge file. Save it and gendered the cord, and now you see our two five stars appeared under FARC. So now, if you try to edit something here, you cannot save it. You can see that these files are marked as read only five by the crown too. You cannot edit anything here. There are two ways to edit the files. What you have just created is using an external ID, such as this ID. This is an external I.D. So if you want to edit the files here, then you have to mark these files. Five External. I have to select externally here. For this also external. So if you mark these files as external, then you cannot open these files under this software because this is an external file, so you have to edit these files using external IDs. That's why if you want to edit the file using some external IDs, then you have to take this external option for the files. So we have created two files. Now let's understand how to generate the code for that, do you? How to exploit code generation directive? This will be understood by going through the documentation. Here, go to product documentation and to a modeling tool. This is the whole documentation, so here go to core engineering and here upon this core generation directors. So this is nothing but some directives. I mean, directives to the QM tool to generate the court. You can fine tune which court you want to generate and which code you don't want to generate. All those things you can fine tune using these directives. These directives give direction to the tool to generate the code. There are three major directives one you could declare to define a director and define one director.

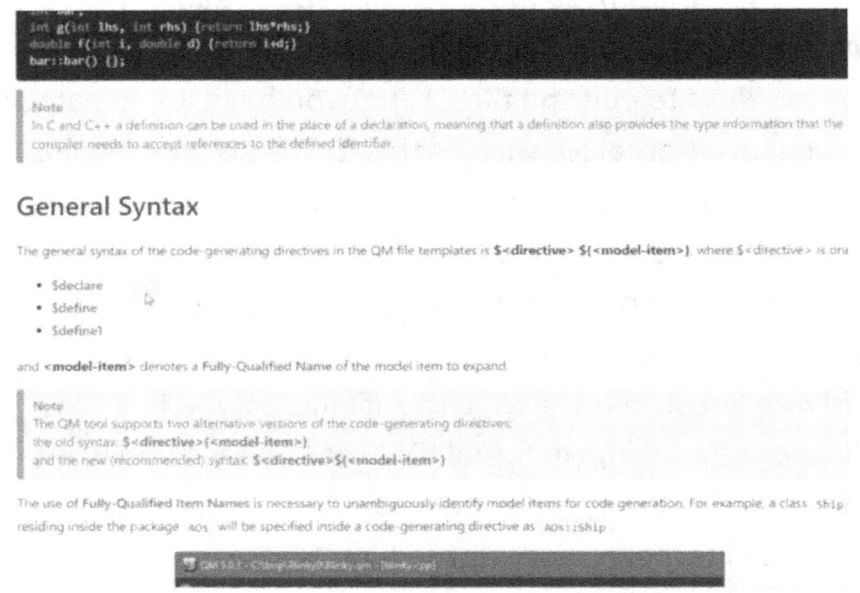

So let's say you want to just generate the function, declaration or function signatures, then you can use Declare Director. Suppose if you want to generate the function definitions, then you can use a defined director so you can explore them. Do you find directors specify the recursive definition of an element could be anything. It could be a class and operation of a state machine, a state or a free operation. Or three attributes like that. Syntax up using this directive, as mentioned here, you have to start with a sign mentioning the director and this directive, and after that, another dollar sign. Then you had to mention that element, name or item name in the curly braces. You have to mention. Let's start with our doorstep pile. And here we want to create or we want to put a state handler function declaration for our signature. Let's see how to do that. But now head over to our I.D. because I cannot edit the file in the queue, I'm told. That's why I have to use my ID and I'm going to the Dart CP file and here I'm going to use it. Fine. Declaring art will do one thing. We'll go to that tool, and for the time being, let us temporarily make this internal to disable the external option. Then you can open this. And here, type declare. I just used their declared director. And then if you open this package, this is a package that just sent me the package. And under that package, this is plus the main cloth or main application structure, or it is also part of an application cloth and the cloth name or structure name is Q HSM test, and it is derived from Hugh Acheson. It's superclass this Q at the about which you will see later. This is a cloth or in C programming it is the structure. And this is a state machine of this cloth because we write a state machine to model the behavior of a cloth or of an application object. And it has got one or two. Now I want to generate a state handler function declaration or signature. Let's see how to do that. So the state machine contains different states. What you need to do is you just drag and drop here this one so that complete the code generation directive. Or you can manually write it, declare this is the package name. And this is a main class and under which this is a state machine and we are going to generate now the signature our declaration of all the state handlers of this state machine. So then save it and generate the code. I just agenda to the court. Now let's go back to Heidi. And here you can see that under Dr. CWP file, we just created the state handler's declaration threat. Now we have to include the kewpie nano Arduino Library into a project, that's why it is showing so many errors. What you have to do now is to edit your flat from the ipod identified in our previous project in the platform iReport and nine. We actually added this liquid crystal library and this variable actually points to our environmental variable points to the various library dependencies. So that's why you have to copy this variable and go to your platform. I walked in and paste that.

A quarter now, where is the library, the coupon Arduino Library? That part you had to provide here, just open the sketchbook location. This is a sketchbook location. My sketchbook location. And. Go to the library and kewpie and underscore where we are in this pot. I'm going to copy. Let's go back to the ID and paste here. After that, you have to include the coupon and. We'll see that later. So after that, you can get it off all these areas, but we just generated the state handler's declaration. And now let's go to our next step. That is now let's see how to create or generate the code for state handler functions and definitions. Again, let's go back to the tool. So please note that you can only add this file when it is not extended. You can also directly write these directives in the external light itself. That also works. Now let's copy this past year and let's change this declaration to define. Save it and generate the code. You can see that here. Let me close this. That's the open again, and you can now see that these are the signatures of the function and these are the definitions of various state handouts. If you check here, we just implemented the code related to the state machine. For example, if you want to declare the main application class or structure, then you can do that. We have to do that. Anybody can do that. So let's start at the beginning. So just write. Declare and I'll drag and drop this May an application class. And now let the court. Here you can see that the main application structure is created. So now, instead of using these three separate directives, you can just use, declare and define over this main class because this state machine and the class attributes are the structure attributes are all part of this main class. That's why you can just use, declare and define over this class name. So that will generate all the required courts, including the underlying state machine code. But it won't create a court related to this operation. This is basically a function constructor function. It is called pre operation since it is outside class. The code will not be generated, so you may have to define a separate directive for that. That's why instead of using these three, I can just write something like this: declare and define. This much is OK, now let's generate the court.

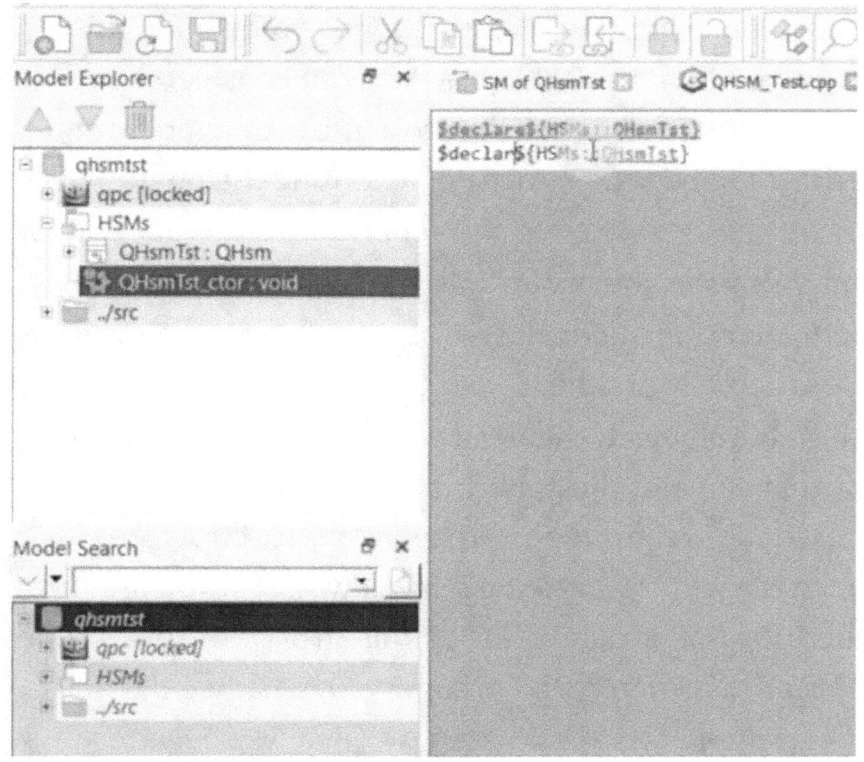

And it has generated all this court yet again, see, that is the main structure which corresponds to this class to at some test. Under this class structure that is one private attribute or a private member element. This is a private member element, and this structure is derived from another structure, a super structure related to a superclass and a super class name is Q HSM. When we create this class, we also mention the super class here. Super class is nothing, but it is another structure. So basically it was structure embedding. One structure is embedded in another structure when you embed this structure inside this structure. You can consider it as inheritance. That means the structure is derived from this structure. I'm in the structure, inheriting the operations and attributes related to the super class and a super class. What we have chosen for this application is Q at USM. So there are other super classes as well. You can select here that is actually another Super Cathcart Q MSM. If you are using act to object, then you can use Q Act two, etc. It's like that some of the generic attributes and generic operations are included in the super class structure, which is given by the kewpie framework. So you are just inheriting that structure inside this structure. This is your application structure. So in summary, what we did in this video was we actually created two five AQ seven test underscore 7.2 CP and Q at some test underscore as edge in the Dark CP file. We actually kept the code related to these things, so we kept the code related to the structure declaration that is this one. And after that, a code related to the state handler of declarations. As you can see, it is limited to the file scope. So use of the tardy storage class persists here. And also, we kept the code related to state handlers definitions. These rest of the codes are related to the standard definition. All these things are limited to five codes because they are encapsulated in a file and it is not shared with the external world. In the next project, we will generate the code for Smart Edge. Here we can keep you and the declarations in the form of items because events have to be shared with other files. So other files need to know what events can be posted to the state machine. That's why that information you have to share with other files. So that's why we will keep event declarations in the form of enum or macros in the smart act. And we can also keep any export declarations of variables to our functions asymptotic in the next project, which ended the court for 7.8 hours in the next project.

ADDING CODES TO FILES USING QM TOOL

Welcome back. Now let's call for a test drive, so this I have marked as external. But for the time being, that very modest distinction and make it as internal. First of all, let's include guards. Here, let's create an enum. To include all the events up the state mission, if you just click on that state machine, you can see that it actually takes many events and events are from eight to eight. And there is also one more event called Terminator event. Now, let's call that here. He underscored, think you have to mention this under thick with an event because as you can see, when it has generated the court for the state machine model, you can see that this framework used a boundless thick to underscore thick prospects with every event. That's what you have to use that cell. You went out from A to I. And after mentioning all the events at the end, you had to mention a Micromax signal, Max underscored That this enumerator constant actually indicates the total number of events supported by the application, so keep that at the end. The framework may use this macro, I don't know, but this is required.

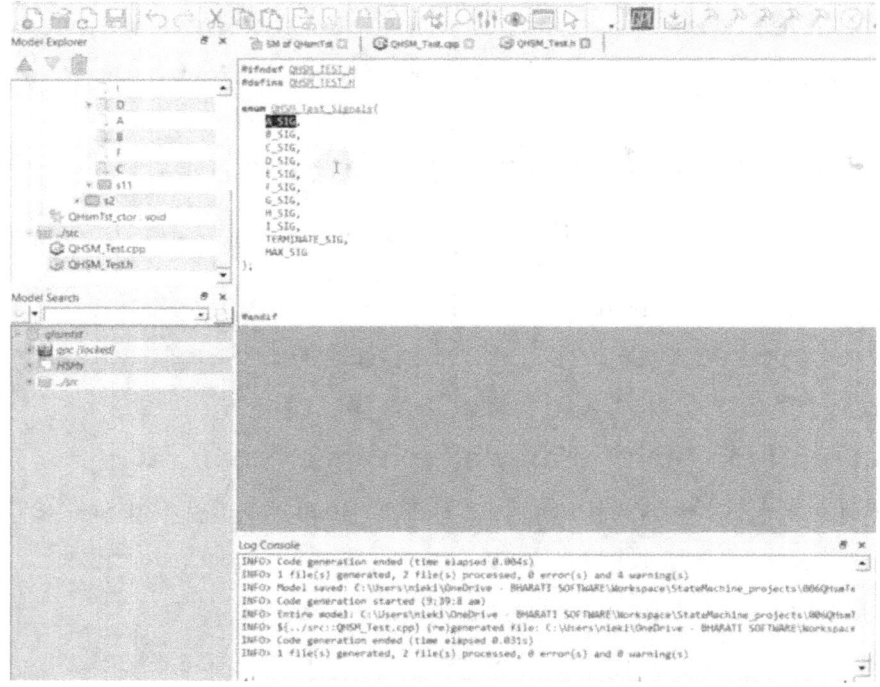

And after that, this is the beginning of the first user event in the documentation. You can go to nanostructure meditation files, and here in £Q, there are some results. Signals of the framework like Q underscore entry seek, experts say in its SIG signals related to the timeout, etc. The cue user thing is a macro, which indicates the beginning of the user signals Are you you? That's why you have to equate this event to Q user think. Its value is actually eight eight is assigned to this, which marks the beginning of the application for how to use the signal. This is to distinguish between the result signals because the first radar signal starts from one here that the Q and two signals. If you don't do this, then the value will conflict with these results signals. Now let's generate the code. I just learned the court. And let's go to the debt file, and here you can see that it is already here. Now, let's work on resolving some errors. First of all, let's go to Dr. TPP and here you have to include some header files. Let's go here. First, what you need to install is a hash. That includes the header file of the Arduino framework. Are being underage then they had, in fact, related to the Q financial framework. Q P Dot H. And had to fight related to the.

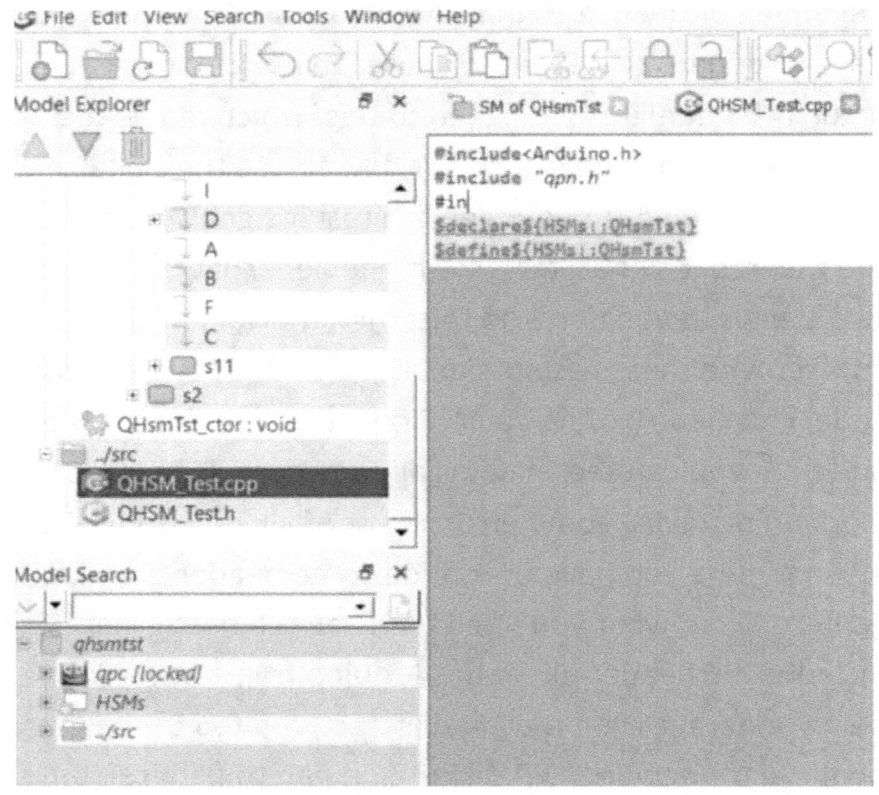

This had, in fact, to some test. Dart. Now let gender at the court. Here it is. You can see that, so we resolve most of the ads. There is one at it. I'm not sure why it is showing this remark here because I have already included the library here. During build, it may disappear. What's our next task? Now in the model, if you check the model, the state machine model, you can see that it uses different actions for different transitions. For example, if you consider the state that the model has defined entry action as well as egg detection, now we have to give the implementation of this function BSB display.

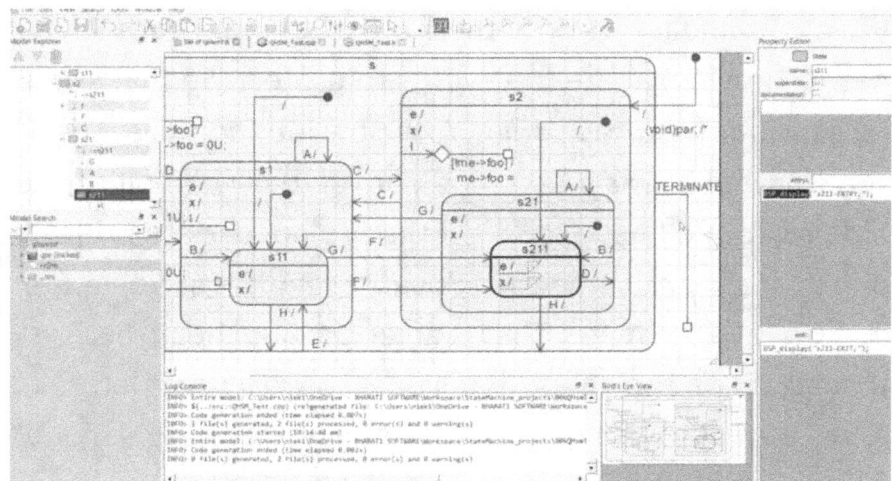

Let's do that. Let me just create one five here. New file. I'll just call the VSP Dart CP. And another fire. Here you can keep any petrol related or BSP related code, but because this has BSP dot edge. The courts for these are not generated by the QM two. This is our BSP court to try various methods in the BSP. Dorchester includes guards. Let's create these two functions. BSP display and BSP exit. There's one more function out to get the BSP exit. Just ride this train. FDR. It doesn't return anything. Just give the declarations here, and let's give the implementation in TPP, so just include. Are we now headed for? And here we just use cloud print. So just print some text on the.

Clear that. Now, let's include this had to be a speech shortage. And that's generally the cold. It appeared here. Fine. Let's go to the main door BP for the mandatory BP, probably the government. It takes the event or gender to the event and it is sent to the state machine. That's why it has to know what are the events to protect. So that's why let's include test, test, edge. And now let's compile. We'll see whether it was fine or not. I am actually compiling the old project, so I have to select the project back to project directly to fix. At some test. You can see that as you enter it. Now let's compare. That is an error. But check this function is on the news, that's fine, so we'll use it later. And it says that this macro was not declared in this scope. This we used actually, and this had in fact, what do you do is in the major step before including this had in fact used to include kewpie and undertake. That. Now it was prime. So far, we have completed all these steps. And in their next project, we will explore some of the API Kewpie Nano to post the event to the state machine. Now see the next project.

ADDING A CLASS ATTRIBUTE

Now, our next job is to post the U.S. to the state machine. Now for this, we have to explore the kewpie nano API. Let's do that. Just head over to Amazon.com slash coupon and here you can read for API reference. These are the APIs we have to use or have to first call the hierarchical state machine that is queued at your firm there. That is the constructor. And after that, queue at your firm. And if you have any events, you can use this macro view at the from dispatch to dispatch the event and also some helper functions to get the current state, etc. These things had to be called in this order only. First, you have to call them and then the Q. I just I'm in it. So the framework is based on the superclass Q adjustment, if you just explore that. Q SFM is in our it's super tough. And you can see that this cloth Q SFM contains these attributes as data fields. Mythical infrastructure and our application structure, our application class is derived from this super plot, so we have already embedded this superclass in our application structure.

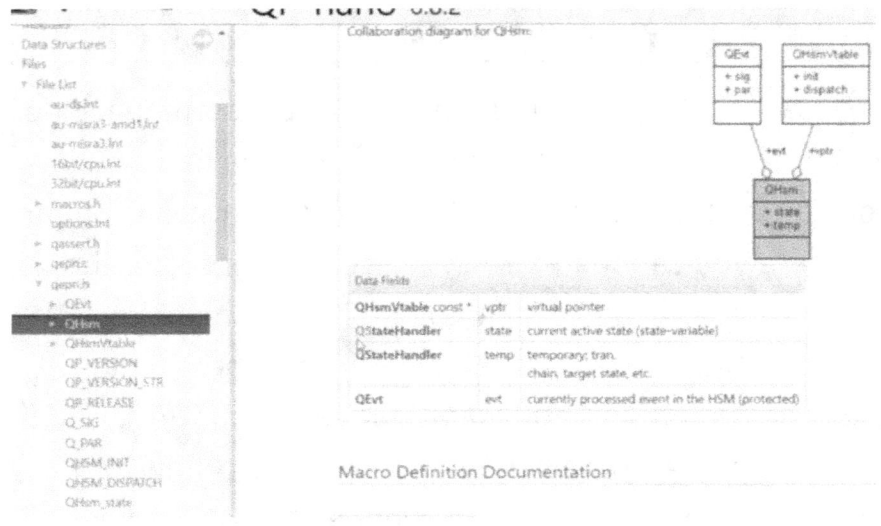

You can see that. So we have already done that. Here this is our structure, and here we are already embedded in that structure, that means now this structure inherits the attributes of this structure. What are the attributes of this structure? You can see that it has one important feeling that is the state handler, which is used to hold the pointer to the current active stage handler. This is a state variable. So our cloth inherited this or our structure inherited this, that's why now you have to initialize this state variable off the queue at the same cloth queue at the same cloth. Our structure for which is our super cloth. This is provided by the framework. How do you initialize this state? I mean, the initial state has to be an initialized question that you can do by using the constructor queue adjacent constructor. You have to call this function. Q at just the tr, this performs the first step of each of them initialization by assigning the initial pseudo state to the currently active state of the state machine. Basically, it initializes that state data field. I think you have to call this function since you may not see BP, you can call that from the of function, you can call that for this API. You have to provide two fields, so you are to provide the MI pointer, which is nothing but a pointer to the superclass. And you had to mention the address of the initial state handler of your state machine. Now, let's head over to our I.D. and let's go to the main door TPP. And from here, you can call that tar. Just copy this. You want a pointer to the superclass, which is embedded in your application structure. Now, how do you do that because in the queue at some undisclosed test participe, we have not created any instances of this structure that create that. You can do that using the tool itself. Go here. Now we have to create an instance, or you can call an object of this class or this structure. You can do that by right clicking on this and selecting add attribute. You can do that or you can add manually, that is also possible. Now before that, let's understand about attributes like adding attributes using the tool.

Adding a Class attribute

1) Static class attribute
- Static class attribute exists in one copy only, regardless of the number of class instances.

2) Non-static class attribute
- Non-static class attributes correspond to data members of a **struct/class**, present in each instance of the struct/class

Source : https://www.state-machine.com/qm/bm_attr.html

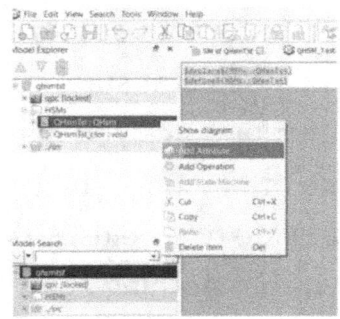

There are two types of attributes. One is a class attribute and another one is a pre attribute. What is a classic, as this name signifies adding an attribute to the class of class attribute? Very simple. I mean, you can see that you have to right click on the classmate and you have to select that you would add an attribute option. This is like adding a tough attribute. What is a free attribute? You have to click on the package. This is a package. And if you select Add Attribute or that, then that is adding a free attribute. First of all, let's understand what is a classic tribute in the classic tribute, there are two types. Static classic tribute and non static rather tribute. They are all well documented in this link. Let's understand what exactly the static trough attribute and a non-started class of Typekit are. These technologies are being taken from the C++ programming language because in C++ programming language, when you write a class, you can define static class attributes or non-static graphic Typekit. But let's understand what exactly these are? By analyzing a C++ class, for example, here this is a class in a C++. And you can see that here is some data. This is a non-static class attribute. Why? Because that is not a static keyword present here. That's why it's a non-static class attribute. And here this attribute is a static class attribute here, because that is a static keyword. What's the difference between a non-static attribute and a static attribute? The year when you create a number of objects of this class, each object will contain its own copy of non-stop attributes that are not static data. The object one will have its own copy of some data, that is, this variable object two will have its own copy of that non-static data, etc.

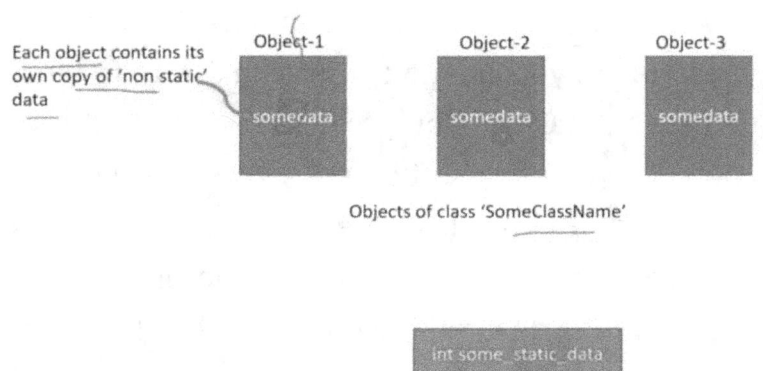

But you see the object will not have that one copy of static data. Static data is common for all the objects. That's right, that will be only one copy for all the objects of the cloth. This one will be only one copy of this static data created in the memory. How to declare and define this fatty attribute in C++. You see, this is not a definition, actually. This is a static attribute declaration. Now the definition you must do outside the class. This is a definition here. You see, it's just like in C. It's just like defining a global variable. But you cannot access this straight away here or in some random functions because H2 visibility is protected by the private keyword. That's why the static and non-static class attribute concepts are taken from the C++ programming language. And if you want to implement a similar thing in fee, then you can create one global variable. And you can treat it as a static attribute of a structure, and you can use that global variable to share information between different instances of a structure. In C, you can do something like that and you'll see that next. Okay, how to do that using that tool? I hope you get the idea of static class attributes: a non-starter class attributes static properties in only one copy and static attributes are used to share common information. Among different instances of the class are different instances of the structure in C, whereas non-static class attributes correspond to data members of a structure class president in each instance of the Class R structure. Let's move forward now. Let's do some experiment with a tool to understand that, for example. So here that is a variable pool and this is actually inside this class. Correct. But that is marked as non-static. The static checkbox is not checked, hence it is a non-starter. If this is not checked, this is considered as the member element of this structure or of this class. You can choose this option, so this option is not that relevant in any programming language. It would be useful in C++ language because the member element can be segregated into Private Public Protector. You can create one more attribute if you want. I'm creating a class attribute, which is static, so I'll call this bar and I'll keep this as private and I don't check the static, generate the code. I have not defined the type here that defined Typekit attribute int birth, gender, the code, and let's see what happens. You can see that two variables or remember elements have been created under this class. So these are non static. That means if you want to create a member element inside the structure, you've non option. What happens if I select static? For this bar. Let's see what happens. We just produce the court. And you see, now it disappeared from the structure and it went outside. You can see that now it is considered as a global variable in this fight. This is automatically attached by the QM tool for this variable name. This is a static cliff attribute. We're going to get more information in the user manual of this tool. You can go to state machines here and you can go to attributes not here. Sorry, go to basic modeling and working with attributes. Now, what are three attributes attached to a package are called three attributes in C or C++. Such three attributes correspond to variables defined directly at bioscope, either using static variables or global variables, so three attributes are some variables either static variables or global variables for which are not confined to the class as static or non-static attributes. The pre attributes can be limited to five copies using static keyword, or you can define three attributes as. Global attributes, OK? So that's why you don't see static checkboxes for free attributes. So because it is not confined to a class, you can make that variable. Files are global. OK? You can select that in the tool while creating the preclearance that also you can create by using the tool itself for that.

- **attribute type** drop-down box (NOTE: accepts also user-supplied types)
- **attribute visibility** drop-down box with options: public, protected, private
- **static checkbox** (for designating a class attribute as a *static class attribute*)
- **attribute documentation** for documenting the attribute (see also generate comments)

Free Attributes

Attributes attached to a package (as opposed to a class) are called **free attributes**. In C/C++, such free attributes correspond to variables defined directly at file scope (either static variables or a global variables).

Adding a Free Attribute

A *free attribute* can only be added to a Package. To add a *free attribute*, in the Model Explorer right-click on the Package to which you want to add a new *free attribute* and select Add Attribute from the popup menu.

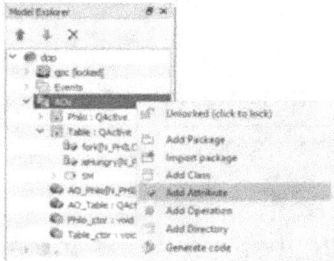

Just click on this package and create an add attribute. I'll just add one attribute. That's the name of the variable type. Let's take a cat. And you can control the visibility. Whether you want to make it as a global variable or a file variable that's using five variables. And you can give some documentation here and any initialization values that say 10 here. Let's see what happens. I just generated the code, and now you can see that that variable is not created. That is not created because this is outside this class. You use the code generation director to generate the code for that will do one thing after this line will define that variable. Define and drag and drop this and say, What is the code? And you can see that that is created at a static variable initialization that I have not used properly. I think you have to use equal to 10 and terminate this with the semicolon that is required. So as you can see here, since there is a free attribute, this tool doesn't attach the class name to it where it has attached a class name to the class attribute. This was the class attribute which I attached the class name to. Here is the structured name that is about attributes, adding attributes and for timing. Let me delete this thing or delete bar or delete this. So now our job is to create an instance of this structure. We have to create an instance of this structure. We just need one instance or one variable of this structure type. Let's go for a tribute to a classic attribute. Add a tribute to the name I call Jeff Kill at just in intense area objects I call just object types of this type. Type, I will add it as Q at GSM TFT, a structure name, and it is a static type class attribute, and I'll keep this as private and let's generate the code. And here you can see that the instance of the structure is created, which is the object of this structure that divides. I would just mention the object here that generates the code. So now we have to use this in our main doorstep. How do you use that with the question? He taught you how to use it. One thing is you have to do this. I can extend this in Maine and RCP. But that won't work because you can see this structure now. It needs to be exposed outside this file because this structure is declared in Doctor Sleep. Here it is defined here. You have to export this structure.

Exposing this structure to the outside world breaks the encapsulation, and it exposes all the private variables, our product and variables to the files that will definitely break the encapsulation. So how or concept data encapsulation is implemented in C++? If a class attribute is private and then functions other than member functions of that class cannot access them, right? So here this is wrong. So how do you implement something in C, for example, here? You have not exposed the structure to main dart CP. Hence you cannot do something like this, right? So this will definitely throw an error. Also, none of the functions of main Dart CP know about the private attributes of the structure. So if any function wants to access that supports the upper class or structure, it needs the midpoint pointer here. So the ME point is nothing but a pointer to the instance of the main class or structure. That's why this is not a good idea to extend that variable. What we can do is we can just expose the pointer to the super class which is embedded in this structure, just expose the pointer to this super class. For that, let's create one variable or pre attribute using a tool. How do you create the attribute? Why I'm creating a pre attribute is because I'm going to share that attribute with the external file. That's why I'm going here and clicking Add Attribute. And I call this the Super Q HSM Test. Typist pointer up the superstructure, what's the superstructure are Superclass Q at AFM plus monitors pointed of that the type must be a pointer type, a cost pointer type and visibility is global because, as I said, it will be shared with other parts and will internalize this to be to this object. Our main application object. Dart Super hadrosaur after event percent First of all, value declared this will declare this in Dart because it is shared with other quals using the declared director here. Just drag and drop. And I define this in Nazi occupied, maybe after this line or maybe at the beginning or after this line of do. Save it and produce the code here now you can see that we just created a pointer variable of this type and we saved the superclass pointer of our main application object here, and at this point it is shared with other players through Dart Edge Fire. Here you can see that this is extant and now it is not required because you are already in that file here. You can use that super. This one, that pointer and far fewer jsem is taught you how to provide the address of the initial state handler, but that is a problem. Address of the initial state handler is this one, but that is starting. This is not exposed to the external world. That's why the better approach here would be to create the theater for our application object. And from that, we will call the superclass theater. That's why this application has already been created. You can see that queue at some test, underscores Peter.

ADDING ASSERTION FAILURE CALLBACK

We met with this para que on a third. So let's go and explore that. You have to check this file to a third stage, and here you find to expand this queue on a third queue on a third for the callback function in case of assertion failure if any of the API has a framework. If that is any assertion, failure due to you are invalid arguments or if there are too many nesting archetypical state machines, then that could be an assertion. Failure to assert failure may happen due to many reasons. And if that is any assertion failure, it will be notified to you.

QP-nano 6.8.2

Function Documentation

● Q_onAssert()

```
Q_NORETURN Q_onAssert ( char_t const Q_ROM *const module,
                       int_t const              location
                     )
```

Callback function invoked in case of any assertion failure.

Description
This is an application-specific callback function needs to be defined in the application to perform the clean system shutdown and perhaps a reset.

Parameters
[in] *module* name of the file/module in which the assertion failed (constant, zero-terminated C string)
[in] *location* location of the assertion within the module. This could be a line number or a user-specified ID-number.

Note
This callback function should not return, as continuation after an assertion failure does not make sense.

The Q_onAssert() function is the last line of defense after the system failure and its implementation should be very **carefully** designed and **tested** under various fault conditions, including but not limited to: stack overflow, stack corruption, or calling Q_onAssert() from an interrupt.

It is typically a **bad idea** to implement Q_onAssert() as an endless loop that ties up the CPU. During debugging, Q_onAssert() is an ideal place to put a breakpoint.

Called by the following macros: Q_ASSERT, Q_REQUIRE, Q_ENSURE, Q_ERROR, Q_ALLEGE as well as Q_ASSERT_ID, Q_REQUIRE_ID, Q_ENSURE_ID, Q_ERROR_ID, and Q_ALLEGE_ID.

I mean, to your application through this callback function that you have to implement in your main Dart CP. Let's go to the main Dart CP and here let's implement that. What is provided here using these parameters? The first module containing the name of the five arm module in the attachment has failed, so this is our null terminated fifth string. You can directly print that string will do one thing here. We'll just use our serial. Print and land to print this model name, so just a third. Assertion failure, and we'll just print the module at which the assertion failure occurred, just bring this module. And after that, also let's print. The location. Let's hang here. Now let's compare. So the world is fine in the next project. Let's explore other APIs, that is to address them in it and you adjust them dispatch. I've seen the next project.

QHSM_INIT() AND QHSM_DISPATCH() APIS

Welcome back to the project. Now let's explore Q at the end. This morning, more quickly execute the top, most initial transition in the state machine, so now you have initialize the state variable with the initial state handler in the previous step, and now you have to execute the topmost initial transition in the FSM for that, you just have to call this function with me pointer. You can see the example here. So that is the pointer to the Super Cross. Let's do this. This must be called once after the constructor, after the constructor Q patch in it. So you already have this client in the US just shows that. Compile. Now you have to do one thing here. You have to define this macro. Q Define this fire. Just use this macro in the main Dart CP, which actually defines this variable, this model variable, which I think what it then already stole the name of the file, a module name which stops the module name. Just make sure that you use this macro and recompile. So that went well. And now let's go back out, we have to collect what you rent and dispatch it using the queue at GSM Dispatch. This dispatch of the event to the dispatcher of the framework and the framework then calls the appropriate state handle. And that's how event execution happens.

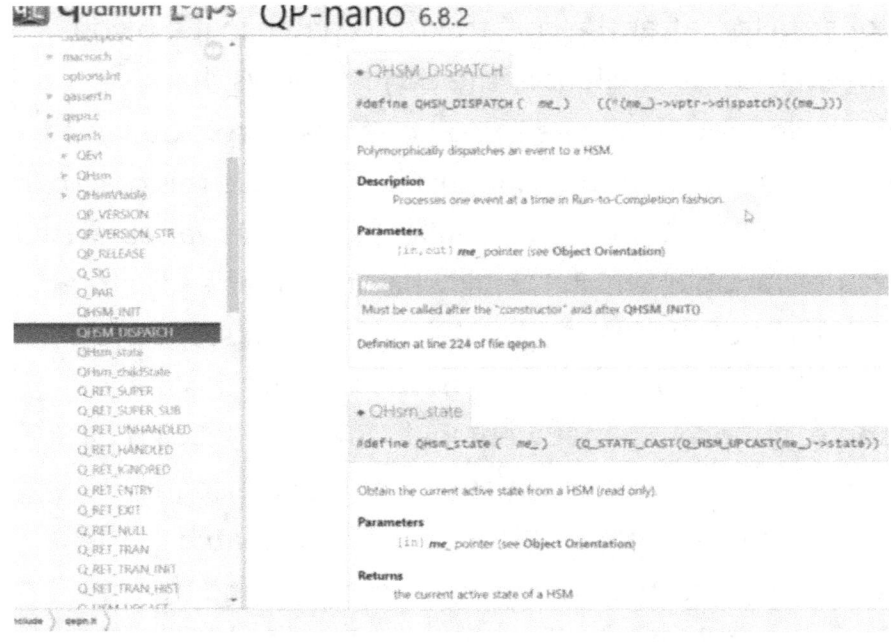

It processes one event at a time in the run to completion. Passion, artistry, passion just provide me with a .38, which is a pointer after Q in superclass. Here, let's take the event. Let me take the events from the city of port. The U.N. far from the eye, isn't it? Let me just write this course about Syria. Available safety data is available at Serial Port, still available greater than zero. Let's take one. Wearable Art Fair User Event. User event is equal to let's read the serial port one bite. So let's read one bite. And if. The UAE is equal to or a UAE if the quota is equal to capital, let's say. Then we have to dispatch the event. So the event name is Ithink that we have to dispatch what you do now". Take this pointer. And data from that event, dark, thick is equal to. Which type is the kill signal? Like that, basically this point itself holds the signal. So, Alpha. You eat like that, do you have to write up? I ate, too, I. So instead of writing like this, you can just do something like this. You can just use the macro Cusick. After some point too. So you can just do this that you can find in Kill Biotech. Here it is, Cusick. Like this, you have to add different events, as per the user event, to the superclass point to. And if the user entered a character other than these values, then you can just invent one event called ignored, think you can add that here? Just add one more event. Ignore the fake. After that, at the end here you used the function, Q HSM Dispatch. And you just use this point too. After that, just print a new line character here to push the next message to the new line and here as well. That fit. Now let's. Compile. It went well. Competition is fine and in the next project. Let's test this completely up to here.

EXERCISE-006 TESTING

Welcome back to the project and the previous project, we completed this exercise. And now let's test this before testing in effective function, please add this line, which can fix the portrait of the heart. And also, I'll send one message. Now let's compare this. Let's download. Let me open the Arduino cereal. Time to go to tools and open that. See, they'll monitor. But before that, you had to select. The board that is not. She doesn't want it to. Here you can see that the application ran and the initial transition. I mean, the action related to the initial transition has been executed in this order. Now let's analyze that. Let's go to the model. You can see that model starts from here. This is our outer shell. First, it executes the action related to this initial transition. The action is just printing, topping it. That's why you see top in it here, that action is executed. After that, it enters two states. As we discussed in the previous part of the course, while entering the nested states, the entry actions are executed from the outermost state to the innermost state. Here you can see that the outermost state is, if so, the reaction of this will be executed fast. Just like that, and you can see the entry and exit ActionScript if the entry is printed next. And after that, this date is entered because the initial transition points to F2 here. That's why after this, the state machine entered this date F2. So F2 entry action will be executed. F2 entry. That's correct. And when the state machine is in F2, so this transition shows the next stage, this transition actually signifies which state has to enter when the state machine is in F2.

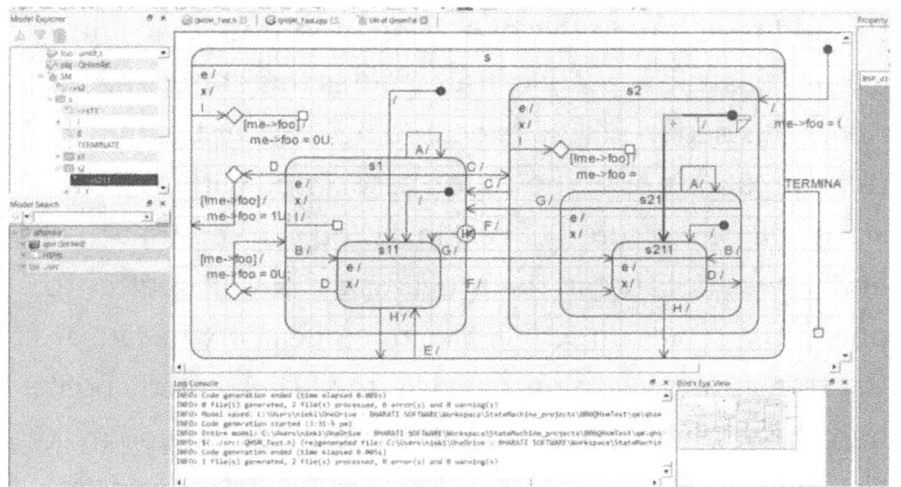

That's why the action related to this initial transition is likely going to next. You can see that too in it. So this is still in it. After that, you can see that this transition is entering here. So any reaction to this first? That's why you can see four to one entries. After that, it is directly entering this state and reaction off as to one one. No reaction like that. So now the state machine is settled at two one one. This is not the current state of the state machine. Now what would happen if this transition is? Up to here. How do you analyze this question? As you know, this is the initial sort of date. Everything starts from here. This will be printed first. And after that, this is pointing to this. Why are this batch violent reaction of this end reaction of death after that, this initial pseudo state pointing here first, the action associated with this initial state? And after that, this is pointing here. So obviously the end reaction on this one. When the state machine is in one, this initial pseudo state guides this state. That's right. This action will be executed next. After the initial reaction of this one, the action associated with this Utah state will be executed to one in it. You can see that to one end. It was not that in the previous output after after to one entry, it was directly if two one one entry because the transition was something like this. This directly points here. That's why this entry got executed. But if you make like this if to one entry after that, the action associated with this pseudo threat. And after that, the reaction of this one has two one one. So we'll see that just generate the code and let's test it. Well, that is an error. While applauding because the port is already busy here, we had to close this. That's open. And here you can see that after a two one entry is two one eight, it got printed. Prime, now let's send one event. So I have a couple of snapshots here. Let's test that you went deep. Now the state machine is in two one one. Now let's send the event and let's see what happens. De Jeff, Type D and send. This is a sequence of execution of different actions. That's the end like this. So the state machine was here, it was the current active state and it received that you went deep when the event was received. That is a transition. This is actually an external transition to 2-1-1, and this is a local transition, but as to what? The action associated with. This is executed fast. So this is a little different from the human specification classification phase, first detection has to be executed. But the implementation is different here with this framework. The action associated with the transition is executed first, so if two one one be either executed first. That's why you see as to 120 and after that it is an external transition. So exit action is executed next. Like this, this is fast. This is my second Kent. Two, one, one exit. As to one exit after that, it enters here. But as to one one is not entered, remember entering a statement when it has to be entered from the outside world. That's why f two one is not entered here. The control went to f to one state here. Entry action will not be executed because its two one was not entered from the external world when it is here. It is a super class of F two one one. The state machine cannot settler's superclass. It has to finally go and settle at the state, a concrete state, or it has to settle at a simple state as to one one is a simple state. F two one is a super state or as to one is a super state and as to one one is a substitute. It has to settle at a substrate. This will be executed next, because when it is here, it will be guided by the initial transition that is guided by the initial pseudo state, the action associated with two one in it is executed. So that's why you see us wanting it here so as to end it. This action is related to this initial pseudo state. And after that, this is two one one is entered from the external world. So that's why the entry action of this state will be executed. At the last. That's why you see, yes, two one one entries like that. It actually goes something like this. Goes like this. Execute this and it executes this. Let's move forward. Now, the state machine has settled that as to one one, you can see that in the output as to one one entry the state machine used in two one one when the state machine is in two one one. What happens if you want to be sent? It is here. And what happens if you rent B.S.? Let's analyze this. When the state machine is in two one one left tender, you won't be right to see what happens. I'm sending that you won't be. These are the actions. So how to analyze this? First of all, if 2-1-1 doesn't handle beat when it doesn't handle be, the event will be propagated to its 8:02 its 8:02 as to one. Please note that the event is propagated. There is no transition. There is a propagation event here. And if two one actually handles that event B, you can see it hand to be. There is a local transition from Earth to one to two one one. This is executed fast. The action associated with a transition, this is executed fast. That's what you should see. Something like this f to one b f to one b is printed fast, which is right here. After that, this date is entered, the reaction of one one has to be executed. Now the end reaction of this has to be executed. But the current state is still two one one. The current state has not changed. It is after one one when it is in two one one. How can it enter again unless it exits first and then re-enters? So that's why what happens here? The exit action is executed first and then into action is executed next to three. Like this, it has to exit first, then it has to re-enter the device. That doesn't make sense, right? So now again, the current state, if 2-1-1, the current of this 2-1-1 and what happens if I send the event a what happens when the event is sent? Let's see what happens. These are the actions that they like. It wasn't. It is not handled by the state. So the event is propagated as to one now is to one hand of that event. You can see that that is a self transition. This is a self transition that means the super state after one was left when a super state is left. So all the exit action had to be executed right from the innermost state to out-of-state trust. The action associated with this transition will be executed. You can see that if two, one eight, then exit action, this exit action has to be executed next as to one one. Exit. Innermost to outermost. That's why this is next. You can see that. And then it re-enters as to one percent reaction, then ultra monster innermost. This is the fourth. As to one entry. And when it comes here, the next state is guided by this initial state, and it has got its own action here, so two to one in it is next. After that, it enters the port, is this one fixed? Like that? Finally, the state machine has featured at this substrate as two one one. Now, our current state is the two one one. And what happens if it receives what you went at? Let's send it. And these are the actions that they have written here. First of all, this handles edge, the substrate handles that you can see. The action associated with this transition, so as to one one edge as to one one edge after that, is leaving this state when it is leaving, all the exit action had to be executed from then most to the outermost state. This is the second. As two, one, one exit.

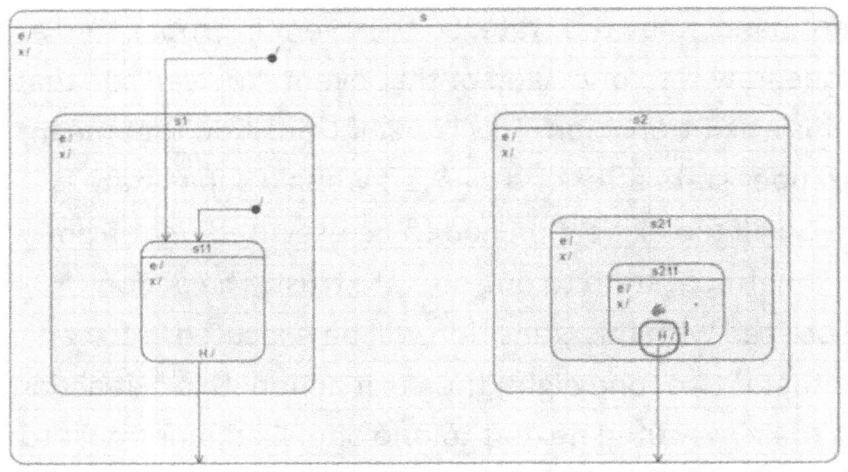

State ➔ S211
H➔s211-H;s211-EXIT;s21-EXIT;s2-EXIT;s-INIT;s1-ENTRY;s11-ENTRY;

State ➔ S11
H➔s11-H;s11-EXIT;s1-EXIT;s-INIT;s1-ENTRY;s11-ENTRY;

So this is third as to one exit. After that, this is what. To exit. So the transition is to if that transition is going to f but for as it is a local transition. And the state machine comes to this super state now, if it is now guided by this initial 2.8 for the action associated with this will be executed, that is fifth. Ethnic. This is in it. And after that, it is directly guiding you to this state if one one. Now the entry actions will come into picture. That's one entry next. As one entry. If one one entry next. Now, our state machine has settled at one. Yes, one one. Now what happens if it receives it here? Let's send it. You can see that it came to one one. Let's analyze this. When the state was, yes, one one, it received each event. This one. If one one edge after that exit action, exit action. To agree to action. You can see that to exit action. It comes here to the superclass. And again, it is guided by this initial pseudo state that is thin, it has thin it. And again, and reaction and reaction. It again said let s one one substate. Now, our state machine is in fact, one one to remember that. So now let's analyze the event I. We are here. And what happens if it is received when it is in F1 one, first of all, it is not handled by the state so that is why it is propagated to it, superstate. It comes here, as you can see the super state F1 handles. It's an internal transition for F1. That's why this internal transition will be executed. When the state eases one one, when I extend, yes, one is printed, yes, one I. Correct. This is printed. But there is no transition. That's why the state has not changed. The state is still one one only. This is the current state. The state variable will hold the address of as one one. The state has not changed. The event has propagated to the next level. And if there is any action defined, then it was executed. For one, it was just an internal transition. That's why one is printed. Please note that there is no entry into the f one. Why? Because the state variable has not changed its value. The third variable is still holding the address of F1 one. That's why when the state machine is in F1, one, if you send, I let me send I. Just Princess, when I have, again, just princess when I. You can keep sending I hear it just print as one I. Now, the state machine is in F1, one substitute. Now let's go to F2 one on one. And let's see how AI behaves here. What I will do is ask for the state machine I can send to the event to go from F1 one to two one one. That's why I was sent here. So now I'm going to analyze how I respond here. First of all, I just look at this AI is not handled by this, so it propagated to the next level. AI is also not handled here, so it is propagated to the next level. AI is actually an internal transition for Eth2, but the action is not defined here. We can see that there is no action. If the action is different, then your flashier flash is not. That for action is not defined here, but it has got a guard. It verifies the value of the CPU variable, so initially the pure variable is zero. You can see that in the initial transition, the variable value is set to zero. So not zero is one. That means the God condition turns out to be true. If it is true, then this CPU variable will have the value one and. It displays to me, that's why I asked to be printed and there is no change in the state. The state variable still contains the address of one one, so just two are printed here. Let's see, how can I? As to is it not what happens if you send the I again again, it is not handled properly to the next level, probably to the next level. I know the pool variable value is one because it was set to one percent, not off one is zero. The God condition turns out to be false. If it is false, then these actions are not executed, so it doesn't print anything. That's why Esther couldn't handle me. Esther couldn't handle me in this case because the guard evaluates to false. So that's why I use propagator to the next level. When it comes here again, the guard condition is checked here. The poor value is one guard, Errol Louis, trying to safeguard evaluations to true. That means she handles it. So if it is printed. That's why you, CSI, when you send it a second time. First time you see eye to eye because it's to handle it when you send the eye. Next time I couldn't handle it because the guard had failed. That's why it propagates to the next level and this f handles it. So that's why you see if I. And now, if you send it again, you can see that dance actually makes the pool variables zero again when it is zero again. This handles like that. Alternatively, you see eye to eye and see here. I hope that is clear if you do not understand. No problem. We are going to draw the guard conditions and other things and will understand how to define the guard for a transition. Using this tool is a little different because this is a choice, not actually for the guard. You have to use the choice. Not. But we learn that later. Let's move forward now. Let's understand that you won't see that. Let's be in the state of two one one. I'll just reset the board. We are in two one one now in the one 2-1-1 and the U.N. three isn't here. It doesn't handle seats so it has been propagated to the next level. Yes, one doesn't handle it, so propagate it to the next level. Yes, to handle it, you can fear it. The action related to the transition is really good at first. That's why you see to see if to see. And this is an external transition, so all the exit actions had to be included right from the innermost state. All these are executed. You can see there are three exits. Exit, exit, exit. And then it takes a transition here, so. Entry next is entry. And the next state guided by this initiative will state its action is executed next S1 in it. It has one in it. And as one entry. It happens like that. So this is first and then all the exit action. And reaction. And this one. And this one. We are now here. What happens if the state machinery that you rent sees here, so it is not handled by this state to probably to the next state if one handles it? This is fast. This exit, second, third. It's one exit, and after that and the reaction of this. This and this. So any reaction to it as to one entry? And if 2-1-1 entry, we are here. Now what happens if you find that you went, gee, first of all, if two one doesn't have to go so it is proper to the next level, he is handled by two to one. So fast this one. And followed by the exit action, this one. This one, you can see that. And after that, this transition is going to leave this too. That's why they exude action up to. It comes here for the past, the entry, action and reaction as one entry and Wednesday's hearing guided by this initial transition as one in it and then as one one entry. Let's discuss the history straight.

EXERCISE-006 TESTING HISTORY STATE

Now we understand there are two types of history: a shallow history and deep history and each class what I think it's a deep history. When you first reset the world, the state would be as one one. Initially, the history of if one is absent, it does not have any history because it was never entered, the history was absent. Let's first analyze when there was no history. Let me take you to this model, and let's add one more state here in this one guest remote. If I let me modify the internal transition, I'll just cut that. I just make some space here, and I will add one more state here, I'll call this as yes. One two. Yes. One two. And after that, I give one transition from here to here. I'll call this transition due to the trigger I.

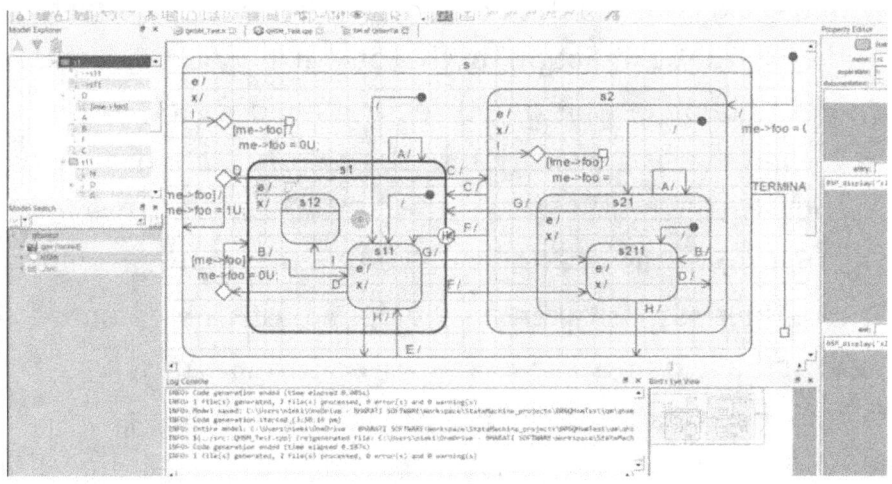

I will define the transition action for this, I'll call this as yes. One one I. Let me just read the quote. Let's discuss the history threat. I just made these changes, I just introduced, yes, one two. And let me also define entry action and exit action for S1 two. I call this as if I want to. Entry and, yes, want to exit? So now this looks something like this. First, let's reset the board, I just reset the board when you reset the board. The state machine will set it to one one. It never entered S1. That's why history for F1 is absent. There is no history for F1 here. I attended the event. If let's take this case, no history. Let's say you send the event f when the state was to one one. What happens? First of all, F is not handled by f two one one four. It is propagated to the next level, f to one that is also not handled, and it is also not handled here. Propagate it to the next state as F2 f to handle c f action associated with F is executed first. S2F, you can see that this is fast. And after that exit action on this one exit action, not this one exit action on this one three exit actions exit, exit, exit, then that is a transition to the history state history of F1, but the history of F1 is absent. There is no history for F1. That's why history is ignored when history is ignored. The default path is taken on the deep part. The default path actually points to S1 one. This is just like this, just don't look at that history. It is just like this. What's happening in your entry? S1 after that entry of F1 one.

But when history is absent now, the state machine is here. Let's send it to this, first of all, let's verify this output. Let me go back to the idea and compile it because I have made some changes. Let me just download it. I stand here. It is in F1, one entry, it is here as one one. And now let me send I. I.

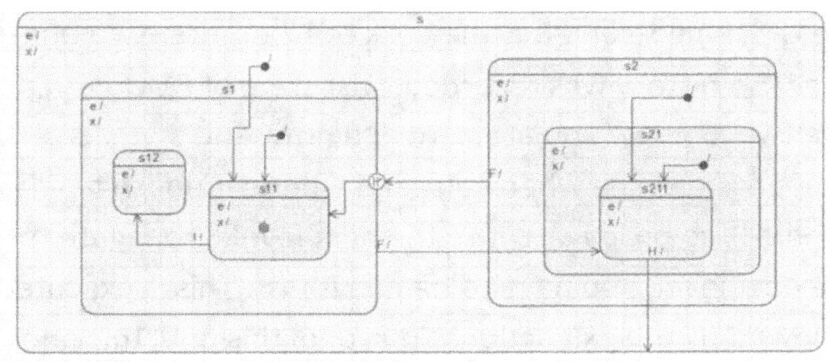

State → s211
F→s2-F;s211-EXIT;s21-EXIT;s2-EXIT;s1-ENTRY;s12-ENTRY; (If History)

State → s211
F→s2-F;s211-EXIT;s21-EXIT;s2-EXIT;s1-ENTRY;s11-ENTRY; (If No History)

Now it prints. That is a problem, I think I have not downloaded the cold, the latest cold, because I actually added exit and entry actions here. Let me again reach into the court. Let's open the CDL monitor. Let me send it. Now I am here as one. And let me send I. When I feel I hear it now, I have handled it by myself. It goes to F1, to

F1 to enter, reaction is executed. The state is the F1 to now, the state is the F1 to so now execute f to come back to us to one one, execute f here and come back to F2 one one. If we came back to one one, we are one one. Now send F here, when you finish up here, it will go to the history state of F1 and history is already dead because it had previously visited F1. History was recorded in F1 and the history of F1 was F1 two when the state was the F1 to the U.S. Empire and it came back to F2 or after two one one. The history was recorded. Last state of F1 was, yes, one two. So now you are here and now, and if what happens, let's see when you send F here, it doesn't handle F, so propagate it to the next level. Propagate to the next level. You have to handle it fast. This is executed, followed by the exit actions. This one, this one, this one, and that transition comes to the history stage. History is already there, so it goes here. It won't take this default, but now the line looks something like this. That is the first entry action of one. Look, here is one hand and reaction of F1 to let's check that we are in two one one. We had already visited one two here you can see that.

```
QHSM Testing...
top-INIT;s-ENTRY;s2-ENTRY;s2-INIT;s21-ENTRY;s21-INIT;s211-ENTRY;
s2-F;s211-EXIT;s21-EXIT;s2-EXIT;s1-ENTRY;s11-ENTRY;
s11-I;s11-EXIT;s12-ENTRY;
s1-F;s12-EXIT;s1-EXIT;s2-ENTRY;s21-ENTRY;s211-ENTRY;
s2-F;s211-EXIT;s21-EXIT;s2-EXIT;s1-ENTRY;s12-ENTRY;
```

Stand up here and you see that it comes to Earth one two. It will not go to Earth, one one, it will go to Earth, one took because that was the history record of it all. We have one that covers history and will use this history in our exercise later. So if you don't understand now, we'll understand later what happens here. Let's say you are in yes, one one and you received the event. E e is not handled properly to the next level. E is not handled here as well. Here to the next level F handles e four f e the local transition first. This is executed the action associated with the transition and then that is a transition to this. What happens? All the exit actions, how to be executed fast. Why? Because the f one one is getting reentered. What does that mean? It has to exit first to re-enter the exit of F1, one exit of F1. And that entry, action and reaction is from the outermost state. That's why F1 entries are like that. What happens here? First of all, let's assume that we are in, yes, one one state if one, one and four variable values are initially zero. What happens if you can be authentic? First of all, if one one handles d, the action associated with these executed. But that is no action defined for B because you don't see that flash market. That means no action is defined. That's OK. Here, the guard is evaluated. The poor value is zero. Initially, the guard fails. If the guard fails here, that means if one one couldn't handle the when it couldn't handle the the D's propagated to the next level. If one has one hand as deep and the pull variable value is zero, not of zero is one guard evaluates to true and purely becomes one. And yes, one be printed. That's why everyone gets printed first. And that is a transition. When the guard evaluates to true, that is transition. Transition is to if there's a transition, if the state machine is here now, which is now guided by this initial pseudo state and in it is executed first next, which is here and now it is getting entered into. If one one, when it is getting reentered into one one, its exit action has to be executed first from the innermost state to outermost state. This is executed next after one one exit. F1 exit next. And then it will get re-entered again from here if it is executed in the next F1 entry. F1 one entry like that. And remember that when this happens, the full value is set to one. So now the state is F1 one again and the full value is won and now B is received here. The event is sent here again. F1 one handles RD only if this car develops to true, but fuel is already set to one so gardevoir to stay true.

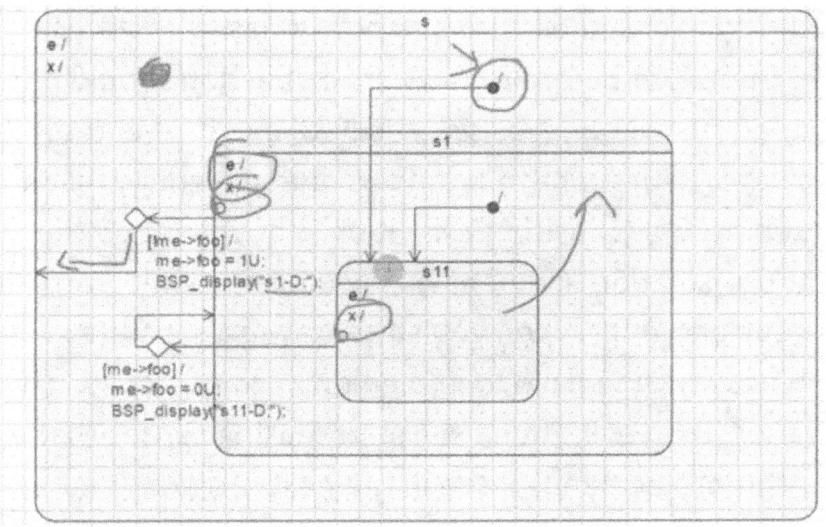

State→s11, me->foo = 0
D→s1-D;s11-EXIT;s1-EXIT;s-INIT;s1-ENTRY;s11-ENTRY;
me->foo = 1;

State→s11, me->foo = 1
D→s11-D;s11-EXIT;s1-INIT;s11-ENTRY;

That means the F1 one has successfully handled that event. That's why the action associated with that transition is executed F1 one day and then this transition is taken. This is not a self transition. Remember, this is just a local transition to F1. This is just like this. The car was successful. You can consider this just like a straight line from F1 one to, yes, one. That's why this is actually a local transition for S1. F1 was not entered from the outset. This is a local transition for F1. That's why after F1 DX, the control comes here and now it has to re-enter into F1 one. But before reentry, its exit action should be executed first. S1 one exit is executed, and it re-enters from here. He has one in it. And as one one entry, that's about different transition execution sequences and the event propagation, if you have any doubts. Don't worry, it will get cleared for when you start drawing the state machines and you have to implement a couple of exercises, then everything will start making sense. That's it for this project, and I'll see in the next project.

EXERCISE-007 CLOCK ALARM INTRODUCTION

Let's do one more exercise. So the exercise number is zero zero seven and the exercise name is Clark a lot in this exercise, we are going to implement a real time clock using the software. That means we are not using any RTC chip and the requirements of this project will be you have to show the current time of the day to the user and you should allow the user to do modification to the clock that if clock setting, alarm setting, alarm notification and you should also show day to month your day of the week this I have not implemented. You can extend this project later .

I'll give you an assignment and outlook. You should give the provision to fact and modify the date information. So the circuit diagram of this project is pretty much similar to the previous one. Now there will be two buttons on the button pad.

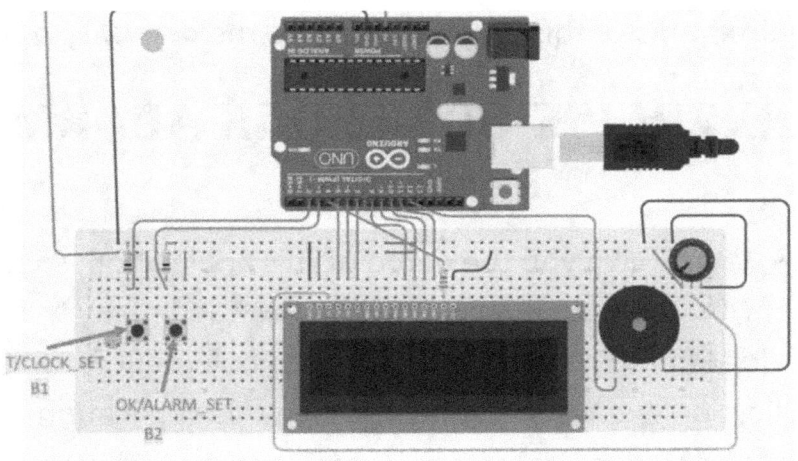

The first button is B one, which is a multi-functional button, which can be used to fact and clock set functionalities. If you want to execute that functionality, then you can use this button and to enter into the clock fighting mode. You can't use this button. The second button V2 is also a multi-functional button, and this is used for approving that is OK. If you have done some setting, you have to approve that. Then you can use this button as OK. And this button can also be used to enter into the alarm setting mode. He had the digital pen for Arduino connected to the LCD anode of the LCD backlight wired to this resistor. So this is to control the backlight after the LCD. Those are just two changes in the socket compared to the previous socket. Now let's see the demo of this application so that you get more idea how the application looks and you will come to know about other requirements of this project. Let's see the demo.

EXERCISE-007 CLOCK ALARM DEMO

Now, let me give you the demo of this application, so now when you see the demo, we will understand many things. So a lot of requirements you have to implement for this application and we are going to solve this application using the hierarchical state machine approach. I have reviewed the earlier circuit and components for this application in the pro time and application, we actually use three buttons. But in this application, you just need two buttons and that is the LCD. The connection between the LCD and the Arduino board is exactly the same as before, and that is optional, but there is potential for me to set the contrast for the LCD. And there are two buttons on the button pad. Now let me explain the functionalities of this button for this exercise. The first button is called Fat are clock fat button and the second button is or key slash alarm set button. These are multi-functional buttons, so I'll explain how to use this button in a moment. Don't worry. First of all, I have downloaded the application to the Arduino board and the application is currently running. And let me just reset the Arduino board, and when you reset the board, as you can see here, the application is currently showing. The current time of the day, the current time of the day is presented to the user. As you can see here, and the display format for the time is minutes second. And this is supplicants. So this also you must show. And also here you must display whether it is a 24 hour format or whether the time is in 12 hour format embedded in 12 hour format. You have to show whether it is MRP and there's also a thimble, as you can see here, the alarm symbol, which indicates that the alarm is currently on. So what you're seeing here is taking what? In their thinking, what the application takes and the current time is presented to the user by calling this as are taking what? Now there is also one more mod, and that mode is clock fact mode. Suppose if I want to modify this time or if I want to adjust this time, or if I want to change the mode after time or time format, then I can do that.

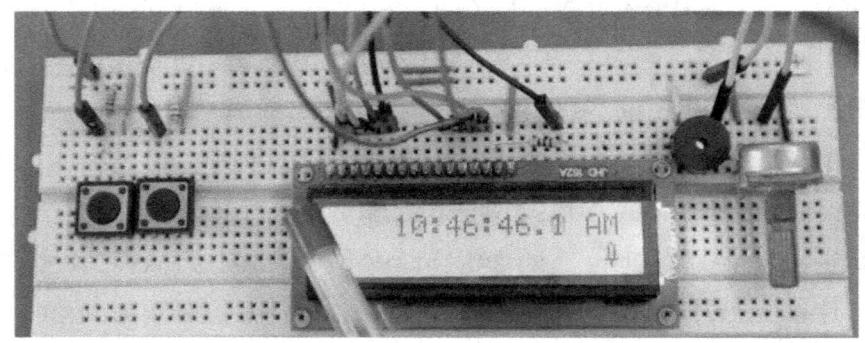

So I have to go to the clock set mode. When the application is in ticking mode, and if you press this first button that is four bar clock sets. Then the application morphed to clock fact mode. Let me show you that. So here you can see that now the application is in Clark set to Mort, in which you can change some settings. And you can also see that the cursor is blinking on the first field after odd information. This is the first digit of the. This is the second digit of the art like that four digit wife. You can enter new values here. Now it is asking you to modify the odd information. And you have to use that button if I press the start button. You can't change it to different values as you can see it. Let me select two if this is OK. Then you have to press OK. The Kurds are most of the next digit where you can feed another value if you want. OK? It goes to the next field. If you don't want to enter anything, just press OK. It goes to the next field like that. Here I enter fifty one. Oh, let's say you want to abort everything so you don't want to set anything, then you can do that. So to abort this operation, you have to press these two buttons simultaneously. Let me press these two buttons simultaneously. So which abort that operation? And it comes back to taking what? Right. So as you can see, the clock is not delayed, OK, so the clock will be ticking in the background, maybe using interrupt or timer interrupt or something. So the current time of the day is never disturbed. It will be ticking, always in the background. Maybe you think the timer interrupts? Now, let me again and turn to the clock setting mode. I practice and it takes me to the clock set mode and I enter some value here. OK, OK, OK, OK. And I enter some value here. And then press OK, and now it asks you to set the mode, whether you want a 24 hour format or 12 hour format. I would go far to allow for it. And then you can press, OK. So when you press OK, it actually comes back to the ticking mode. For now, the time is modified. It actually took you 30. Now let me again press the button. Now it is in clock set mode. So OK. OK, OK, OK, OK. And now let me change something here and press OK. And now let's say I. Thirty two am. Now, let me press, OK. And now it says it's an error because the time is in 24 hour format and you are trying to set that 2:00 a.m. or p.m. information. That's why this format is wrong. So that's why it says edit when it is in the airport. You can see that. There is no response to this or Kabataan. What you can do is you have to go back and modify this information, what you had entered here. That's why OK, Button will not work here and you have to press the button. And when I pressed the start button, it took me back to the setting and now I have to modify it. So now let me make this 24 edge and then press, OK? So now it takes the new 30. So that's about the ticking more and the clock set what? Now, I think you understand what are the requirements you have to implement for this application? And now let me explain one more feature of this application that is alarm set mode that is provision to set the alarm when the application is then ticking. What if you press this button? OK, but the alarm set takes you to the alarm segment. Now let me press this button. Right here, you can see that now the application is in Harlem settlement. So the first line shows the current alarm. This is the current alarm set by the user. The second line must show the current time of the day. And you can also see that at the second line, the current time is displayed, and in the first line, the cursor is blinking at our feet. And these symbols indicate that the application is in alarm, set more. Now, I pressed the fat button again to change in this field I set for, let's say, zero. OK, eight, OK. Thirty four fifty four. OK. And then. OK, and I change this to p.m.. And then, OK, and then it is asking me whether I want to turn the alarm off or on so you can use the set button to either turn on the alarm or turn off. I go for an alarm. OK, now the alarm is set for 08:54 PM. Now, let's see why that alarm happens or not. It is close to 854. Right now, the alarm happens, and when the alarm happens, it has to blink the alarm message and it can add some other effects. Now if I press OK, it goes back to the ticking. What? So now let me show you once again. So now the application is in ticking mode, and now again, I press, OK, bar alarm set button. And here you can see that at the first line, it shows the current alarm set. That is 08:54 PM. Now, let me set the alarm once again. So let me set it for eight, 55. Sorry. So now if you did something wrong here, then you have to abort this here. I made some mistakes, so I wanted to enter something, but I moved to the next field. I cannot come back now to that feature you can provide. Of course, but I have not provided that feature. So now I have to abort this. I pressed the two buttons simultaneously to go back to taking more and I can come back to this mode. And as I said, this symbol indicates that is actually an act to allow. So if you want to be modest, then you have to go to the alarm setting. And press, OK, OK, OK, OK. And make this alarm off. Press OK. So now you can get rid of that symbol now the alarm is off. There is no alarm set. Now let me explain one more requirement that you need to implement that is coming back to the history state. For now, let me demonstrate that let's say there is an alarm that is an act to alarm, so I'll set the alarm. Let me know about this, let me set it to nine. Sorry, again, let's abort. Nine, nine p.m.. So now the alarm is set for, as you can see, if I press this alarm set button, it shows that alarm is set for nine p.m. Alarm is on. You can see this button indicates that the alarm is on. Now I am setting some clock. I'm changing some feet, and while doing this, the alarm may trigger right for now, the alarm will trigger. As you can see now, when I am doing some, setting the alarm could trigger an alarm at any time. So now we can see that the alarm triggered here, not only by press, OK? It should go back to that setting. What you are doing. It should not go back to the taking, what are some of what it should come back to you, City? This is like coming back to the history state. So this was the earliest date and it moved to the alarm display or alarm notification state. And when I spoke, it came back to the earlier state. So this is also one of the requirements of this application. That is, while you're doing some things, if an alarm happens and after the alarm notification, it should come back to the previous state. The same is applicable while you're doing the alarm setting. For example, let's say I'm doing some alarm setting here.

I've changed this to. Ten alarms on. So the alarm is set currently and that I can see here, alarm is set for 9:00-2:00 p.m.. And I am making some changes to the alarm, as you can see here. I'm currently modifying this digit here, but an alarm triggers that fire alarm trigger. You see the alarm triggered. Now if I press the OK button, it should come back to that field that you are doing some setting, let me know about this. So these are the requirements. I mean, you can implement it in your own way. No problem. I mean, I have just explained what the pictures I have provided are. So if you think you can provide some better options, then you are welcome to do that. But for this exercise or for this application implementation, we will consider these requirements and we will try to solve this using the hierarchical state machine approach. And one more thing you have to observe here, when I go to the clock segment, it actually snapshot the current time for the city. And when I press the button, it starts from there, most of the next digit from that, if I press that you can see it, it goes to the next digit that is zero one two zero like that. OK. And it goes to the next digit from here. It starts from two now. So start from four now. When I pressed the start button. So that's about this application, and I see in the next project, so from next project onwards, let's start to implement this.

EXERCISE-007 STATES, SIGNALS AND DATA STRUCTURE USED

Now, you just saw the demo of the application by, I think, the demo you can imagine a few states in the application. Sometimes the application was just presenting the current time to the user that will call it as a ticking mode or ticking straight up the project. And the user can also do a clock setting. That's why we can't introduce one more state called clock fatigue, and the user can also do alarm setting. That's why we can introduce one more state that is alarm setting. You can imagine such states or you can write it down on the paper before you model the software. So let the tiki state be our initial state whenever you give power to the application. Our application will be in ticking mode, showing the time cut on time to the user. When the application is in ticking mode, if you press the button, in fact, let's say, then the application state changes to talk setting because the user wants to do clock vetting and whenever that application is in ticking mode, if user pressed the button, OK, then the applications state changes to alarm setting. That's why when the mode is ticking.

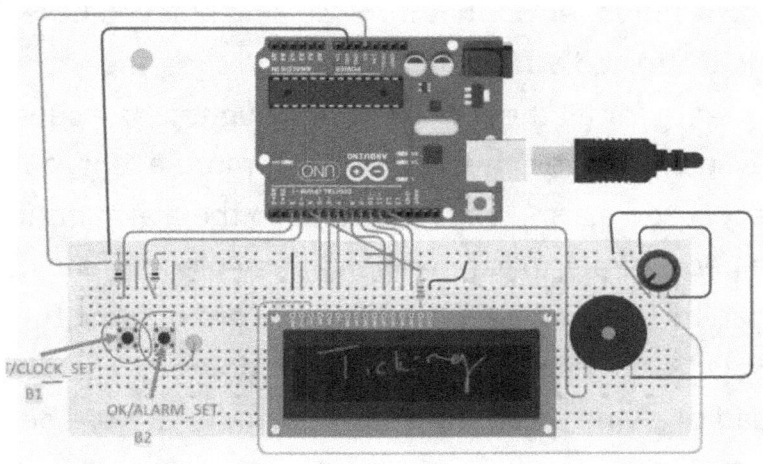

User can press this button to enter the clock setting mode, or the user can press this button to enter the alarm set. What's it like? So that's why there are two events the Sept. and Oct. events are signals that are necessary like when the application is in ticking want. When the application is in a clerk setting or an alarm setting, the user can abort the setting at any time. That's why we can also give one transition from setting mode to ticking mode. Instead of, you know, drying individual

Abbott like this. You can just draw a super state for these two states, and you can give one common transition from setting state to taking state so that actually they are blocked. And also we can give one more transition from here to here. If a user is done with the thete, then the user can come back to that taking mode. So the only difference between this one and this one is here. The setting is uploaded so that if the setting is saved here, it is not. It is aborted. After that, we can. Create one more super state for all these states that caught it as a super state clock and we can introduce one more event, our signal caused alarm, which takes us to the alarm notify state because alarm can happen at any place. It can happen here. It can happen while you are fighting the clock. Or it can happen while you are doing Alarm City instead of giving three transitions from here. Here here you can create one superstate called clock, and then you can just give one common transition from here to here. That is four alarm signals. When the application is in an alarm notification state, it can show the alarm notification to the user. You just saw that in the demo, and whenever users press the button or OK, the alarm notification ends and. The application now goes back to the history of this clock state because when it took place, the user might be doing some clock setting or alarm setting or something. That's why it makes sense to come back to the history stage. I hope that makes sense. And in fact, the clock setting, we have to draw some more substrates to configure the art information, related information, second information and other things which we'll see later.

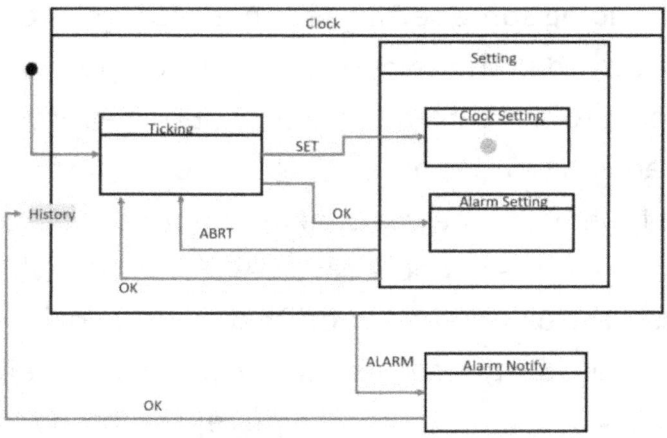

This is just a zoomed out picture of our whole state machine. So our main application structure, we had to create one main application structure for which we are drawing the state machine. And this main application structure is obviously derived from a thumb because this is actually a hierarchical state machine. That way, we will derive our structure from a thumb and to introduce a couple of attributes to the main application structure. Let's say the current time attribute, which is used to hold the current time that is the real time. So this variable is actually updated by the time horizon for every 100 milliseconds. Let's say we are to implement our time at

IFR, which we'll see later. The state machine never updated this variable. This is only updated by that time horizon, so that will be one more variable called temporary time. This is used to hold the fitting time while you are doing some settings so that settings information will be stored in the temporary time. Temporary time will be copied to the current time only during approval. That is, when you say OK, otherwise it is not copied like that. Alarm time holds the user's alarm information and that will be one more variable called alarm status, which holds whether the alarm is on or off that is active or deactivated. State and also users can select different times. Most, like the time, can be represented to the user in 24 hour format or to allow for it that information that the user collection is stored in time variable and there could be some other variables or other attributes. We may be using it while drawing the state machine, so we'll see that later. If you want more attributes, then we will keep adding those attributes to the structure. Currently, I can think of only these attributes. Signals, as you saw in the previous picture of a state machine.

Main application structure

```
/*Main application Structure*/
typedef struct {                          Derived from
                                          QHSM
    /*Updated by the timer ISR every 100ms*/
    uint32_t curr_time;
    /*Holds time information during clock/alarm setting*/
    uint32_t temp_time;
    /*User configured Alarm time*/
    uint32_t alarm_time;
    /*Alarm on/off status*/
    uint8_t  alarm_status;
    /*Time mode: 24H or 12H */
    uint8_t  time_mode;

} Clock_Alarm;
```

These are the signals I'm going to use. OK, I bought a lamp and that will be one pick you run to, which is sent to the state machine for every 25 milliseconds. The sticky rent we can use to update the display or if you want to blink some warning messages, error messages, alarm notification method just so we can make use of the tick, which is posted to the state machine for every 25 milliseconds. Now, before going to the next project, the total for this project, you have to create a new project: the regular seven clock alarm in We Have Scored and copy paste, LCD, dark and LCD data displays attached with this project in V is called Project Folder SRT. These are the same LCD files that we used in the previous exercise. Just download it and copy it into the source folder after we scored Project, and I will see you in the next project.

EXERCISE-007 DRAWING AN HSM

Welcome back to the project. I am in the exercise zero zero seven. Let's create a new folder. And I can't m. Now here we have to keep the new Model five, which you are going to create using the cu.m tool that launched the curium tool. Go to file new model and select coupon none and give a name for your project or model, let's call this clock alarm and provide the part of this folder. I'll just click and I will. Hoping that in the File Explorer, I'm going to copy this part. It just opened that location and selected him. And click OK. You mafia QPR. After that, before creating a state machine model first, you had to create a package just right click here and select Add Package. Package is nothing but a group of different elements and by means of a package you can provide a namespace project that may have different packages. Project may contain any number of packages. And if you have any plan to reuse certain variables, name or attribute names or function names and different packages, then you can assign a different namespace. You can get more information about packages here in this user manual. Basically, what it says is it is used to group elements and to provide a namespace for the group element. A package may contain other packages inside of the package. You can create classes. You can create three attributes that we have already seen, and you can create three operations, directories, etc. It also provides a namespace option here. You can assign a name for a namespace if you are planning to use more than one package of prostate or type option. Just select components here, and you can give a name for the package. I'll give each of them. That's how you create a package. And under the package, let's create a class. Had class. This is our main application structure name. Let's give the name, clerk and alarm and select the superclass classes Q at your farm. Our clock alarm is derived from queue at the then say, so now we can create our tribute at a tribute concert tribute is current time Taipei's you and 32 and difficulty and visibility. I'll keep it private. This is a non-static attribute. And after that, let's create one more. I'll call this half term time. You interject to difficulty. Private like that, let's create a couple of attributes. I just added all these attributes and now also add rectory here and add five to keep the generated code Goodyear package here and right quick, and you can select a directory. Let's give the part for the directory. Dot dot slash. Yes. Ah, see, we are going to keep all of our source files here. FARC is here. Let's add fine. Let me call the thought file clerk. Alarm underscore as Sam Dot CPP that the CPP by and again adds another five. Clock alarm underscore AFM got edge. Currently, I'll keep them as internal files. And now that's provided they include guards for the head file. Fine. Now let's get the court. GPL files are generated. Now let's check.

We got to file here. Now let's add the state machine, state machine we add to the class. Right click and our state machine double click on this here you get the canvas to draw your state machine. Let's open this one first. Let's create three simple steps. You can get all the required state machine components from here, like state transitions, try segment, initial transition, etc.. So now just click on this state, then you need to drag anything. Just come here and just click the outfit that drafts the state and you can copy and paste. To make another one. Make another one. And we need one super state, let's say, draw the super state like this. These are tough states of this state and you can also draw one more super state like this. You can make this canvas bigger. Let's give the name for this state. You can change the name here. I'll call this as taking. This is called a clock. This alcohol dies. Thanks. This al-Khatib dies. Clark, thank you. This is a death alarm set. Now, let's draw some transitions. First of all, the initial state, when the application starts, will be tikki initial state. How to draw the initial state is very simple. Here it is. It is already ready. An initial transition is available. Just click on the initial transition and you are to draw like this. This is our initial transition. Initial Utah State and is the initial transition. Now let's draw a transition from here to here. When the signal threat arrives, it should transfer to the clock setting. Just take this transition component and just draw like this. By default, it names the death trigger one, you can select that component and you can change the name here. We'll use capital letters for all the signals that and when OK arrives, when the state is ticking. Then a transistor alarm setting. I will draw like this. And you give one superstate, then let's draw about. From setting to here, she's aboard a BRT. And after that. OK. We need one more state for alarm notification. I will draw that here to just expand this, expand this canvas. Let's draw one state here. Like this? And how to assess the alarm. Notify and it happens with the event alarm. When it is in the alarm, notify, it will be showing notification, saying user, hey, alarm has happened, so users say OK.

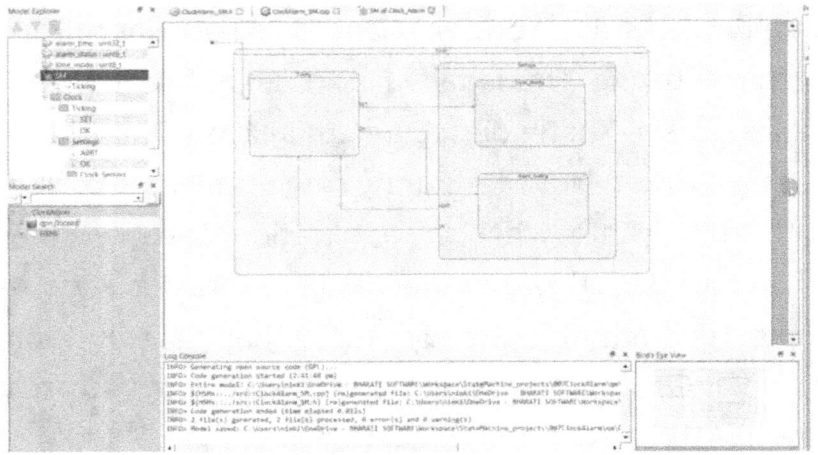

And when the user presses, OK, here it should come back to this clock, but it should go to the history stage. Let's define the history of clocks. We need deep history. History for clock history for clock can be achieved by using a history state on state, any of the boundary lines. I take the history and I put that on the boundary. You have to put that on the boundary, you see. It does not allow you to put here the meaning of this in our history of a state. Let's try once again, let's take the history here and then draw something like this. This is a history of the clock 's default transition. If the history is not available, then it's a default transition. This signifies the default transition and we'll take one transition from here to history. I'll call this OK. Favorite complete up to here, and I'll see you in the next project.

EXERCISE-007 ADDING MAIN APPLICATION OBJECT AND CONSTRUCTOR

So now let's generate some code to go asymptotic and let first define the signals. These are the signals that create an inner clock alarm signal. And don't forget to initialize the first signal to cue. User fake. And after that. Let's go. Yes. Dot Copy. And here let you declare. And let's give the declaration. They can just drag and drop this class named here. And after that, just add the required file here. Cardinal George. Include. Kewpie and shortage. Include LCD dotage and include. So the Hagin file clock alarm underscores FM. Generally, the court. Cody generated let's see. Here you can see that in their 7.8, we already have this. And. Darts Corp.. We got the structure declaration.

```
007ClockAlarm > src > C ClockAlarm_SM.cpp > ClockAlarm
34          uint8_t time_mode;
35
36      /* private state histories */
37          QStateHandler hist_Clock;
38      } Clock_Alarm;
39
40      /* protected: */
41      static QState Clock_Alarm_initial(Clock_Alarm * const me);
42      static QState Clock_Alarm_Clock(Clock_Alarm * const me);
43      static QState Clock_Alarm_Ticking(Clock_Alarm * const me);
44      static QState Clock_Alarm_Settings(Clock_Alarm * const me);
45      static QState Clock_Alarm_Clock_Setting(Clock_Alarm * const me);
46      static QState Clock_Alarm_Alarm_Setting(Clock_Alarm * const me);

TERMINAL   DEBUG CONSOLE   PROBLEMS 2   OUTPUT                    powershell + ∨

Windows PowerShell
Copyright (C) Microsoft Corporation. All rights reserved.

Try the new cross-platform PowerShell https://aka.ms/pscore6

PS C:\Users\nieki\OneDrive - BHARATI SOFTWARE\Workspace\StateMachine_projects\006QHsmTest>
```

And the signatures of all the state handlers that it has not added any definition yet. For now, let's resolve the edit. Go to a previous project, go to the platform ISO, file the order to have this part. Just copy that and come to your current project platform. I'll start and I find this variable. If you don't have one, you can add the LCD library from the previous project. After that here, create a second line and paste that. Now, let's build. That is a mistake here. Our double quote was mixed gender, the court once again let us compile. So the bill is fine. Now let's go to the next step that generates the definition. Defined. Safe and gender, the code.

Here you can see that we got the definitions of all the state handlers. And now let's create an object of this structure. Our main application object. So we will add that as a static variable closeup tribute on the class, right click and click on Add Attribute. I'll call this f, o j. It's the type of this type clock underscore alarm, just type, that clock underscore alarm. And it is a static variable. And keep the visibility private.

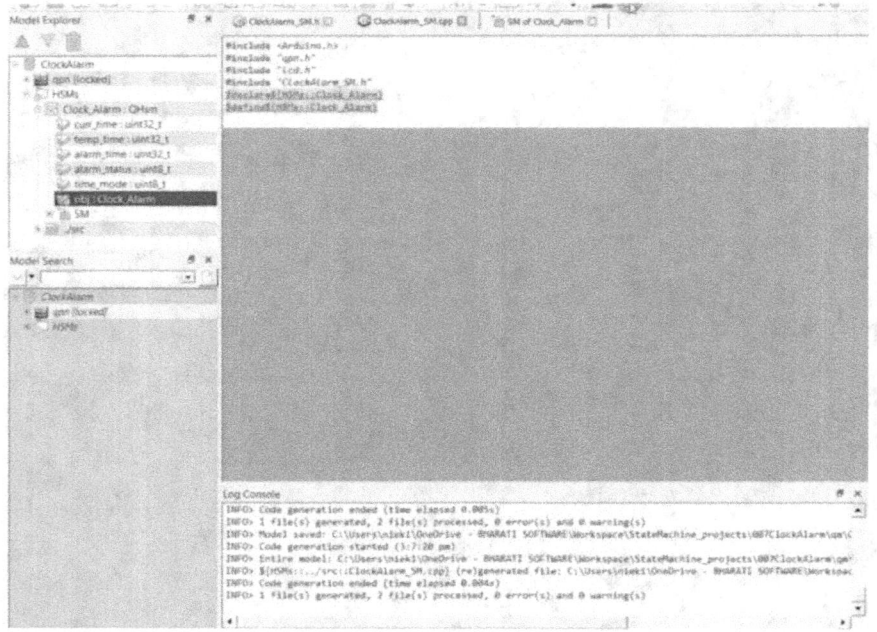

Now, let's say and generate the court here, you can see that we created an object of this type. And now let's provide a constructor for our class or structure. Let's add a constructor; constructors can be added as a pre operation. So now let's create a constructor for our class in the constructor, you can initialize any of that trigger to the object if you want, or you can use that constructor to call the constructor up to superclass, as we did in the previous exercise. And remember that the constructor should be shared with the main darts. That's why we will create the constructor as a pre operation. Let's go here, click on this package and create an add operation. We will just give the name part of the constructor. Just type the name of the class here, clerk. This car alarm and of course, see tar and run time. Let's keep it as wide because we don't type up. The teacher must be white. After that, you can keep this as a global function and you can put any chord here. In the code section. You can call the constructor up to superclass Q AFM underscore C Todd. And here the first argument is a pointer to this upper class that is I just off our object. That is Clark. Alarm underscore object super. Karma's second argument here is addressed after the initial state tournament for the initial stage handler in our code, which is different. So I just copied this and used the macro Q state costs something like, let's check the documentation Q State cost, use that macro and mention the initial stage handle. You can create a couple of attributes or parameters, and by using those parameters, the main function can assign a couple of initial values to the constructor. For that, the constructor can initialize the attributes of the main class object. You can also do that, but save and generate the cord in the F.M. dotage. Let's declare the constructor and in the same dark CP, we can define that. Generate the code. We got the constructor here.

ATMEGA328P TIMER PERIPHERAL EXPLANATION

Hey, welcome back to the project, let's understand the McGarty 28 microcontroller assignment failure because we will be using the time ESR to attract the time in our application. Before that we already had these variables and these attributes in our main structure. And in this application, this current time variable stores the time in number one hundred milliseconds. That means this variable will be incremented for every 100 milliseconds by the time ISA. For example, if the current time is equal to one, that means 100 milliseconds have elapsed, then the display will show something like this. Zero minutes zero second zero The subsequent field will show one, which signifies 100 milliseconds. For example, current time, if it is equal to nine, that means nine hundred milliseconds. That is nine into one hundred milliseconds. That is nine hundred milliseconds. Then the display would show something like this if the current time is equal to ten. That means ten into 100 milliseconds. That means one second. Then subsequent feed will show zero and the second period will show one. So if the current time is equal to six zero five, that means 16 to five seconds, 60 seconds minute, one minute. That's by the minute the feed will show one and point five seconds means 500 milliseconds. That's right, the second field will show five like that. And please note that this variable holds the time in 24 hour format. That means they. Really about will hold the time from zero to 24 hour, 24 mins, 24 into, we have to convert that into second. That is three six zero zero zero two multiplied by three six zero zero. That is one hour contains three six zero zero seconds and multiplied by 10. To convert that into a number of one hundred milliseconds is the minimum value and is the maximum value. When this value is equal to this value then the current time goes back to zero again. And alarm time. This story, the timing is not off, second, because we manipulate the alarm time in terms of our minutes and second, so we don't care about the subsequent field. That's why it just shows the time in the number of seconds and this way they will host the time in a 24 hour format and a temporary time variable starts the time and number of seconds because we don't edit or we don't set the subsequent field. We only modify our minutes 10 seconds.

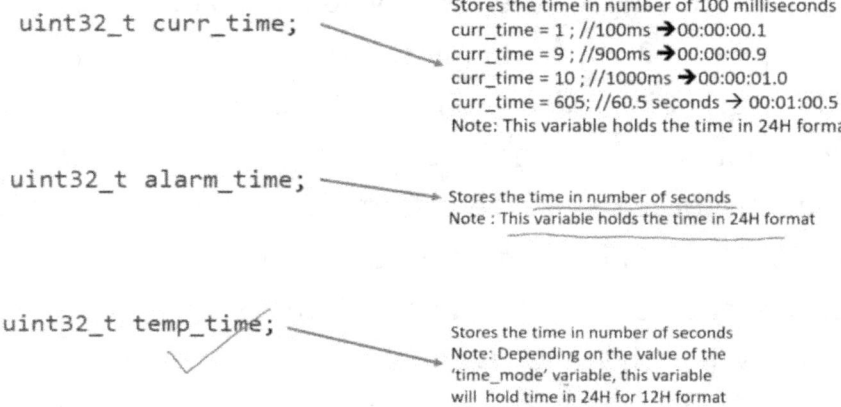

That's why this also stores the time and number of seconds. So depending on the value of the time more variable, this variable may hold time in 24 hour format or 12 hour format. We'll see while calling how to use this variable. This is just for information. And basically, if you see these two variables, they hold the time in 24 hour format. When you hold the time in a 24 hour format, then you need not use one more variable to hold the time format like AM or PM. Because by decoding the 24 hour format, we can come to know whether it is a.m. or p.m.. So that is one advantage of storing the time in a 24 hour format. Now, let's explore the time at petrol, so the mega 320 hp has three timer and counters, purpose timer counters zero timer, counter one and timer counter to the timer counters. Zero petrol is already used by the Minis functionality of the Arduino framework. Let's open the datasheet up the bigger 328 P microcontroller to know more about the timer. Now here is in the data sheet of at Magat 320 hp and here you can see that it has got three timers and counterfactuals. One is eight with timer control zero. Another one is a 16 bit timer. And at that time, what better? Eight with a timer counter to. So the time count comes to zero and the timer counters to eight with a timer and timer counter. One patrol is a 16 bit timer. It would timer count to zero. Petrol is already used to buy the Arduino framework to implement Milly's functionality. The Middle East variable is updated using the all flow intercept after the eight time timer counters zero parts, so it will not be using that. Petrol will use a 16 bit timer counter. Here you can see the block diagram of the 16 bit timer. And here's the important thing. What we should notice is this field. So this is a place where counting takes place. And this is driven by the county clerk. This is a county clerk or time of clerk. And this is again derived from this clerk's election engine. So you can supply a special clock to tick the timer. You know, you can provide the clock way the external pin up the microcontroller will not be using this method. What will you do? Will use the main system clock off the microcontroller and we can slow down that clock using this preschooler. Basically, we'll use the clock this way. You can use the killer to slow down the clock to increase or decrease the time of regulation. Let's go. More on that later. And this time it also has got to compare registers will be using these comparative stuff so whenever the counters value. Matches with the composite registry value, then that will be a composite entrapped. For example, let's say you have stored some value 200 here and you start this timer when the value of this tea count register reaches to 200. Then. This competitor detects the match when the match is detected. Interest can be generated. You can see that here.

ATmega328P Timer

16-bit Timer/Counter1

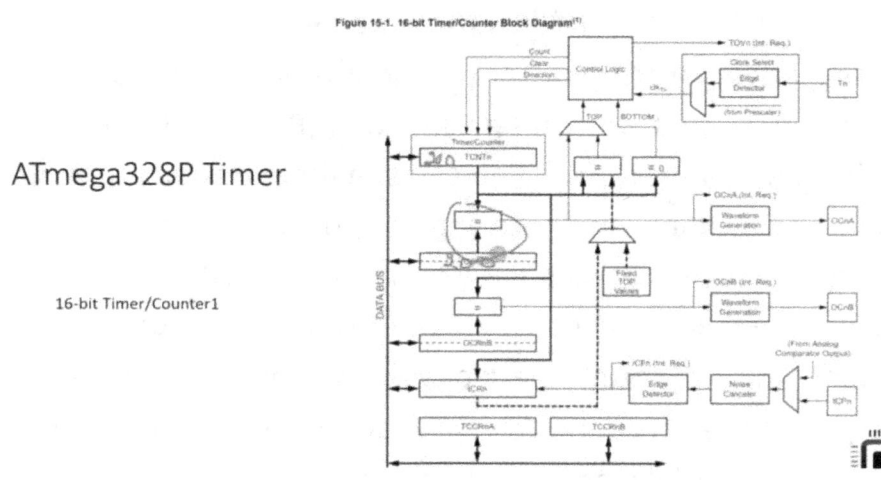

That is a compound interest, and we will catch this interest in our application to implement this variable value. You can explore more on that in this section. In the datasheet output compassionate. And you can see that it is clearly written here. The 16bit competitor continuously compat. This is a competitor compared to count one, with the output comparative to that output compared to Adjustor A or B. If Ti count equals or C R1 one register, the comparative signals to match a match will set the output compat flag at the next time clock cycle. If any about the output, compare flag generates an output compat interrupt. Basically, we have to implement the IF output compat interrupt. You can work with this timer in different modes. Explore this section to understand various more top operation. So let's get back to the datasheet. First, go to fifteen point nine modes of operation. You can drive this timer in normal more. Please read here so you'll understand what exactly the normal mode. There are various more factual. We'll be driving this timer in Fitzy mode. That means clear timer on compat match. This is how our timer behaves. If you use the timer in 30 see mode, and this mode can also be used to generate the waveform on some selected pin, but will not be using that functionality because we don't want that. Here you can see that. What does this mean? Fitzsimmons here they have clearly written. In CTC mode, the counter that is to count registry value is cleared to zero automatically when the counter value to count one matches either the OCR one, or air one register. So the way Palm look, something like this, let's say the tea count register starts with zero for every time clock cycle. The tea count registry value is increased like this when it reaches the value of output comparative literature. The tea count value is automatically cleared and interest will be generated like that. Yeah, you can vary that output compatriots to value to generate some waves on the output bin, so we don't need this. We will not modify the output compared with its true value. Now, let's talk about this clock, which is also a part timer count clock. This is a clock which is set to this engine. Please note that in our we don't want, the Admiralty 28 microcontroller is clocked by external 16 megahertz resonator on the board that the resonator that is off 16 megahertz that is used as a main clock main system clock for this microcontroller operation. That's why we consider F Clock underscore Io is equal to 16 megahertz. This is our terminology: what is being used in the data sheet of this microcontroller? You can consider it as frequency off the main clock that is 16 megahertz. So that is represented by the term clock and you. Timer count clock that can be derived from this main clock, so you can divide this clock by using a preschooler value initially, by default, the particular value will be one. That's why there is no division. This is equal to this one. How to control that killer there, the register called PCC Odd One, be that the control register, and you can see that by using these fields, you can control the police, Kelly. You can divide the clock by eight, 64, 256 or 2024. So we will use the pre-schooler of 256 for this application. So then what happens to our timer count clock? This one, this is equal to the main clock that is 16 megahertz divided by 256. That means the timer count clock will become sixty two point five kilohertz, so the timer count clock looks something like this with the time period of 16 microseconds. That means the count will happen for every 16 microseconds. Now we have to calculate the output to match the value.

Timer/Counter clock (clk_{T1})

- In Arduino Uno the ATmega328P MCU is clocked by external 16MHz resonator
- $f_{CLK\_I/O}$ =16Mhz
- Timer1 count clock (clk_{T1}) = $f_{CLK\_I/O}$ / 256 → 62.5KHz

16µs Time Period

What's the value we are going to keep in the output compared register? As per our preschooler, the preschoolers had to have to fix the TIC resolution to 16 microseconds for every 16 microseconds. The counter means to take once it needs 16 microseconds, then to generate the time base of, let's say, one hundred milliseconds, how many tics are required if you just calculate with simple mathematics. Will arrive at this value of a six, two five zero. So that's why you have to consider this value minus one as output compare to match value and you have to keep this value in the output compat register. And if you are wondering why this needs to be minus one, because for the simple reason, the account to start from zero now let's say you want to interrupt for every 32 microseconds or you want time based generation for every 32 microseconds, 32 microseconds divided by the resolution that is, 16 microseconds will give you the value to. If you just talk to in the output compared to just that said out would compare, register and use told the value to year, then that would be wrong because there. And let's set the timer count clock. And this is that 50. Can't register when you start the timer initially, this is a fast clock cycle. This is a second clock cycle. This is the third. When you start the timer initially here, what happens? The key count registry value will be zero. And for the second clock cycle, it becomes one. The change to this system happens here. And in the next baroque cycle, the change will happen here, it becomes to hear. And when that happens here, the comparison Typekit degenerated to equal to two comparisons would be generated here. But what is a lapse of time? Sixteen profits in profits so that if 48 microseconds what you wanted it, what microseconds? That's why you have to store minus one here. Can you do that? The comparison chart to be generated here. Because here it is written, I can see a match will set the output combat flag at the next clock cycle. So here one became two here. But the match will be reported at the next clockmaker. And in the software, we have to define the time in one comparison. You define that IFR in the clock alarm underscore feminazi as just how to use DSR macro and the vector address. The vector address is this one time on one underscore compat, an underscored reset. You have to write exactly like this.

ATMEGA328P TIMER REGISTERS AND SETUP CODE

Hey, welcome back to the project in the time where Wonder CP, I just added a function timer on underscores setup, here we will configure the time one part of the microcontroller to generate interrupt for every 100 milliseconds. As I explained in the previous project, I will be configuring the timer on Petra in CTC mode now to configure the timer and theboard. You have to explore the register description that could be a registered description. First, let's start with the first register of the timer. One bathroom that is the odd one is that if a controller registers eight here you can see that these are the bits we need not to use because in our example, here, let's start with the right field. Let's start from here. You can see that the bit zero and one, which stands far away from generation Mont W.G. PM.

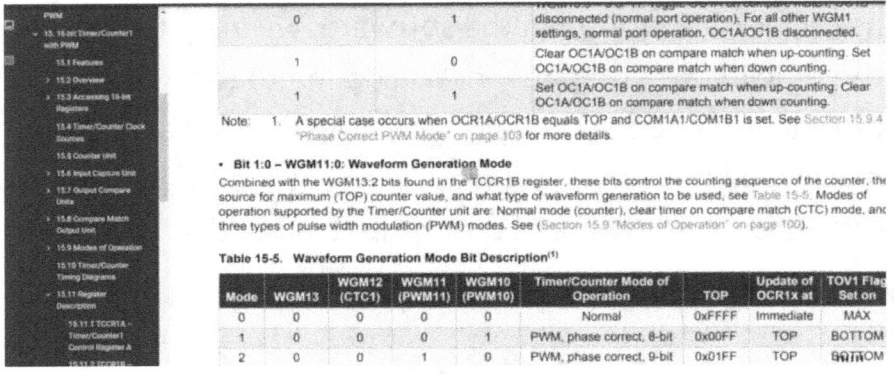

And this can be used to choose mode I. I'm going to keep these bids to represent the CTC mod for that. These two bids must be zero. You can thea and WG one to bid must be one and one. Three must be zero. Here you will get 10, 11, 12 and 13 you get in the next register, so we'll see that aspect, that table. It is confirmed that we have to keep these two bits filthy at zero. Now let's see four, five, six, seven, four and five. Here it is Compat output mode for Channel B. Actually, these bits are not required because these are used to control the O31 and we'll see one pin pin. I want it to be disconnected, so that's why we will select zero here. So we'll select zero for these poor Whitfield, because that is something to do with the wave generation. That's why it turns out to be zero. So that's why I just copied this register name and went to our main dart copy paste here and made that zero. Now, let's go to the next register, the next registries are one, here, you can configure the preschooler and also you should configure WG 12 and WG 13 fields. Here you can see that WG 12 must be one. So travel must be one thing, you keep zero. And this is something to do with input capture, so we are not using input capture.

Table 15-5. Waveform Generation Mode Bit Description[1]

Mode	WGM13	WGM12 (CTC1)	WGM11 (PWM11)	WGM10 (PWM10)	Timer/Counter Mode of Operation	TOP	Update of OCR1x at	TOV1 Flag Set on
0	0	0	0	0	Normal	0xFFFF	Immediate	MAX
1	0	0	0	1	PWM, phase correct, 8-bit	0x00FF	TOP	BOTTOM
2	0	0	1	0	PWM, phase correct, 9-bit	0x01FF	TOP	BOTTOM
3	0	0	1	1	PWM, phase correct, 10-bit	0x03FF	TOP	BOTTOM
4	0	1	0	0	CTC	OCR1A	Immediate	MAX
5	0	1	0	1	Fast PWM, 8-bit	0x00FF	BOTTOM	TOP
6	0	1	1	0	Fast PWM, 9-bit	0x01FF	BOTTOM	TOP
7	0	1	1	1	Fast PWM, 10-bit	0x03FF	BOTTOM	TOP
8	1	0	0	0	PWM, phase and frequency correct	ICR1	BOTTOM	BOTTOM
9	1	0	0	1	PWM, phase and frequency correct	OCR1A	BOTTOM	BOTTOM
10	1	0	1	0	PWM, phase correct	ICR1	TOP	BOTTOM
11	1	0	1	1	PWM, phase correct	OCR1A	TOP	BOTTOM
12	1	1	0	0	CTC	ICR1	Immediate	MAX

Let's keep these two Whitfield's at zero. And after that, this is four clock flexion things like the clock selection bit. By default, it will be zero zero. The timer is disabled. Part timer counter is stopped. If we want to stop the counter, then you have to make these Whitfield's as zero. And you can also use this with filth to select the police killer value to go with 256. That means the main clock we are going to divide, that is the main clock is clock ill, that one, we are going to divide by 256. So we are slowing it down. So the struggle has to be won here. We just do that. Just copy this register name. And I'm just making those two bits of one here that fit. I'm just storing the value in binary. And after that, we have to enable the intercept for the compat event that you can do in this register. Let's go to the register timer counter interrupt mosque register and will be using output compare register a. You have to enable this bit, i.e. arguments interrupt any output compact and enable far register a. You just have to make this one. I do that here and out of that, keep the value in OCR one a register. This is the output compared. Register A. That fits. And after that, go to the state machine darts TPP that is aimed at TPP, and here we must implement DSA for that. Use the ESR macro here. And you have to give the vector address here and that you can take from here, go to interrupt. And entrapped vectors in this microcontroller and ours, this timer come out. You select this. And let's go to the cord here, just paste that. So just right. Timeout one. Underscore comparé underscore we.

EXERCISE-007 ADDING CLASS OPERATIONS

We have defined what I thought and thought we have to implement that current time variable. But there is one problem. Currently, you know, we have selected it as a non-static variable. I mean, whenever you create an object off the main structure, every time, one copy of the current time variable will be that. I mean, currently we made it current time as a private attribute of the object, but that is not actually a good idea. We'll make some changes here to make it a static variable. That means a single copy variable, which is generic to all the objects of this main structure, because that makes sense. The current time variable can't be a private variable of each object because our current time variable tracks the time time is the same for all the objects of this main structure. Let's consider a scenario. You know, you have created two objects, object one and object two of this main structure. Let's say an object with one drive displays one and it displays time zone x time in 25 format, let's say, an object to drive another display, and it displays time zone wise time in twilight format. No matter how many objects you create, the time is the same, this time should be generic to these objects. Object one takes this time and it converts that into our time format and a display that likewise objects to. Does that mean that we will keep this attribute outside this object? That means we will make this current time attribute as a static variable.

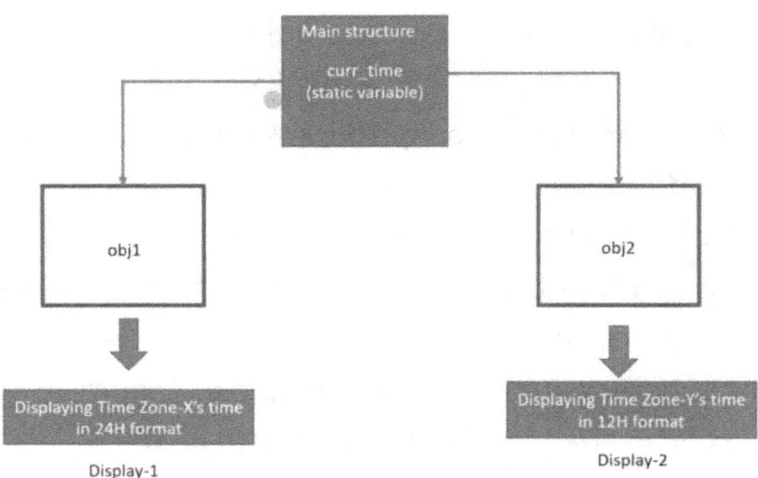

That could be a good idea. That's why what I'm going to do now here, select the current time and make it as static. And let's give one class operation. This is a class operation to get that current time, so get cut on time. This class operation? I want to make it as a static one because it uses this tactic attribute that we just added. That is the current time. It just returns the current time. I will keep the return type as you ain't 32 on difficulty and you can make this as public. No problem with visibility. It doesn't matter. Actually, here I am in Thi. It can keep this public. This doesn't affect this function and the court will put it later. Actually, this, you know, returns the value of current on time. We will now generate the code quality generated. Let's look at the court. As you can see now, the current time variable should disappear from here. How close this is and let me generate the call once again. Here you see the current time now went outside. So now it came here. This is a get cut on time, get cut on time. Static function to retain the value of this variable will implement this function later. Now let's implement another function or another class operation at operation. And here I'll call this as. Update quarantine time, but type is wide and also a static function white, the static function, because it cannot access any private variables, are private attributes that a clock alarm can only manipulate the static variables like current time. And also not that, as I mentioned in the previous video, the static class operation will not have access to the MI pointer. Now let's generate the code. Let's go back to the court, and here you see we got this function clock alarm update current times. Here we put some code.

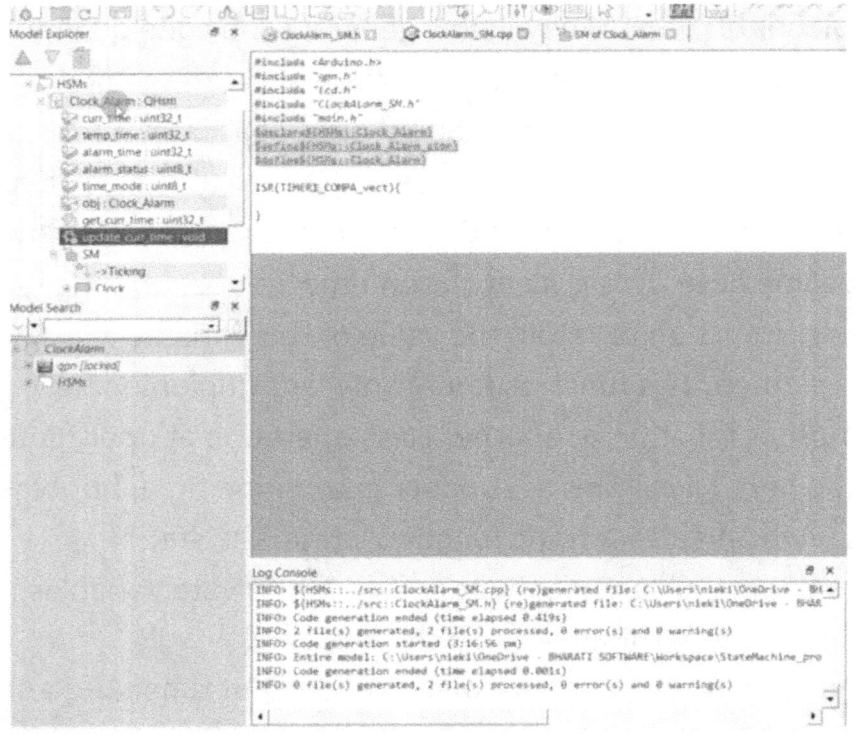

If we have to increment this current time variable plus plus is equal to equal to, let's say, max time. Then we'll make this add zero. And the max time variable I just defined in the clock alarm underscore some dark age and this is a max time. This is actually 24 into three six zero zero into 10. That's a max time in the assembly or take place to find that micro. And this clock alarm update current time this function will call from the introductory throw chain will call that from here. Let's go to 2013, and you just called that from here. In the function update, current time, you have to add the code here, because since the file is managed by this software, I cannot say anything here. That's why this court has to be that of the two tools by the update current time function. I'm going to add that code here. Now, let's build the code. So now, whenever an interrupt happens, this variable will be updated.

EXERCISE-007 DEFINING INITIAL TRANSITION ACTIONS

We just completed the time record in our previous video. And in this project, let us display something on the LCD. Let's go to our model, our model and for the model, we already know that that should be one starting point. This is a starting point, though the initial state. And this is the initial transition. Let's define some action for the initial transition. That action you can mention here the quote real quote where you had to write here, whatever you write here, it will be copied to the file during the core generation and whatever you write here will be considered as a pseudo code and whatever you write here will not be considered during the core generation. This is a pseudo code section. This is a real code section. Initially, we will set the current time variable to some value. To set the value of the current time variable, let me create one more class operation. I would make it as a static class operation, I call this as set current on time. And the return type is white and visible, just keep it as public. Generally, the code and for this function will add one parameter. Add parameter here, you can set the name of the parameter. I'll just give the name of the new code on time and type, as you intended to underscore.

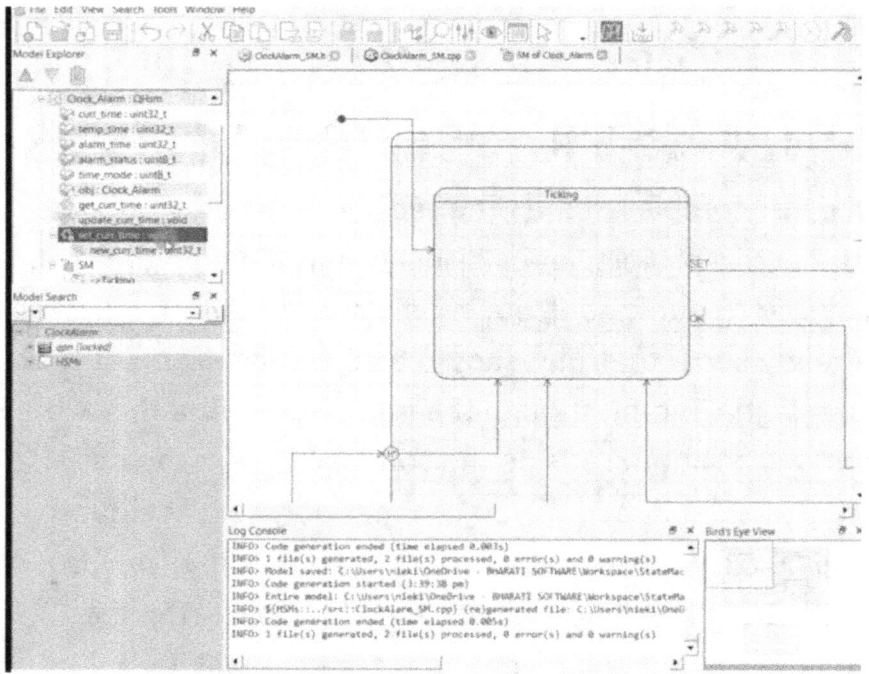

Now let's go to the set current time function, and here is the court. After that, let's generate the code. Here, you can see the set current time in this function we have to modify, or we have to set a new value to the current time variable. But you cannot do just that because that variable is being shared with the user. That's why before modifying the current time variable so you are too fast, disable the interrupt, modify it and then reconfigure in Chapter four that we can make use of f regular gesture your search for asterisk in the administrator sheet and you see a threat area. It's a status register and it has a bit of seven, which is of global interest. And this bit can be manipulated using if the AI and the alliance structure in the program cost will disable the interrupt.

SREG – AVR Status Register

The AVR status register – SREG – is defined as:

Bit	7	6	5	4	3	2	1	0	
0x3F (0x5F)	I	T	H	S	V	N	Z	C	SREG
Read/Write	R/W	R/W	R/W	R/W	R/W	R/W	R/W	R/W	
Initial Value	0	0	0	0	0	0	0	0	

- **Bit 7 – I: Global Interrupt Enable**

  The global interrupt enable bit must be set for the interrupts to be enabled. The individual interrupt enable control is then performed in separate control registers. If the global interrupt enable register is cleared, none of the interrupts are enabled independent of the individual interrupt enable settings. The I-bit is cleared by hardware after an interrupt has occurred, and is set by the RETI instruction to enable subsequent interrupts. The I-bit can also be set and cleared by the application with the SEI and CLI instructions, as described in the instruction set reference.

- **Bit 6 – T: Bit Copy Storage**

  The bit copy instructions BLD (bit LoaD) and BST (Bit STore) use the T-bit as source or destination for the operated bit. A bit from a register in the register file can be copied into T by the BST instruction, and a bit in T can be copied into a bit in a register in the register file by the BLD instruction.

- **Bit 5 – H: Half Carry Flag**

Before that, we will save the status of this status register before doing any modification to this register. I'll just create a variable you date and go affair as drag is equal to a threat and then disable Vayntrub. See a light just to use this function. See a light or match that inline function or its macro actually do that and intimidate Edge, which executes the inline assembly code, which executes the instruction field. And after that clock alarm clock So you have to make modifications to this variable. Third, the new value. And after that, you just restored the status of ethnic. That fit. I'll just copy this code, and I'll put that code in the model under the current time function. Let's go to the model and call that function, that current time we assign some new value, I call this as the initial cut current time macro, which will define this macro later and after that for the alarm time. Also, we've assigned some initial value. I call this initial alarm time, and after that mod for this mod will use some initial value me of. Time on this commode is equal to our just initially keep more as to allege and alarm status will keep the alarm status as off. Initially, alarm status is required to alarm off. We can create all these macros in their symbiotic state. Let's create an enum here called Time Mode 24 X. Moored to a ledge and that creates another enum in alarm status. Alarm off.

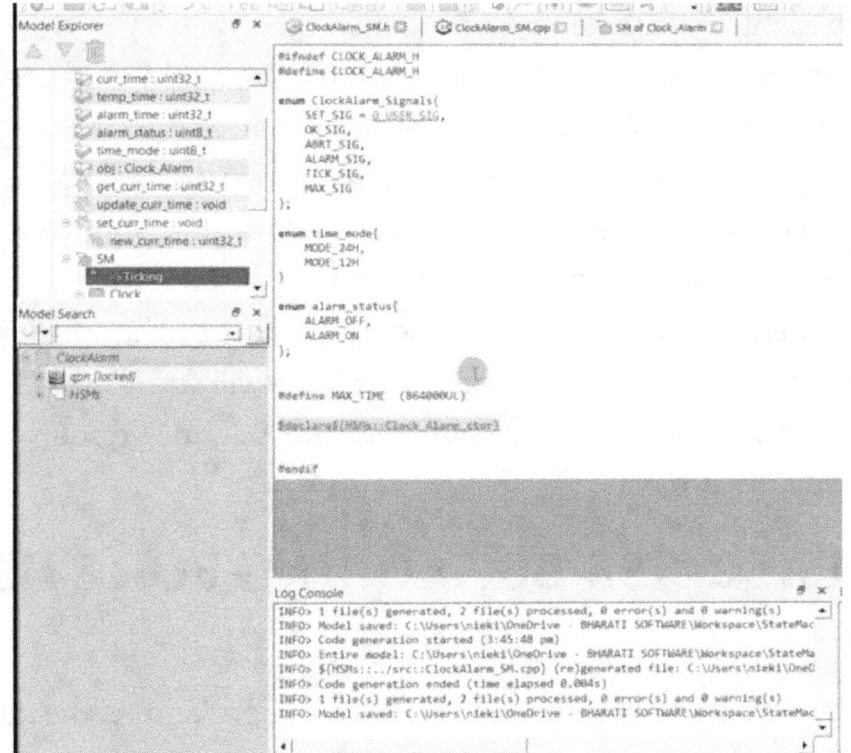

Alarm on like that, and after that, we'll keep some more macros here defined. Let's define this initial current time and your current time. Let's keep ten hours, ten hours. That means 10 multiplied by three six zero zero plus 10 minutes. That is, 10 multiplied by 60 plus 10 seconds. And this value should be multiplied by 10. Let's multiply that by 10. This is the standard 10 minutes 10 seconds. All are unsigned long values and for the initial alarm time, you just outlined some values. I'll keep it as a dodge. I'll just say a modest eight dollars that fits the initial alarm time of eight o'clock. Remember that all these values represent the type of format, and for the alarm, you need not to multiply it by 10. Just remove that. So this is the initial value you can give anything you like. Let's save this and generate the code. And now you can check in the initial transition function. This is a function which implements the initial transition. You can see that these codes are here. In the next project, we will see how to display this time information on the LCD, and I've seen the next project.

EXERCISE-007 CODING FOR THE TICKING STATE

Hi, welcome back to the project. In the previous project, we added the initial transition action and now in this project, let's call for this state to key. So the people of the taking state are to show the current time or display the current time whenever the control reaches the state. We have to show the time to the user on the LCD display. That's why let's define some entry action for this date. When you click on that state, you can see that at the right hand side, you see the entry and exit section here and here you can add the actual code. And you can also add to the quote here. This is a space for pseudocode. Like that, so when you define what entry and exit actions, you can see that the letter E and X appears here with a flash character, which signifies that the entry or exit action has been defined. First of all, in the entry action of the ticking state display, the current time. And Latham functions for that. So with this project, I have attached a five card clock alarm and of course, as Sam underscored to the doorstep, so you just download that and the file contains various functions, helper functions and other housekeeping functions to display various information on the LCD. And you can just refer to that code so you can just study that code and you can copy that code to your project. First of all, let's look at a function called display current time, which is very simple. This function actually converts the current time into string, and it uses the function display right to display it on the LCD. What I'm doing here is very simple.

```
 * param2 : row number of the LCD
 * param3: column number of the LCD
 */
void display_curr_time(Clock_Alarm *me, uint8_t row, uint8_t col){
    String time_as_string;
    uint32_t time_;

    uint32_t time24h = Clock_Alarm_get_curr_time()/10; //convert to number of seconds
    uint8_t ss = time24h % 100;                        //extract sub-second to append later

    time_ = (me->time_mode == MODE_24H)?time24h:convert24h_to_12h(time24h);
    time_as_string = integertime_to_string(time_);  //hh:mm:ss
    time_as_string.concat('.');
    time_as_string.concat(ss);

    /*if mode is 12H , concatenate am/pm information */
    if(me->time_mode == MODE_12H){
        time_as_string.concat(' ');
        time_as_string.concat(get_am_or_pm(time24h));
    }

    display_write(time_as_string,row,col);
```

I'm just taking one variable time to switch this. Variable stores the current time, and I'm getting the current time using this function, which we created earlier, and I just divide that by 10 because I just want to consider a number of seconds. I'm not interested in milliseconds. That's why I'm dividing that by 10 now. Time 24 each variable contains the current time, a copy of current time. Then, if the mode is 24 edges, I will display that as it is, I'll just copy this value into a time variable. If the time mode variable is not 24 h, then we have to present the time in the form of a large format. Please note that the time whatever this function returns, it will always be in a 24 hour format. That's why we have to convert your 24 hour format to allow format. This is actually a helper function, which is defined in this file. It can take a look in this function to convert to 24 hour format and convert to file format to allow it. It's just a simple logic to convert. So you can just study those functions. So once you have that time information, then this function, this is another helper function, integer time to string this function, convert the integer time, which is this time to a string value in this format. Heart, a colon managed colon second. Integer two string is another free operation. It's just a helper function which takes integer time and converts into a string. In this format for that, they just extract our information minister information and the second information using this macro guitar to get it, get second. These are simple macros.

```
lcd_set_cursor(c,r);
lcd_print_string(str_);
}

/*
 * Description: converts an 'integer' time to 'String' time
 * param1 : time represented in terms of number of seconds
 * return : time as 'String' value in the format HH:MM:SS
 */
String integertime_to_string(uint32_t time_){
    uint8_t h,m,s;
    char buf[10]; //00:00:00+null
    h = GET_HOUR(time_);  /* Extract how many hours the 'time_' represent */
    m = GET_MIN(time_);   /* Extract how many minutes the 'time_' represent */
    s = GET_SEC(time_);   /* Extract how many seconds the 'time_' represent */
    sprintf(buf,"%02d:%02d:%02d",h,m,s);
    return (String)buf;
}

/*
 * Description: Converts given integer time in 12H format to integer time 24H f
 * param1 : Integer time in 12H format
```

The macros are defined here. For example, let's see how this works. Get out. It takes a number of seconds and is divided by 3600. That fits that number of us. And four minutes. Divide by 50 first and take the mod of 60 like that. Very simple. After that, we also had to show the subsequent field. This is how the 30-Second Field is obtained and that is concatenated to the value which is returned by this function. Since I'm using the string object of the Arduino framework, you can't access all these matters. Can Cat is a method up the string object. I just do that. And after that, if the mode is to allege, we should also print or concatenate the airmar pm information so that I do here. And this is just another helper function to extract whether the given 24 hour format is am r.p.m., then display right is another helper function display varieties mentioned here. And for that, since the exact location is based on a display. The display current time also takes two other parameters: the row and column number of the LCD. You have to mention that here. And display, right, is just another helper function, it just calls these two functions of the LCD dark TPP. They already have these functions that just caused that. First, it sets the cursor and then prints the string. I want you to download this file and take a look into these various functions and helper functions. I'm going to create this function. This function has access to the ME pointer, so I'll create this as a class operation, which is non-static, because I want to have access to this MI pointer. That is why I go here and class. I'll call this display the current time. Return type, wide visibility, you're going to keep it as public or the non static, so don't check this. And let's add parameter first parameter is the U.S. aid and difficulty role. Another one. You are under 60. I thought of this, but I made a mistake. Name is Robert Fine after that for the court. Here are just copy paste this court. Save it generally, the court.

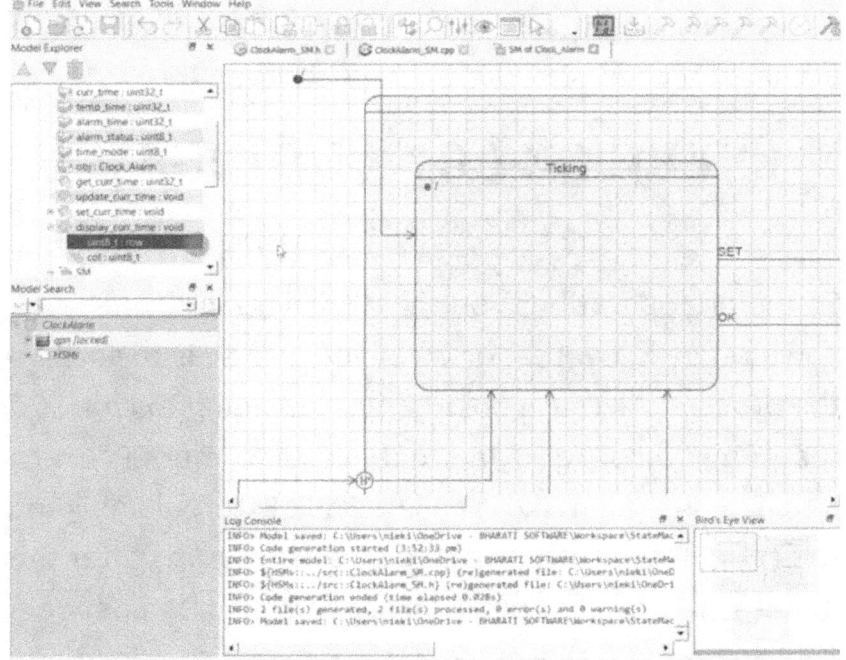

So here this clock alarm display, quarantine and dysfunction. I'm going to call from taking state as a reaction. I just paced here. Provided me a pointer to comma, row and column number. Let's go to the smaller stage, and here, let's define some macros. Define, let's say, taking. Current time raw, the Raw is zero and column. Column for the column position, I will select three. So we mentioned that here first, you mentioned the roll comma column. Generally, the court. And you can see that dysfunction now causes these. Helper function, so these helper functions you can create as the free operation, and

I hope you can do that so you can get the code from the attached file. I'll see you in the next project.

EXERCISE-007 ADDING FREE OPERATIONS

So the pre operations you can either create from here, you already know that or what you can do is to speed up the process. All these possibilities I'm going to copy. Copy that. And you have to add that in as a former CP. Go to S.M, Dot CP and make it an external. External and gender, the court. Now you can paste all those chords after this mark. You should not edit any code which is in between. This marker and this marker, please keep that in mind. Here it is mentioned that do not edit the section between this marker and this marker.

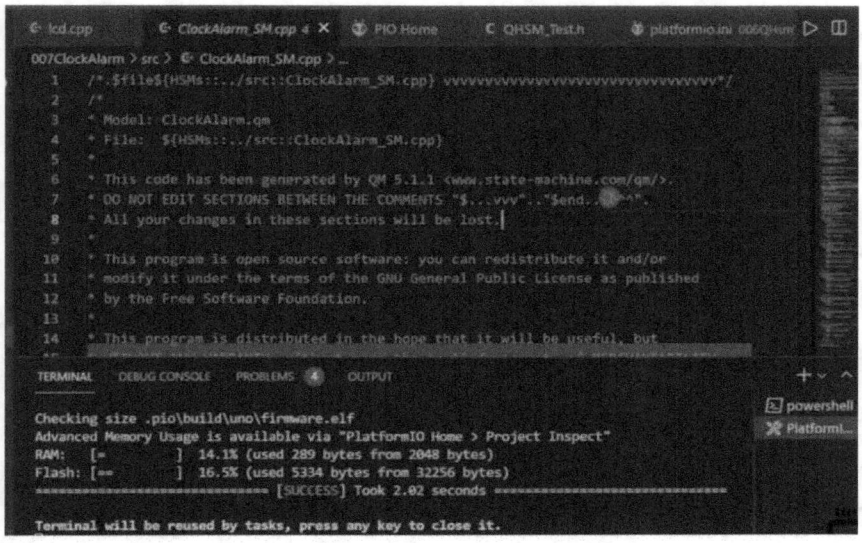

You can edit the code, which is outside this marker. That's why it will go at the end and we will paste here because we are doing that outside this. I'm going to paste all that code here. And now you can even add the prototype at the beginning, just copy the decorator and you can add. So maybe after this, you can add that here so you can add any court after this marker here, I'll paste the prototype. Just like that. You can copy paste like this. I hope you can do that and. In the next project, we will test this on the LCD I see in the next project.

EXERCISE-007 READING CURR_TIME THROUGH CLASS OPERATION

So you're in this function displaying the current time we get the current time using this function, which is not implemented. Let's implement this function. What I'm going to do here is you have to use the same thing here. You just have to return the current time variable that is this one. But before returning that if you are reading this variable, so you have to disable the interrupt, OK? The same technique. We'll read that into a temporary variable. A return to camp.

You should not save here. You can save here, no problem, because I actually made it as an external file. The same court also needs to be cockpit in the modern era. So you have to. Put that cord in, get the current time function, go to the get current time function and paste here. Fair and gender, the court. The compulsion was fine. So now in the next project, we will test this core on the LCD before testing and have to add LCD initialization code to do that in the next project.

EXERCISE-007 HANDLING TICK EVENT IN TICKING STATE AND TESTING

Welcome, come back to this project, lead the ticket, go to this state machine and update the display with real time here. Now I will introduce myself. An internal transition. So this is how you draw an internal transition in this tour. This signifies the internal transition just like the transition and just draws a line. So now I'll call this event our Signal AV take. This is a tick signal Arctic event, and you can see that it is saying the target is internal. The target is not going anywhere else. It is just an internal event, our internal transition. Whenever the Typekit rent is received, let's say that rent is sent to the state machine for every, let's say, 50 milliseconds, it should update the display.

That means whatever you do in this entry action, so you should do it here as well. Select that internal transition, and you can define some action for that. So I'll call the same function to display the current time that fits. Now let's test this. I'm going to save this. Generate the code. Now, let's go back to our code and from the main doxy, we will send that event. So let me define one variable you are in difficulty with. Tick time. Something like that. I didn't realize that to me, this must be a static variable. And why? Malaise that is the current time, minus the previously saved time. If it is greater than or equal to, let's say, 50 milliseconds. We will send. Typekit rent. How do you farm an event? So we did that in the previous exercise. Let's go to the previous exercise. We should use cue at some dispatch and the signal name we have to store inside this point. Let's do that. I'm going to my main Darcy, and here let's get the pointer up to the superclass class.

```
007ClockAlarm > src > C main.cpp > ⊘ loop()
 19
 20    void loop() {
 21        // put your main code here, to run repeatedly:
 22        static uint32_t tick_time = millis();
 23
 24        while(millis() - tick_time >= 50 ){
 25            //send TICK event
 26            super_ClockAlarm
 27
 28        }
 29    }
 30
 31    static void Timer1_setup(void){
 32        TCCR1A = 0;                    //CTC mode
 33        TCCR1B |= 00000100;            //prescaler=256 CTC mode
```

TERMINAL   DEBUG CONSOLE   PROBLEMS 1   OUTPUT

avrdude: safemode: Fuses OK (E:00, H:00, L:00)

avrdude done. Thank you.

=================== [SUCCESS] Took 6.36 seconds ===================

Terminal will be reused by tasks, press any key to close it.

Que sigue que sig la superclasse. Is the Goldwater signal to the name Dixie? And queue at dispatch. Just use this pointer here. Now, this dispatch, if the tick signal for every 50 milliseconds and we should reach like this tick time variable. Tick time is equal to me less. And make sure that you keep this event court in that new function? Now let's test this. Let's say you want to locate the cord associated with this element. Here is how you locate that code. Very simple. What you should do is select that element, for example, in this case. This is an internal transition. Select that element. And here there's an option copy link. So just copy the link. And go to your ID and search here. Paste that, and it takes you to that core block. Yet he can see that when we are in the ticking stage handler, when the tick fig is received, this call will be executed. So now there is some problem with this code. First of all, our calculation was not this much. This is just six two five zero. I have mistakenly written some other values here. Now another problem. What I'm facing here is in the data sheet that TCR will be. Register says the default value is zero.

```
Q_SIG(super_ClockAlarm) = TICK_SIG;
QHSM_DISPATCH(super_ClockAlarm);
}
}

static void Timer1_setup(void){
    TCCR1A = 0;              //CTC mode
    TCCR1B |= 800001100;     //prescaler=256,CTC mode
    TIMSK1 |= B00000010;     //Interrupt enable for OCR1A compare match
    OCR1A = 6250-1;          //OC match value for 100ms time base generation
}
```

```
Removed .pio\build\uno\src\ClockAlarm_SM.cpp.o
Removed .pio\build\uno\src\lcd.cpp.o
Removed .pio\build\uno\src\main.cpp.o
Done cleaning
=================== [SUCCESS] Took 1.19 seconds ===================
```

But it was not the case when I tested it right up to the reset of the Arduino board, only showing the value three. That means even though the data sheet says this value, the Arduino bootloader code may be changing this registry value, which maybe I don't know. That's why what we do now is we will initially reset this to zero. Or you just write this whole value into this register because I was thinking the initial value of this should be zero. But that was not the case. And I also thought of some problems and this code displays the current time. So here they feel extracted. Actually, we should not do our by 10 here. First, you get the current time, then extract the second field and then you can. And after that, you can convert a number of seconds. So now with these modifications, let's test on the hardware. So now let me just compile this. And now let's download. Now you can see that. The display is getting updated for every 50 milliseconds. So you just can't predict here, and I'll see in the next project.

EXERCISE-007 DRAWING CLOCK_SETTING STATE

Hey, welcome back to the project. Now in this project, we will talk about this state clock setting. Currently, let's say this is our state, the current state taking state and then the fact signaling that a third there is a transition to clock setting state. These events are set and are generated by the button that we already know how to interface the buttons to the Arduino and how to do it. All these things that we have covered in the earlier exercise, the same debone sync function you can use to send fat and OK signals. So I'm not going to explain that once again whenever the Thatto render the food as, but the demo how to do the clocks setting in the clock, setting fast or how to modify the outfit. And then we should mortada minutes failed and to the second speed. That's why in this state now, let's draw some substrates to take care of individual digits of the different fields like art minutes and second. So I'm going to draw one state here. Just expand this, this state I call this has. Thief Croc fitting. Ah, digit one.

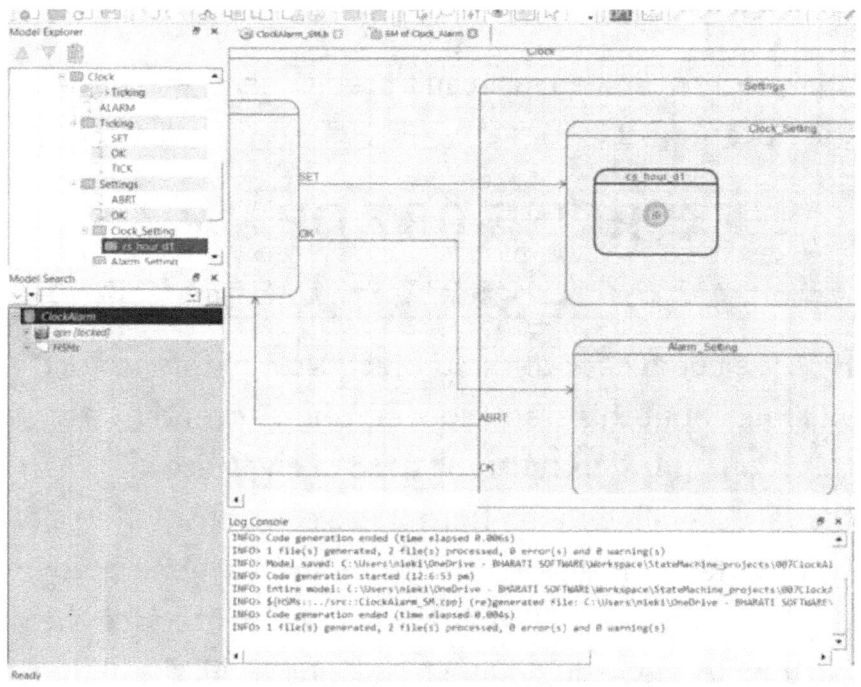

Here we modify the digit one after it is filled and we need another one. Are you going to copy and paste that? I call this D2. And I will make this as the initial substrate and whenever you enter this state, this is the initial state and whenever you are in this state, whenever the threat signal is received, you have to change this degree. That's why that can't be the external transition. That should be the internal transition to this. Let's make it an internal transition. I'll give the signal the name asset and I will do it, you know, you just keep changing the digits and whenever OK is pressed, you should move to the next digit. This is OK. When OK is pressed here and again, the set here will be the internal transition. Fat, this is internal transition, and when OK is received here, you should mortada a minute filled. I hope you can now do the rest of the transition from our two minutes, minutes to the second complete rest of the diagram for this state. I'll see you in the next project.

EXERCISE-007 IMPLEMENTING CLOCK_SETTING STATE PART-1

Welcome back to the project. I just completed drawing these substrates inside this clock venting. I have used a separate state to configure each digit of different fields. Actually, you need not to use two separate states to configure two separate biggert of the field, let's say. You can even use one state, but you can use one variable to distinguish between digit one and digits two. That also you can do because when you use more variables, then you should also take it off, initializing them, digitizing them. Sometimes it's better to use one more state rather than using a variable. Sometimes it makes sense to use a variable. Now let's call for this. So now let's talk about some pseudocode. I'll be just briefing what we'll be doing to hand out the set signal. Let's say you are in a key state, and the current time is being displayed to the user. And let's say the set signal arrives, that is actually an indication that we should go to clock setting mode. Let's define one action for this signal, a transition action. Here we will copy current time to the temporary time variable. And then this enters this stage.

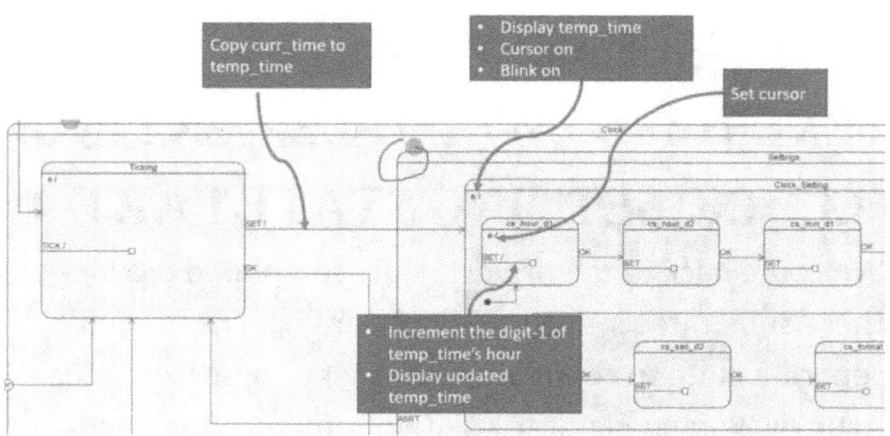

The interaction of this debate together, followed by this followed by this, but we don't have any interaction here. The end reaction of this will be a reaction of clock setting. Here we will display the temporary time warp we captured here. We will display that and we will make the cut on and blink. Because as you saw in the demo, we should blink the cursor that will do here. And then at the initial stage of this super state, the state machine enters the year here. In this interaction, what we do is we will set the cursor at the appropriate digit and will do fact cards. And when the state machine is in this state, whenever the fact signal is received, we have to change this digit d one. We will increment the digit one of the temporary time odd fields. We have to then update the display with a new temporary time that will do here. And then when the state machine is in this state and when the all clear signal is received, it will be a transition to the next state. Here again, this will have one reaction, and you have to set the cursor to this digit on the display. And whenever the signal is received, increment the digital after temporary times are outfitted the same thing you had to do here and then, OK, more here. And again, you have to set the curve here and implement that digit one of temporary times a minute filled. I hope you can do that. This is just my logic, and you are free to implement your own logic to do what I have attached. I have given some cause and effect. You can refer to that. For example, let's call this set a transition action. The Tudou file, you can see the code. This clock alarm state machine ticking set the action taking that action. And here you can see that I am copying the current time into the temporary time and then the mode is 12, which then the temporary time should be updated with the fellow format that I do here. And then I use one more variable called temporary format. This variable will be used to capture user format selection later. Just create one class attribute called TAM format that I captured. What exactly is the time format, whether it's the AMPM or 24h? This is required later when we have to display the time format. What I'm going to do now is I'm just copying this code and I'm going to the fact transition and in the action, just paste that this code actually needs to format a variable, create that a class attribute.

```
141     }
142
143
144
145     /*.${HSMs::Clock_Alarm::SM::Clock::Ticking::SET} */
146     me->temp_time = Clock_Alarm_get_curr_time()/10;
147     if(me->time_mode == MODE_12H){
148         if(get_am_or_pm(me->temp_time).equals("AM")){
149             me->temp_format = FORMAT_AM;
150         }
151         else{
152             me->temp_format = FORMAT_PM;
153         }
154         me->temp_time = convert_24hformat_to_12h(me->temp_time);
155     }
156     else
157         me->temp_format = FORMAT_24H;
158
159
160     /* ${HSMs::Clock_Alarm::SM::Clock::Settings::Clock_Setting} */
161     Clock_Alarm_display_clock_setting_time(me,0,2);
162     display_cursor_on_blinken();
```

I'll call this TAM format off, tie you into eight and copy. And this is I'll just keep it as private. Say that. And after that, when we reach here, we should display that captured temporary time. For that, we will be using one function called display clock setting time. It displays the clock setting time. What it does is it just converts that temporary time that you had saved in the earlier step, just to convert that into string. And then it concatenates the Hammer p.m. information if it is required. You can see that that is the concatenation and a right to the display. Let's create one class operation and just add this name display clock setting time that 10 types are wide visibility public. No problem. And this has access to the point. I would just consider it as a non static function and copy all this code paste in the code section. Save. We are going to call Clark Fetty here, whenever this state is entered as a part of any reaction, we are going to display that clock setting time. You have to supply me a pointer and the location where you want to print that. I'll just select rule number zero. And here this half hour, I'll just provide the macro hash, define Clark setting time roll, which is zero hash. Define Clark fitting time column. I'll just select two here. Column number two and I'll just use this macros here as row and column. Let's go back to the state machine, and you should also turn on the curtain and turn on the blink off the LCD. For that, I have given one helper function. You can use that and its name is display Carteron blink on. It does nothing actually just cause the underlying LCD is just called the LCD dot, CPC function, LCD cursor show and LCD called Blink. You just call this. And after that state machine enters here and we're going to set the curtain at the D1 position, we should call that cadre of just youth display, said Carter, with just cocktails to the third quarter.

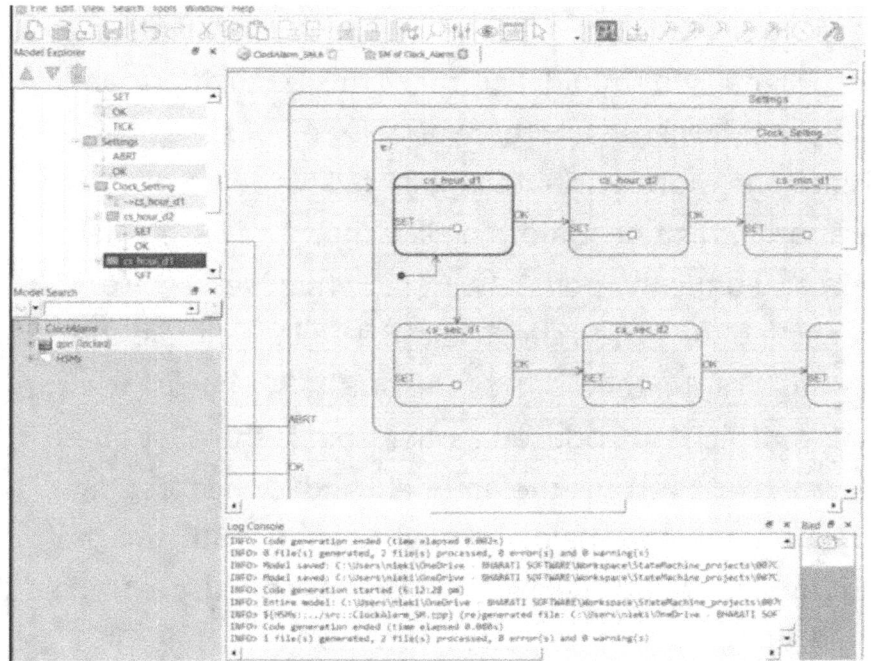

What's the position that coordinates, you have to mention draw and column. No, I'll just use the macros that I used before. So I just define clock fitting time or one column. This is to produce that display set cursor the ROI. Same this one and the column. This is a column for which the next digit column would be different. Clock setting time G2 column will be three like that and then next column is after an hour or minute and one column will be five. This will be a six minute detail. Column will be six. And then after that second second one eight two two eight and then it will be nine. D2 row will be the same. That is zero. So now let's get back to the state machine.

Here we set the cursor and whenever a user sends the fetch signal, we should increment this D1 digit. What I'll do here is I will use another variable to hold the digit. I'll create one more attribute and I'll call it a temp digit or temporary digit or something like that. They use you in debt and difficulty privately. Here, whenever a state machine enters the state. Me of 10 digits will hold the first digit of the temporary time outfit. But I'll just use the macro, which I introduced earlier, that is the digit one macro. It just returns the unit field and 10th street digit 130 10th, the 10th field and digit to every 10th and the unit field. Here I use a digit one off guitar. I just extracted the digit of one of the guitars of temp time. That's it. I just captured the first digit of the field of the temp time. And after that, whenever the fact is reviewed, I'm just going to increment that temp digit plus plus for the digit one, the allowed values are zero one two. That's why I'll just do it for a temp. Digit modulus is equal to three because the digit value can vary between zero, one and two. It can't be three. You have just changed this digit to your digit plus plus whenever the set signal is received. Now we have to update that information in the temporary time variable. You would delete the earlier value and feed the neural. Here is the code. I'm going to do this temporary time minus I have to subtract first the digit one off our field of temporary time digit one is that 10th place. That's why I had to multiply by 10 that many seconds. I'm removing it and then I am compensating with this digit you. I'm taking that digit value multiplied by 10 because it's a 10th place, because this should go at the tenth place and multiplied by number of seconds in one hour, but subtract the old second, introduce the new second. And then you already have created this function to display clock setting time. They just display that the modified temporary time and the cut must stay at the nuance position. Once you do, this quarter will move to somewhere else. You had to bring back the curtain at B-1s position. I do that. Just copy this code and paste here. Display clock setting time he had a row position is nothing but this one clock setting time row, and the column is this one clock setting time column. Please note that this is not the logic you have to implement. You are free to implement anything you want. I mean, that could be some other approaches, but you are free to kick off your own logic and whenever OK is received here, that is the external transition. We come here again where I repeat that whatever we have done here, we have repeated here. I'm just copying the code of this one and I'm going here and here. I'm just pasting that instead of digit one digit two and display that cursor D2 column and set the same code, almost the same to copy here and paste here. The value of data can vary from zero to nine. That's why you have to use tenure and this is a digit too. And the two are actually at the unit place. That's why multiplying by 10 is not required. Same with that here as well. This is required to code the cursor at the D2 column here. This macro is something different. One column this one. Now here. This is a D2 collar. Likewise, you have to modify it. Now I will ask you to compete for this, this, this and this, and we'll see about this format later. After that, we will test this on the hardware up to here.

EXERCISE-007 IMPLEMENTING CLOCK_SETTING STATE PART-2

I just completed adding chords for these states. First of all, let me explain from here. Let me just quickly explain what we did here. Here this is to change the digit one of the outfield whenever we take entry into this state. Very simple. We just said the cursor at this column of the display and we just see the first digit of the AR field of the temple every time. And then whenever that signal is revealed, we just increment the digit and our field. The digit one of the odd field can vary between zero one two. That's why I do a modulus operation with three. And then we update this temporary time. So I subtract these many seconds and then I update with the new value here. And then we just update the display here, and we again set the cards that are back to that position. And for a minute, do you want the same thing here? Digit is equal to digit. One of the minutes filled up the temporary time that the cursor was at this location. I'm going to do one column and whenever the FET is received, you know, increment that digit the D of the minute field can vary between zero to five. That's why I do a modulus with six and then subtract one digit off the minute. Digit one up the minute. Fill up the temporary time. You have to multiply by 10 into 60. Because it's a minute print, one minute is equal to 60 seconds. That's why I multiply by 60 things in tenth place. I have to multiply by 10 and then I compensate for that here with this new value. And then we display and set the cursor back to that location. If it is one of the Kent fields, then the same thing here does it one up the second filter. But over time, we could extract that here and whenever the set is received, we do like this. This is essentially the second field. Just you have to update the temporary time like this. Very simple. And now let's generate the code. The code has been generated. Now let's go back to the idea. Now here we have introduced the three functions. Cluster function is to display cards around Blinken. We have to add that definition to our file, our source file, and we also introduce the two more functions that display that cursor. And also this one display clock setting, timer display clock setting time. We added that right here has a class operation you can see, but we didn't add any parameters to.

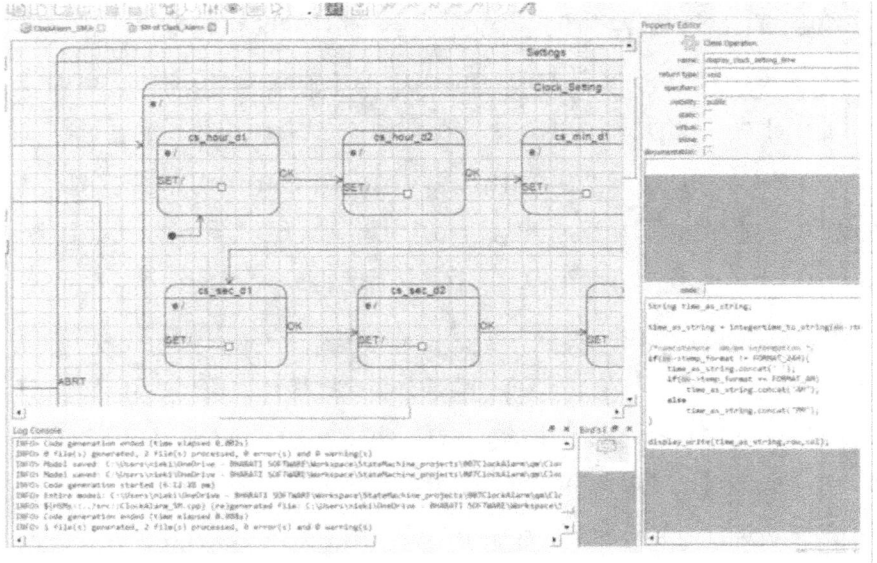

This actually takes the roll end column as parameters. Let's add that the parameter name is row type if you engage in difficulty. And another one adds a parameter column. You end up with eight difficulties. Now let's go back to our To-Do file and around blink on cargo, blink off set cargo. These are all three operations, just some helper functions. We can start to add these functions just to copy them, go to the source file and at the end. I'm just directly adding this to my state machine, dark CP file, because I have selected it as an external file here to add some call when it is an external file, I can edit that but don't edit. Don't put any code in our body markers. Everything should be below this marker. That's why I am adding that here. Maybe I already added that here.

Carteron around. Blinken said. Carter will also add this function blink off. And provide the prototypes of these functions. Here we are provided the prototypes here. Please note that this prototype we added below this marker and about this marker, fine. Now let Fergus. There are a couple of errors, so let's check. Last, generate the code once again. That is one error. You see some errors here. Don't edit. Don't change anything here. If you change anything here, then it needs to be copied to the model. Otherwise during the next generation, everything will be deleted. I mean, you are quoting it will be removed by the model's auto code generation.

That's why if you see some problem here, then you are fixing the model. What do you do? You just copy this. What exactly is this error? The link is here. Just copy this link. The whole link? Copy that. And go to the model, use this paste link, it takes you to that code section here. This is the display clock setting time. Actually, Miss Clark underscore alarm alarm display clock setting time bake off clock alarm is excited by the code generation that's fair and generates the code as you see it is now fixed here. Blood tests on the target. I'm going to compile this. Last download. Let's press the button. You can see that there is some problem. You can see that there is some cleanup issue, you need to take care of this. I think we have to add some cleanup actions here or exit actions. Let's go back to the model. And here you add an exit action to clear the display. I Am sad that I just go back to the cord at the end. Go ahead to the end. I'll just add a wide display. Here, I just called LCD display. Or LCD clear function. And also at the prototype here. And let's call this function from the model here. Let's define an exit action for this display clearly and also well defined when exit action for this settings state. Whenever the setting super state is exited, the display must be cleared. I put that code here to display it clearly. Now let's generate the code. I'm going to applaud this. Let's check. I'm going to press this button. Now it is fine. And now I can keep pressing the set button to change the digit, you can see that the one of the odd fields is just around zero one and two after two, it becomes zero. Then OK, it goes to the next field. Here you can change up to nine and then it goes back to zero and it goes to the next field. Two three four five. Next, I failed. Failed. Six seven eight nine zero. You can abort this operation whenever it is aborted. As you can see in the diagram, that is just a transition back to the taking state. Let me aboard this. You can see that it is aborted. But the real, the current time is not disrupted because it is actually maintained by the interrupt service code complete up to here. And if you have the hardware, just test it. And in the next project, we will take care of how to handle this format and also how to handle the added because the user may enter some wrong values. That's why we have to flag the error in case the user entries are not valid that I would cover in the next project.

EXERCISE-007 IMPLEMENTING CLOCK_SETTING STATE PART-3

Hey, welcome back. In this project, last call for this clock setting format and clock setting edit in the format. As you are seeing in this demo, we should present a different format to the user. That's why whenever the set signal is received, you should present different formats to the user. First of all, what happens in the end? Very simple. Here you can see that I just said the content and I just print the current time format using the variable temp format because the time format holds. What exactly is the current format? The format could be 24 am or PM. I just use that to decode the string. The local variable, the local array, local stringer and I get the message and I just use the display write function to print that at this location. The column number to display is 11 very simple and then set the cursor back to that position. That's the interaction. And whenever the set signal is received, you have to show different messages. AMPM 24 h like that. For example, if the current time format is 24 x, you should show the next format to their user. Let's say I am. You just keep changing this temporary format variable to different values for each set signal. This is just a local variable. And then you just display it using a display, right? This actually displays that Carter pushes the color back to the correct position. Just take a look into this code snippet. It's very simple. I think you know the purpose of this temporary format variable. This is used to hold the user selection for the time format. Whatever the format user has selected, it will be in the temporary format variable when the user fence or signal here that it's over. I mean, everything is over. Our clock setting is almost over, but the user may enter some invalid time. That's what we have to verify. The user enters details. If the user enters details correctly, then we exit this clock fitting composite state. If the user entered details are incorrect, then we should not exit this. Then we should. Mortada error state that we should display some error message to the user saying something is not correct. That's why now we have to use a god condition here to transit from format to edit. Let us draw the transition. I'll just take the transition here. And this is OK. OK, so now you have to assign some Good conditions to this. But there is no place to assign the guard condition for the transition in this tour. There is no guard section. You can see that in this software, the guard condition is provided using the tri fuel state. You have to attack this choice pseudo state to up one end of the transition. You select that. Now the state is selected. You can see here, but you cannot put here. You can only attach that choice to the state to one end of this transition. You can see it. You cannot put anywhere else. Just click on that and drag like this. Now you have attached one guard while this tri state to this transition. When you click on that, you just selected the tri state hard drive segment, and for the tri segment, you can mention the guard as well as action. If this guard is true, then only this action is taken just like that.

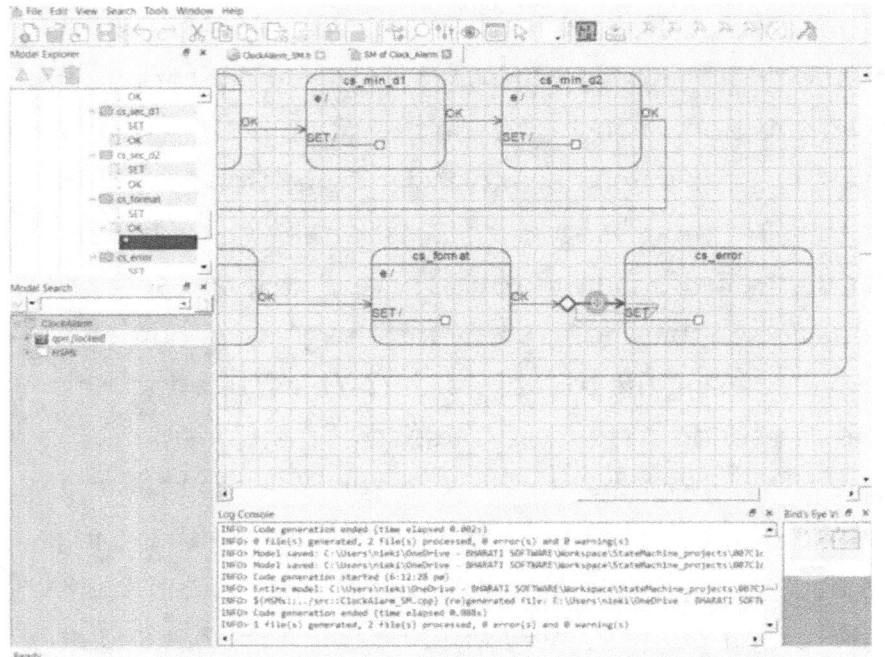

So now collectively, what are you going to say here when you are in this state, when the signal OK is received that it would be a successful transition to a state only if this guard condition becomes true and this action would be taken? Suppose if this guard condition fails, then this OK signal is considered as uncontrolled, then it propagates to its parent, state or superstate here. Now what could be the guard for this tri pseudo state? What we do is we will use one function to detect whether the given time having the user enter time is error or not. I would just call this function e's time set at. This is a function which returns a Boolean value. I would just call that function here. This function returns true if timeThat is an error. If there is any error, it returns true. You just have to provide two details. One is temp time. And temp format, now you can see that the guard is appearing here. What we do here in this function, very simple. We just check, for example. We just get our field. If the air field is greater than 23, then that's an error. So it returns true. Suppose if it is less than 23, then you have to check for some more conditions. For example, if like this, if the article is greater than trouble or if the article is equal to zero, then format should be counted to correct if the format is not equal to 24 age when it is good to to our age is equal to zero, then that you go through an edit like that we just check for. They just take a look into this code. You will understand that. Now let's do the definition of this function. This is just a helper function. Let's go at the end.

And copy paste that here and either functional prototype at the top. So now let's generate the code. I just generated a record. Let's check the code for this signal. Let's see what exactly is the code generated for this OK signal? You select that OK signal and copy the link to that element. Go to the IED and you can trace that paste here. Here it is here. There's a problem: you should not give this semicolon. But the God condition, you should not give that. I'm just in it. I think there is some problem. This needs to be typed to time format and difficulty. Let's say this. Generally, the court now is fine here, you can see that when the walk signal is received. If this is true, then transition is taken to the Arab state. That's correct. But if this is false, then OK, signal is considered as underhanded, then that you rent is propagated to the superstate. If you don't want this event to be propagated to the superstate when this condition fails. Then what you are to do in this tool, if you have to give one damage transmission here, what you do is you select a tri state and draw another dummy transmission here. And in the guard, you just write F. That means if this fails, then this path is taken. But it is ignored. So now let's see what the court generated. Let's assume that the court and you feel now it becomes handled. If this condition fails, then OK is considered as handled. That means the event is not propagated to its superstate. If you don't want the signal to be propagated to superstate, then you should do this. But in our case, the event should be propagated to the superstate. If this guard fails, then what does that mean? The user has entered the correct details, then everything is over. We have to exit this clock setting. That's why the event has to be propagated to the super state because it is handled at the super state level here to exit. That's why I'm not going to give this. I'm just deleting that. This is fine. Let's take it up this out of state in the air. I'll just delete this set. What we should do in the edit state, you should display a message to the user that it can edit as you find the demo. I just blinked at some messages. You can blink multiple messages. You can do anything you want. But I just blink the message errors. What I do here is I just create two states. Yet I call this data error on our error message. One added message to like that I just blink different messages. I just called and this edited it on and edited off. Here's what I do is very simple. Let's add the entry reaction for this display, right? I just printed an error. I'll print this in the second row of the display or just create some macros here. Clerk setting error message roll is one and defining clerk fattening error message column is that therefore I just do a display right here. And I will stay here for the final minutes, seconds. That means I just handle the ticket rent here. We know that the ticket is received for every 50 milliseconds. What I do is I just handle the event here and I'll call this ask take. And I'll use one guard. I guess whenever that happens, I just take some action, I would just increment a variable card timeout, I just increment that variable timeout variable. Let me clear that up later. And the guard condition is if the timeout is equal to 10. That's the God condition. If the timeout is equal to 10, then it goes here, it goes to this state.

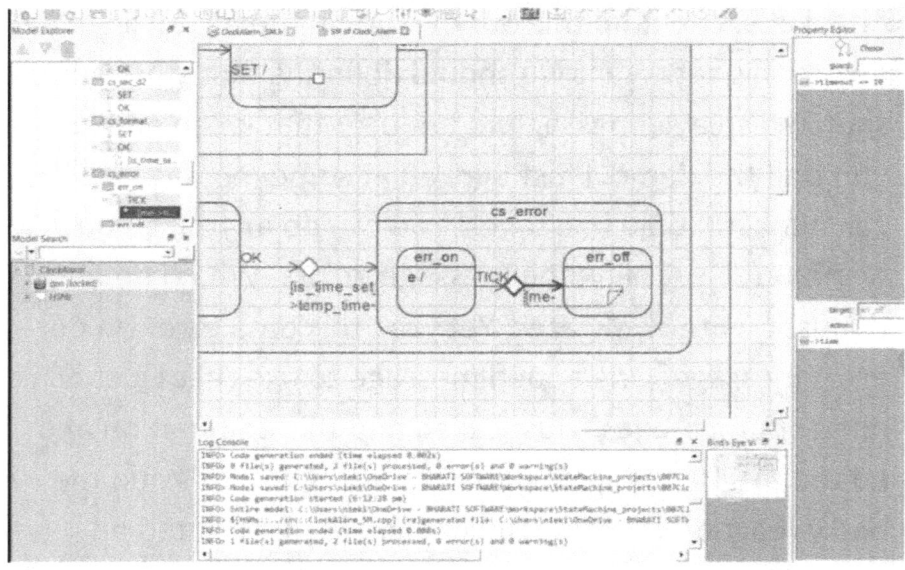

And for this trifecta meant the action will be me if the timeout is equal to zero. If the timeout is equal to 10, then I just cleared the timeout. That means my error message will be shown to the user for finding a millisecond, and then it goes to this state. And here I will clear the display and here I would just make the edit off.

Or you can print any other messages like check your settings or something. Here I would just clear that message. What I printed in this state for this to clear a message on the LCD, I just took the help of another helper function called display. It is blocked. What it does is it just erases our display block. A block is nothing but the number of characters between columns start and column end or column stop. So you just have to provide columns, start in, column stocked. And also the row number erasing means it is nothing but just replacing a character with a whitespace character that is like erasing on LCD. You cannot delete a character. You can only display a whitespace character on that. That is like erasing many lamps. You can take a look into this function. It just goes through different columns of this row, and it just displays the whitespace character of that fit. I will use this function from this state. I will call that function and display it. Erase block. First, you have to mention the row number. It's a message. This one and column start is this one. And column end column. And let me create one more macro here. Column and is that said nine, that's the length of that message. OK. And you should come out of this block op to find it in milliseconds. It's like blinking. That's why I can't use the tick signal here. Is the tick signal and I'll use one guard like this. This is again the tick, the action for this tick. If you have to increment the timeout variable and the guard is me, is it 9:45? That's the guard. And what is the action me off? Timeout is equal to zero.

You are to reset like that. So now it will be toggling, let's say the state machine is in this state and OK is received. OK is not handled here. Users cannot press OK, here, OK is ignored. What if the user tests the fact that the user wants to change the setting? You should take the user back to the aesthetic. That's why I will give one transition. From here to here, this is far fetched whenever facts resume. It will translate to this superstate and everything starts from the beginning. Does that make sense? Yes, because when the threat is received here, the user has the chance to start over again. When you are exiting this Arab state, you should also clean the display. That's why Ireland displays clearly and also the meat timeout should be set to zero. So now let me add this code block to the state machine, dark see at the end. And now let's test this.

EXERCISE-007 IMPLEMENTING CLOCK_SETTING STATE PART-4

Now, let's add that timeout. Tribute, an attribute that is called stealth timeout type is innate and difficult. Private now in this super state, we should also mention the initial state, so let's draw that. This is our initial state. Generate the code, and let's test this on the hardware. Let's download death. So now let's turn to some values here. I'll just make one or two. OK. OK. And how to just enter. 25. OK. The clock is not working.

I'm not sure why you can't see that. OK, it's not working. That could be because of some loose connections here. Let's try once again, one wants to let me in to two. OK. One two three four five six. OK. OK, OK. OK, and now, OK, now let me press OK here. And you see it's an error because the art world is too thick. That's an error. So here it is saying error. And you can also turn this blink off. You can do that. You can see that that message is blinking for every 500 milliseconds. And in this state, OK, should not be handled. So now let me press OK here. You see, there is some problem. I mean, the ox should not be handled, so we'll take care of that. Let's try once again. Let me make it at 20 a.m. So that's actually an error. That's not a correct setting. So this is an error. I would be at that stage. Now, let's press facts here.

Let's see what happens. It should start from the beginning. Let me preface the sentence. That is a problem we can see that actually should start from the beginning, but it's not happening. There have been some problems all day, but this is an issue. All right, so there is some problem. First of all, when we enter this at a stage in the entry, we'll do one thing. Let me get that function. Display cars rumbling, cough left. Turn the blink off. And the exit action for this state is not displayed clearly. You should not clear the display. You should only clear that error segment. I mean, you should only clear that message error.

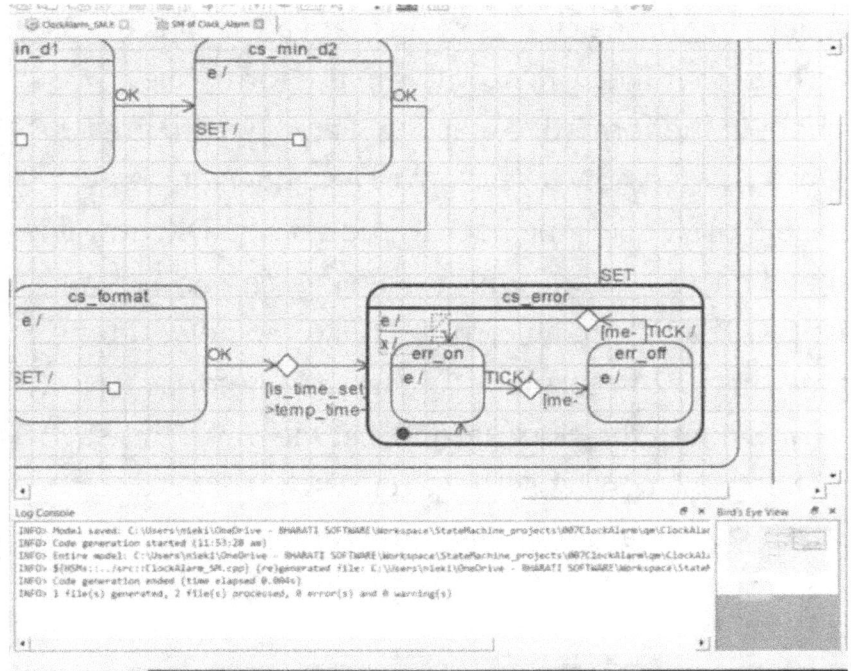

So I will use the display erase block, which I use in the error of state. I just copied this code and I will use that code as the exit action of this state instead of display clear. Fine. And whenever you press that it starts from here, right, it isn't exactly the interaction, the interaction of this is Carteron Blinken. This will not be executed. So start from here. That's why we should turn the cars around, Blinken. Let's do that here in fact. Now, let's test this at the court. Compile this project. There is some problem. This was not declared, it is saying. I think I have not given the prototype up. Cadre of. Blink off. To compile. It's fine now, let's download. Now, let's test this.

First, let's get to the clock setting that I admit has to. OK. Two three four five. OK, now it is in the formative election, in the formative election. I am going to press, OK. And you see now it says error. And now let me preface that. It takes me back to the setting. OK, now I've changed it to 20 20 am, which is again an error. Let me press OK. That is also an error set. OK. And now. Let me change this to 24 years old. That is actually correct. Now, let's go again to the clock setting. Let me make this say 10 pm. That is the correct setting. Ten. 24 h. That is also correct. You can abort at any time. Let me make this zero.

OK. That's an error. I just consider it as additive because when it is in 24 hour format, am pm information should not be mentioned. That's why let me again press the set.

So the user has to set this to 24. Is this the correct setting? So we are not updating the time. We'll do that in the next project. And also please note that whenever we are in error, state or case should be handled, but it should be ignored. That's why we will draw OK as the internal transition for the state. So I'll just draw like this. This is OK. It is handled, but there's no action mentioned. That means it's like, OK, it's ignored in this state. So if you don't mention OK here, then what happens if OK with you there, it propagates to the next state in the next election. Let's update the settings to the current time we look at in the next picture.

EXERCISE-007 UPDATING REAL TIME

In the previous project, we completed testing this, so whenever you are in the format selection, if everything is fine and then OK, it is underhanded. I mean, that is no problem with the user input. Then this guard fails, though, OK becomes untangled when it is handled. Most of the 8:02 so it's super state. Is this one setting and OK, it is handled here. Here we have to update the current time media for how to do that. Here is a code for that. First, we will check whether the user selected the format, whether it is a 24 hour format or not, because this variable contains the user selection regarding the format. If it is not equal to the 24 hour format, then we have to convert that time into a 24 hour format because ultimately we are going to save the value in the current time variable in the 24 hour format. That's why you have to convert that. This is just a helper function. We already have this function.

```
}while(len--);
}

/* $(HSMs::Clock_Alarm::SM::Clock::Settings::OK) */
uint8_t save_sreg;

if(me->temp_format != FORMAT_24H){
    me->temp_time = convert_12hformat_to_24h( me->temp_t
    me->time_mode = MODE_12H;
}else{
    me->time_mode = MODE_24H;
}

me->temp_time *= 10UL;
save_sreg = SREG;
cli();
TCCR1B &= ~(0x70);
TCNT1 = 00;
Clock_Alarm_curr_time = me->temp_time;
TCCR1B |= 0x40;
SREG = save_sreg;
```

And after that set the MOTU 12 hour format, indicating that the display should be shown in 12 hour format. Otherwise, time mode is trying to perform it. After that, we have to update this temp time into the current time global variable. This is how you should do it. First of all, you have to convert this into a number of hundred milliseconds. That's why I am just multiplying it by 10 here. And then I'm disabling the global interrupt because we don't want any more interrupts from the timer. That's why I'm disabling it and stopping the timer. This is. Stop the timer one. So this is how you do it. You should go to the timer one register description, go to TVR one. And here you should keep these three bits at zero. You can see that if these three bits become zero, then there is no clock. So for the timer and timer stops. That's why I'm just clearing those bits and then making the count register zero. Update this variable. Provide the clock though. So I'm just selecting these values. Clock thought with the preschooler 256. Now here the clock will be applied to the timer and the timer will stop ticking again and just restore the value of yesterday, which will also restore the interrupt. Enable Bit a partisan about this code. I'm going to keep in settings. OK, let's paste that here. And then we already have one function called that current time with the new current time. So we'll use this function, but this function was wrong, actually. This is not a correct way of changing the current time variable. That's right. Instead of this discord, that feels difficult. So this is the correct code. I just copied this code block. So this is actually a new quarantine.

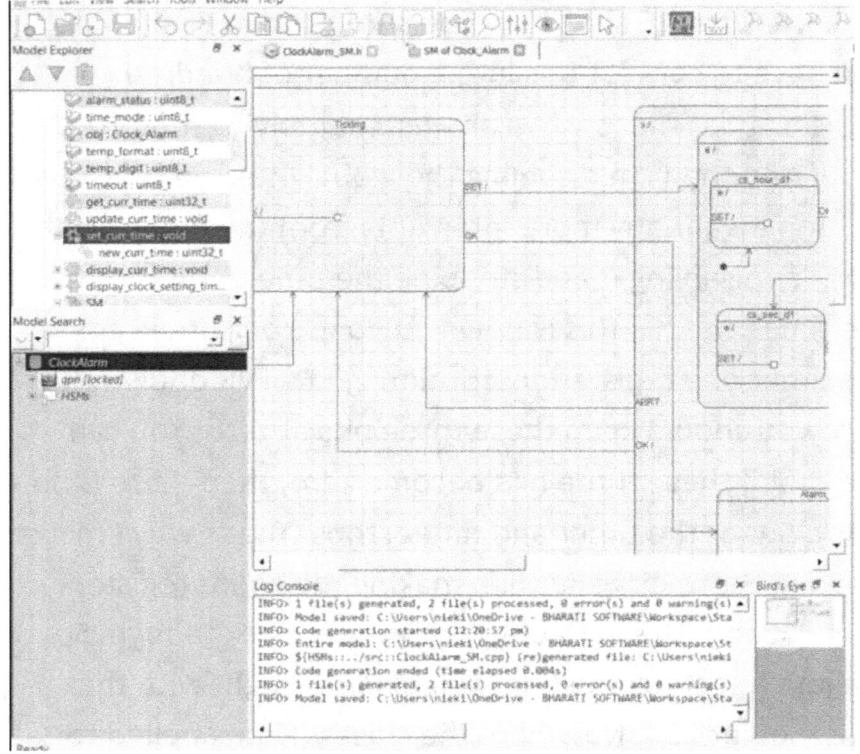

And let's go to the OK. Settings, OK, here, you should keep this correct about temp time multiplied by 10. Then you just call this function to set the current time. Clark underscores the alarm. Current time. And you just provide this value. And one more thing, we need to take care here, see, whenever you are leaving this settings state, you should also make cars that often blink off so the exit function of the setting stage. I'll call that function here. Now, let us have this generator code and let us compile. That is one problem with the cord. That it is here right here.

Large search for this element on the model. It actually takes me here to hear the variable is not defined. You entered and Scotty T. Yes, right? Compiled. The compulsion is fine. And now let's test this. Let me just. Download Discord. It is working. And now let me just set some time, let's say, I would just set it for 23 59, OK. 24. OK, now you see the new time is updated. So let's modify once again, let me make this as one. Let's say 10 p.m.. OK. So let me make this as to forage when it is displaying and trying to protect you from it, it doesn't show that quadrant. Now, let's see some invalid entries. OK, now it is an error. And when it is in error, the OK has no effect, you can see that. You had to press the set. That's it for this project, and in the next project, we will see how to handle the alarm setting state. I've seen the next project.

EXERCISE-007 ALARM_SETTING STATE

I believe this is an assignment to you. You have to implement these alarms heading straight. I think now it is pretty much similar to what you have already done in the crock setting state. I think you have to repeat these internal suspects here as well, and you can provide your own features, or you can take a look into the demo video where I explained how alarm settings should be presented to the user. As you can see, when it goes to the alarm setting mode on the first row, the user should be allowed to make changes to the alarm time and in the second row the current time. That is, the real time should be displayed to the user. And you may display some custom character like an alarm symbol or something like that. And also, please note that that is something called submachine by using submachine. You can reuse any part of the state machine. For example, let's say I want to reuse this cloth setting inside the alarm setting because in this project, we know that the alarm setting also takes a similar pattern of substitution. In that case, what you can do is you can create a submachine of this and you can then reuse that submachine as submachine instances. Let me show you how to do that, but it is not possible with a pre-tour. It needs commercial licensing, so you have to obtain the commercial license to use that feature. But I'll just show you how to do that. First, you are to select this state. Let's see. I want to create a submachine for this. And right click and select Add submachine from state. So now you have created a sub. You can see that you can give any name for that submachine.

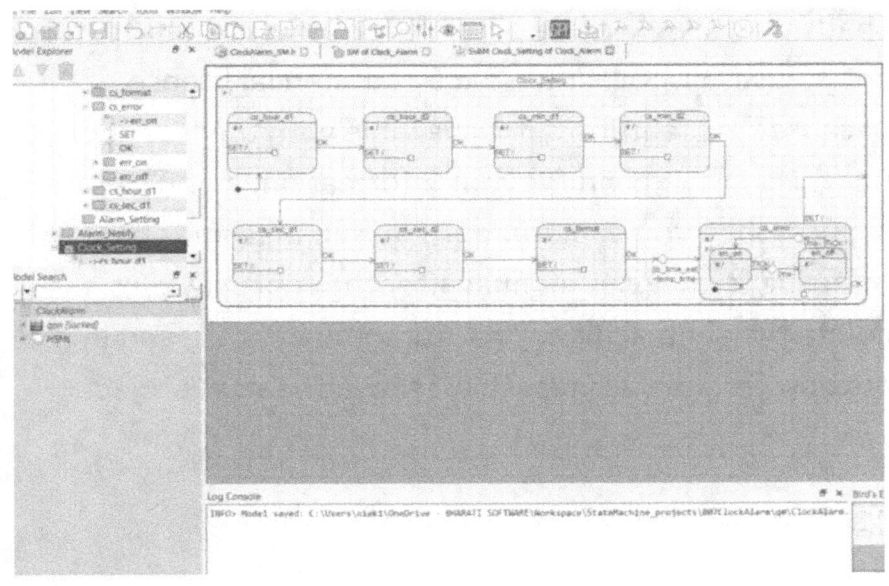

And also, you can use this entry and exit points to define the interfaces. And after that, what you can do is you just say that and you can use the instance of this submachine. Here, for example. Just add the submachine state and the link, this submachine state to submachine, what you just created that is clocked fetty. Now this is the state of this machine. Ah, this is an instance of this machine. It actually inherits all the details of this computer state like that you can do. But to use this submachine, state and submachine, it has to be based on cue MSM, not Q at GSM. Here you need to select Q MSM, but Q MSM is not available in Kewpie n Kewpie Nano. It is not available. That's why it will not be possible for us to use this feature and to use Q MSM. You need a commercial license because that feature is not available with the free tool. But this I just explain for your information. If you get any chance, then you explore more on sub machines by referring to the user manual after the tool. Now, let me delete the submachine. You just complete this, and in the next project, we will test this, I see in the next project.

EXERCISE-007 IMPLEMENTING ALARM_SETTING STATE

In the first project, I actually gave you a task to complete this alarm setting stage. I hope you managed to do that. Let me explain that in this project. I have done a couple of changes here and let me explain that. First of all, in the clock setting stage whenever we are in the underscore format stage. Here we are here. And when the OK signal arrives, the state handles the OK signal. And if this eighth time is set at a function, if it returns false, that means everything is fine. But this God condition fails when that God condition fails. This OK is propagated to the super state and the stage of this clock setting is setting. And from here, we take a transition, and while taking a transition, we also update the current time variable. But that's not the correct way, because the action to take one final OK signal arrives in this state is different, and in this state it is different for the final OK signal. That is a unique action to take here, and that is a separate action to take care. Here, the change at what I did was the call. Whatever that in this transition, I just mode that inside this clock setting state, I just created a new internal transition for the OK signal, and I copied all the code which were here to hear the same code. Because when the final OK signal arrives, we have to take one action here, which is different from the action that you're going to take in the alarm setting stage when the final OK signal arrives. That's why there are two different actions to take. That's why those two actions you cannot manage in this OK transition. That's why we create separate OK signals in both the clock setting state and in the alarm setting state. And after that, I just use one dummy guard state here, which always follows the guard zero. How to analyze this fear whenever you are in clock setting and whenever you are in this underscore format state and when the OK arrives and if this guard condition fails, then or case propagated to the super state that is clock setting state and this super state handles OK here that is already one. Action is defined, that is this action updating the current time variable and then this guard will be evaluated and this guard is always false. That's why this guard is always in space. That's why this OK is propagated to the next super. That is, settings and settings handle that signal, OK, and we will take a transition to the ticking stage. That's the change you have to notice in the Clark setting state, and now let's go to the alarm setting state. I just copy-paste all of these states here. These are exactly the same as before. But just change the state name. I have changed the state name, as you can see it, don't give the same state name. Otherwise, there will be conflict in naming the state handle functions. All these are the same. And here we come to the format. And here what happens. This state is again the same as before. If you sometimes set errors, if it is true, then we just display the error.

Everything is the same as before. The only difference here is this transition.

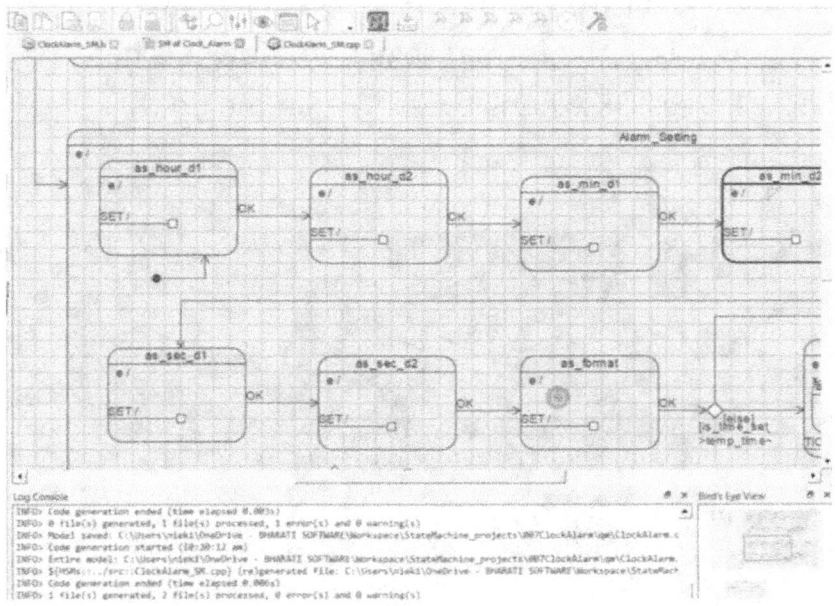

I'll just delete this. I will show you how to draw that. This alarm on off state here you can select whether the alarm should be turned on or turned off. The user does all the alarm settings, and finally, the user has to select whether he wants to turn the alarm on or turn that off. That is taken care of in this state, as you can see whenever the set signals arrive here. I just used one temporary variable, which in the ME points to some temporary variable, or you can use one special variable for this. But I just used the previous variable component of CalDigit, which is initially zero. If it is zero, then I just display the alarm off and make this zero. This is how it looks. Let's say I go to the alarm setting mode. You can see that at the fast line. Our first job is for the alarm setting, and I just press. OK, OK. So now it is in the format selection. Now it is here. And now I press OK when I press. OK, let me do that.

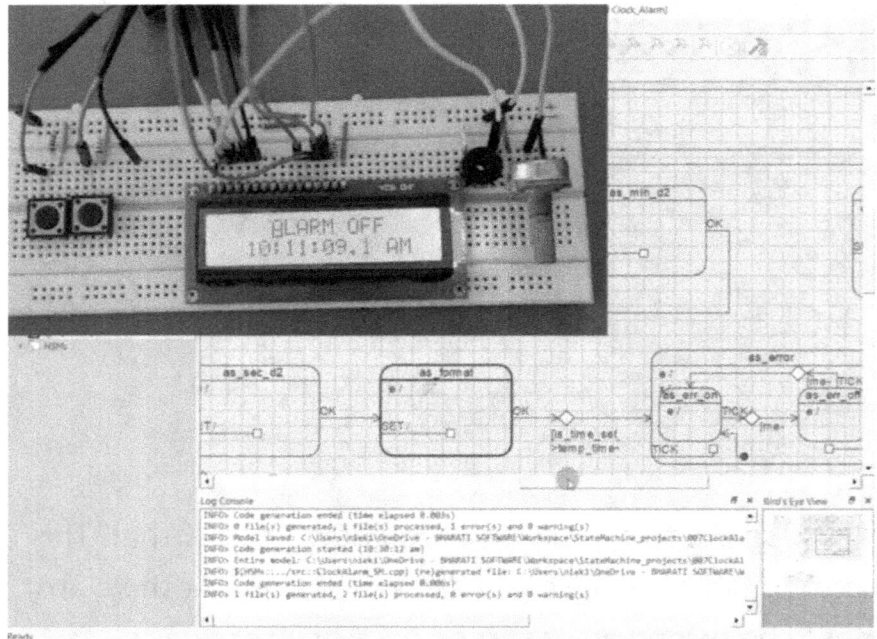

Now you can see that it is asking whether I want to turn the alarm off. I can use this set button to switch between on and off. That is actually handled here. What you do is if this time set error is false, then take one more transition here that you can do by using another chai segment or chai. Not what you do is for the Owls. You cannot draw any transition from here itself from this chair, nor you cannot do that. For example, if I just select the transition and I cannot draw any transition from here to create the elk scratch, what you need to do is you have to again use the chain segment and place it on this chain segment and draw one more transition like this. When you select this it, select that entire chai segment and you can now write the guard and action the negative health. He used the alpha keyword here. He. And you can define any action for this for this branch. There is no action defining this as Grant actually goes here whenever you are in this state, when the signal arrives, the OK is not handled by this state. That's why it is propagated to the alarm setting state. We handle that here. I would show you the alarm setting, we handle that here and what we do, we just copy that users on off status selection to the alarm status variable. And after that, if the time format I mean, whatever the format you selected here in this state, if it is not, is equal to 24 hour format. We will convert the time into a 24 hour format and we'll save it in the temporary time variable. And then the temporary time variable is copied to the main, a long time variable. The alarm time variable is updated here and then we want this OK to be propagated to the next superstate. That's why I just used a dummy card here and I fought to fail by using zero here. That's why this OK becomes one handle here and OK, propagates to the next state. That is the setting. And this settings handles this OK here, and we take a transition to the ticking state. That's how it works. And you can see that I press folk here, and it comes back to the ticking state. And if you want to see the alarm which is set, you can just press this. So now you also see that whenever we get into the alarm setting stage in the second line. The current time is displayed, and in the first line, you can see that because there is blinking. At the first digit of the outfit. Let's see how this is done in the code. Now let's get into the model first in the model. Alarm setting also handles the tick event here when all the current arrives. This is the code to do that. First of all, what we do here is very simple. We just display the current time with a desired row and column number. And after that, after displaying the message, we push the cursor back to the desired location. By using this logic here, what I've done is I just compared the current state handler address by using this macro, which is given by the two adjacent families. The kerchiefs framework gives this macro cue at some undisclosed date. More on that you can learn in this API reference document. Nano API reference. And here there is a queue at just some undisclosed state. That's the macro. This gives you the current active state from HSM, the current active state of H.S.. That current active state, which is nothing but a function pointer, which is compared with another function pointer. I just came out of that with all the different state handler addresses of this alarm setting state. If that is any match, then I use the display set cursor function to set the cursor at the desired location on the LCD. I would suggest you go through this logic. You will understand that better. If you have not implemented the alarm setting state, then please implement. And in the next project, we will explore how to implement this alarm. Notify State I see in the next project.

EXERCISE-007 IMPLEMENTING ALARM_NOTIFY STATE

In this project, let us understand how the alarm notification is shown in this project. For that, I use a separate state called Alarm Note five. And in this state, there will be a blinking message for every 500 milliseconds. What I do is I just use the state and here I just use one variable called timeout. So whenever the tick event is received, I just increment the timeout variable and I monitor that timeout variable using this card when timeout is equal to 10. That means ten in 250 milliseconds, that is final milliseconds. I go to this state and here I will erase that message block. That actually gives the blinking effect for the message. So in the entry action of this state, I just display an alarm when the alarm message is being displayed. If anyone presses the OK button here, then we should go back. So this awkward transition takes us to the history stage of the hat against the history stage of this clock. Super state for the meaning of this is to go to the history of this clock state because the alarm may happen while being in any of these states. That's why it makes sense to come back to the history state. And when the alarm notification is being displayed, and if no one presses the OK button, then we cannot display the alarm notification for eternity for outdoor activities, and the alarm notifies the state after some time. That's why I just use another variable called alarm timeout whenever that tick signal is received here in this state. Current time is displayed because whenever you are in an alarm, notify state, you should also display the current time. That's why that is handled in the signal tick. So I just use display current time, and after that I use another guard condition here and I just increment that alarm time variable and equate to equal to 200 200 men to 100 into 50 milliseconds. So that is around 10 seconds for 10 seconds if no one presses the OK button. This condition will become true and a transition will be taken to the ticking state. Just explore this, the next question is how the alarm event is delivered to this test machine.

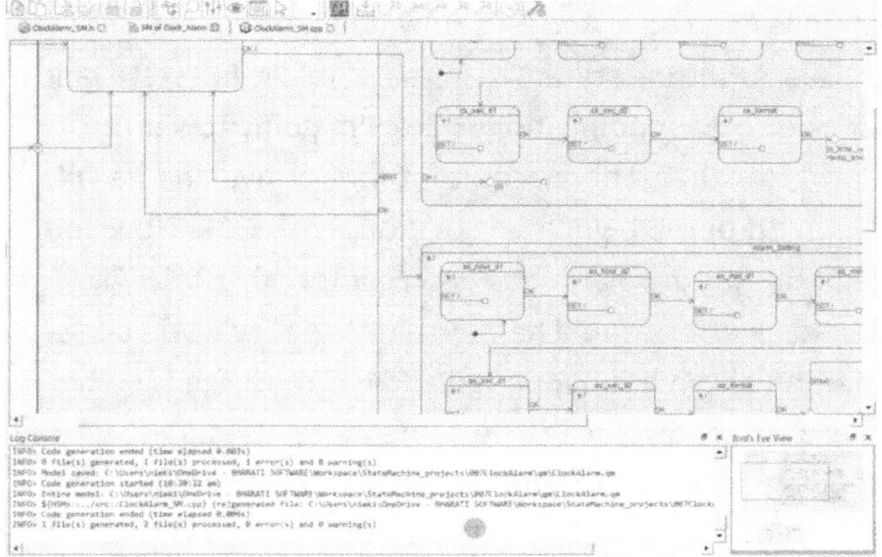

The alarm event is delivered from the main function that goes to the main darts type and the low function I send the alarm event. You can see it for every five hundred milliseconds to see whether that is any alarm or not. Please note that the alarm signal is handled by only this state clock state, so none of this upstage the off the clock state handles the alarm signal when the alarm signal is handled by the clock state. We use this guard to test whether the alarm time is really equal to the current time or not. And alarm status must be on if these two conditions are true. It's an alarm. That's why the transition will be taken to the alarm notify state. Now let's test this project with this change. If I'm going to save everything, I'm going to generate the coat. Let me just compile this code. And let's download. Now, let's get into the alarm setting state. I'm in that, I'm setting state, and let's do some modifications here. I'm going to set the alarm for 10 10. Let me set it for four or five and be OK. Alarm off or on. I would make it on. That's OK. Now you can see that the alarm has been set for 10, 10, 15 Air Canada alarms should happen. Let's see. Yes, you can see that the alarm has happened and the message is being displayed, and you can give some more effects here, like beeping or some other thing. Now let me press the OK and it goes back to the history state, which was this one.

Let me try one more time. Actually, there is one bug. Let me explain. What you do is in your I.D., you just open the CTA and monitor. Just click on it here. It opens the serial monitor. Now the serial monitor is open, and let me just try one more time. The alarm setting. This time, what I do is I send an alarm for 10. I've said it for 11, 11, 10, let's say I'll turn the alarm on and now I get into the Arab states. Let me quickly get into the Arab states. This is an Arab, so an Arab is being displayed, but the alarm happens for the previously set alarm. Let's wait for some time. I can see that a lot has happened. So now let me press the OK, but then it should go back to the history stage. That is the added notification, but that is a problem. You can see that in the Seitel monitor, it is displaying action. VIDEO And that means we actually met with Assad Schnatter here and this function of our main dark zip code. And it has printed a couple of details here, and we are now hanging in this wide one loop. That's why you can see that the application doesn't respond to any of the events because we are now here. Why did this assertion happen? Let's analyze that and this assertion has happened in this module. Queue up in a dark seat. And this is the assertion called FY20. Now let's debunk this. So what you do is just go to any of these functions of the framework. Let me open that to some dispatch, which is defined in Q EP and Dart Edge and on the left hand side, you can see all the thoughts files of this framework. Go to Q EP and don't see and hear just search for that code FY20. And here it is. This is bad, fashion has failed. Basically, the condition was, I repeat, what is IP? The IP is actually a variable. This is a transition entry, the index. Its value is supposed to be less than this macro, some max neft depth that is the maximum depth of the high Caco state machine, a set of five. You can see that, and its value must be less than five. But in our model, what's happening is you feel we were displaying the notification here, right? And the signal arrived and we came to the history state and from the history state. We have to move to this state, the Arab state, the state of the state, what's the number of depth involved? You can see that this number one two three. Four and five. I think this IP value is probably something. That's why that is an assertion failure for now to get rid of this problem. What you can do is you can flatten these states. You can remove that composite state and you can flatten these states or you increase the value of this macro to fix. This macro makes it fixed, actually, including this macro value is not recommended because the algorithm will consume more RAM space if you just blindly increase the value of this macro. But for the time being, I will fix this macro value. And let me save this and let's retest. I'm going to compile this. And let's download Discord, so let's get into the alarm setting. Let me set the alarm for 10 10. Let me set it for five, 10, 10, 50 am, OK? Alarm is on. Now let me get into the Edo State. That notification is being displayed and the alarm happens. As you can see, the alarm has happened. And now let me press the OK button. You can see that it takes me back to that at a notification. Now I can go back to the setting once again, and I can correct that. So this is all seen as a.

Fine. So on that note, I would like to end this project. Please try to reproduce this. If you need any help, you can post your questions. Also in the gift repository, all the source code and model filings available try to refer to that, and I'll see you in the next project.

www.ingramcontent.com/pod-product-compliance
Lightning Source LLC
Chambersburg PA
CBHW052137220526
45471CB00004B/1420